Objective & Short Answer Questions in

VETERINARY VIROLOGY

AF520522

Objective & Short Answer Questions in

VETERINARY VIROLOGY

SECOND EDITION

B.S. Malik
M.V.Sc., Ph.D. (U.S.A.), F.N.A.V.S.
Formerly Prof. & Head, Deptt. of Veterinary Microbiology,
College of Veterinary Science & A.H., Mathura & Jabalpur
and
Dean, College & Faculty, J.N. Krishi Vishwa Vidyalaya,
Jabalpur, India

Meenakshi Malik
M.V.Sc., Ph.D.
Scientist (Sr. Scale), National Biotechnology Centre,
Indian Veterinary Research Institute, Izatnagar (Bareilly), India

CBSPD

CBS Publishers & Distributors Pvt Ltd

New Delhi • Bengaluru • Chennai • Kochi • Kolkata • Lucknow • Mumbai
Hyderabad • Jharkhand • Nagpur • Patna • Pune • Uttarakhand

Veterinary Virology

Disclaimer

Science and technology are constantly changing fields. New research and experience broaden the scope of information and knowledge. The authors have tried their best in giving information available to them while preparing the material for this book. Although, all efforts have been made to ensure optimum accuracy of the material, yet it is quite possible some errors might have been left uncorrected. The publisher, printer and the authors will not be held responsible for any inadvertent errors or inaccuracies.

ISBN: 978-81-239-0872-4

Copyright © Authors

Second Edition: 2003

Reprint: 2006, 2008, 2012, 2018, 2024

First Edition: 1993

All rights reserved. No part of this book may be reproduced or transmitted in any form or by any means, electronic or mechanical, including photocopying, recording, or any information storage and retrieval system without permission, in writing, from the authors and the publishers.

Published by Satish Kumar Jain and Produced by Varun Jain for

CBS Publishers & Distributors Pvt Ltd

4819/XI Prahlad Street, 24 Ansari Road, Daryaganj, New Delhi 110 002, India.4819/XI Prahlad Street, 24 Ansari Road, Daryaganj, New Delhi 110 002, India.

Ph: 23289259, 23266861 Website: www.cbspd.com e-mail: delhi@cbspd.com

Corporate Office: 204 FIE, Industrial Area, Patparganj, Delhi 110 092

Ph: 011-4934 4934 Fax: 011-4934 4935 e-mail: publishing@cbspd.com; publicity@cbspd.com

Branches

- **Bengaluru:** Seema House 2975, 17th Cross, K.R. Road, Banasankari 2nd Stage, Bengaluru 560 070, Karnataka
  Ph: +91-80-26771678/79 Fax: +91-80-26771680 e-mail: bangalore@cbspd.com
- **Chennai:** 7, Subbaraya Street, Shenoy Nagar, Chennai 600 030, Tamil Nadu, India
  Ph: +91-44-26680620/26681266 Fax: +91-44-42032115 e-mail: chennai@cbspd.com
- **Kochi:** 42/1325, 1326, Power House Road, Opp KSEB, Power House, Ernakulam 682 018, Kochi, Kerala, India
  Ph: +91-484-4059061-65, 67 Fax: +91-484-4059065 e-mail: kochi@cbspd.com
- **Kolkata:** 147, Hind Ceramics Compound, 1st Floor, Nilgunj Road, Belghoria, Kolkata-700056, West Bengal, India
  Ph: +033-25633055, 033-25633056 e-mail: kolkata@cbspd.com
- **Lucknow:** Basement, Khushnuma Complex, 7 Meerabai Marg (Behind Jawahar Bhawan), Lucknow-226001, UP, India
  Ph: +91-522-4000032 e-mail: tiwari.lucknow@cbspd.com
- **Mumbai:** PWD Shed, Gala no 25/26, Ramchandra Bhatt Marg, Next to JJ Hospital Gate no. 2, Opp. Union Bank of India Noorbaug, Mumbai-400009, Maharashtra, India
  Ph: 022-66661880/89 e-mail: mumbai@cbspd.com

Representatives

- **Hyderabad** 0-9885175004
- **Jharkhand** 0-9811541605
- **Nagpur** 0-8692091830
- **Patna** 0-9334159340
- **Pune** 0-9664372571
- **Uttarakhand** 0-9716462459

Printed at: Sanjay Printers, Sahibabad, U.P, India

Preface to Second Edition

The first edition of this book was published in 1993. It served its purpose to a great extent. On account of newer information and fast developments in the field of virology, the revision of the book became overdue. The first edition was primarily written to review the subject mainly in question-answer form, ignoring a systematic approach on topics of general information on viruses and familywise description of viral diseases.

Retaining the option of dealing with the subject in question-answer form, the present edition has been revised and enlarged to include general information on animal viruses and familywise diseases. Several topics, including the classification of viruses, viral genetics, virus-host cell interactions, their role in oncogenesis and diagnosis, immunity and epidemiology of viral diseases, have been added. Description of viral diseases includes different types/serotypes of viruses, their properties, transmission, clinical symptoms, pathogenesis and control measures.

Every effort has been made to specifically deal with the viral diseases which are more pertinent to the livestock of Indian sub-continent. It is not claimed that the book is a complete textbook on virology. It is, however, hoped that it will be quite useful to the concerned students and staff of veterinary colleges and will fill up some gap in the availability of virology books of this nature.

We are thankful to the authors of various textbooks and other reference materials on virology which have been used liberally in revising and updating the book. We are also indebted to various authors for Figs. 3.1, 6.2, 7.1 and 7.2. The source of these figures has already been acknowledged in appropriate chapters.

Further we express our thanks to Shri Satish Jain and Shri Vinod Jain for publishing the book and Shri Dharmvir for his meticulous care in designing and preparation of the book in the present form.

The authors will appreciate receiving comments on the book, if any, for improvement and correction in the next edition.

B.S. Malik
M. Malik

Preface to First Edition

Ever since the switch over of the traditional system of teaching and examination of Agricultural and Veterinary Science subjects to Land Grant pattern of USA, in nineteen sixties, the old system has been modified considerably. Under new trimester/semester system, the students are evaluated through a number of quizes, hourly, mid term and final examinations, generally on the basis of multiple choice and short answer questions. This system regularly evaluates the student's learning process. The examinees know their performance and the teachers have chance to see how effective is their teaching. In trimester/semester system, the subject is distributed in a number of courses. The students can review the courses in examination days within a short period without much pressure. The evaluation of multiple and short answer questions is without any personal error or bias. The entire course can be covered which is not possible through a few subjective type of questions practiced in the traditional system.

A number of organisations/institutions now hold regular examinations to evaluate candidates for admission in various degree programmes, award of merit scholarships and appointments on various jobs based on multiple choice and short answer questions.

So far, there seems to be no such book on multiple choice questions in Veterinary Virology in this country. An attempt has been made to prepare and compile 670 multiple choice and short answer questions with their answers. Additional 100 questions, and ICAR Junior fellowship and ARS competitive examination question papers have also been included.

It is hoped that the book will be found useful, both for the teachers as well as for the students in Veterinary Colleges and other institutions.

The author will appreciate receiving comments and printing and other inadvertent errors if any, for improvement and correction in the next edition.

B.S. MALIK

Contents

B. RNA Virus Families

Key to Abbreviations

AAV Adeno-associated virus
AE Avian encephalomyelitis
ASF African swine fever
AHS African horse sickness
ASV Avian sarcoma virus
ALV Avian leukosis complex
AV Adenovirus
AIDS Acquired immunodefficiency syndrome
BVD Bovine virus diarrhoea
BTV Blue tongue virus
BSS Balanced salt solution
BSE Bovine spongiform encephalopahty
BHK_{21} Baby hamester $kidney_{21}$
C Circular
CF Complement fixation
CPE Cytopathic effects
CMI Cell mediated immunity
CAM Chorio allantoic membrane
CNS Central nervous system
CELO Chicken Embryo lethal orphan
CMV Cytomegalo virus
CPD Contagious pustular dermatitis
CD Canine distemper
CVE Coital vesicular exanthema
COFAL Complement fixation for avian leukosis
cDNA Complementary DNA
DNA Deoxyribonucleic acid
DS Double stranded
ELISA Enzyme linked immunosorbent assay
ERP Equine rhino pneumonitis
EBV Epstein Barr virus
EEE Eastern equine encephalomyelitis
EIA Equine infectious anaemia
EDS Egg drop syndrome
FAT Fluorescent antibody test
FMD Foot and mouth disease
FP Fowl pox
GTV Goat tissue vaccine
HA Haemagglutination
HI Haemagglutination inhibition
HV Herpes virus
HCV Hog cholera virus
HIV Human immunodeficiency virus
HTLV Human T cell leukaemia virus
HEP High egg passage
HDC Human diploid cell
ID Immunodiffusion
IF Immunofluorescent
IgG Immunoglobulin G
IgA Immunoglobulin A
IgM Immunoglobulin M
IgD Immunoglobulin D
IgE Immunoglobulin E
ICH Infectious canine hepatitis
IBR Infectious bovine rhinotracheitis
ILT Infectious laryngotracheitis

IB	Infectious bronchitis
IBD	Infectious bursal disease
ID_{50}	Infective $dose_{50}$
I/M	Intramuscular
I/V	Intravenous
I/P	Intraperitoneal
I/C	Intracerebral
I/N	Intranasal
I/D	Intradermal
S/C	Subcutaneous
IFN	Interferon
ICNV	International committee on nomenclature of viruses
ICTV	International committee on taxonomy of viruses
JE	Japanese encephalitis
KFD	Kyasanur forest disease
Kbs	Kilobase pairs
L	Linear
LCMV	Lymphocytic choriomeningitis virus
LEP	Low egg passage
LD_{50}	Lethal $dose_{50}$
mm	Millimeter
Mol. Wt.	Molecular weight
MDV	Marek's disease virus
MCF	Malignant catarrhal fever
MNI	Mumps, Newcastle disease, influenza
MATSA	Marek's associated tumour specific surface antigen
NA	Nucleic acid
nm	Nenometer
NS	Nonsegmented
NDV	Newcastle disease virus
N	Neuraminidase
PI	Parainfluenza
PPR	Peste des Petits ruminants
PBS	Phosphate buffer solution
PAGE	Polyacrylamide gel electrophoresis
PCR	Polymerase chain reaction
RNA	Ribonucleic acid
RIA	Radio immuno assay
RSSE	Russian spring-summer encephalitis
RDV	Ranikhet disease virus
RP	Rinderpest
RVF	Rift valley fever
RBC	Red blood cell
RDE	Receptor destroying enzyme
RIF	Resistance inducing factor
RNP	Ribonucleoprotein
RPM	Revolution per minute
RTD	Routine test dilution
SN	Serum neutralization
SAT	South African Territory
SP	Sheep pox
SFV	Swine fever virus
SS	Single stranded
S	Segmented
TGE	Transmissible gastro-enteritis
TSTA	Tumour specific transplantation antigen
TMV	Tubacco mosaic virus
TSSA	Tumour specific cell surface antigen
$TCID_{50}$	Tissue culture infective $does_{50}$
Temp.	Temperature
VN	Virus neutralization
VE	Vesicular exanthema
VEE	Venezualan equine encephalomyelitis
VS	Vesicular stomatitis
WEW	Western equine encephalomyelitis

PART I

GENERAL VIROLOGY

1

Historical Development of Virology

Historical development of Virology was much slower in comparison to Bacteriology. The main reasons for this development were their submicroscopic size and inability to grow in artificial media. Some landmark discoveries in the development of virology are highlighted in this chapter.

Select the correct answer:

Q. 1. Electron microscope was introduced by:

(a) Antony van Leeuwenhoek (b) Elford
(c) Ruska (d) L. Pasteur

Ans. (c)

Q. 2. Who first observed that foot and mouth disease (FMD) was caused by a filterable agent?

(a) Beijerinck (b) Loeffler and Frosch
(c) Walter Reed (d) Edward Jenner

Ans. (b)

Q. 3. The term vaccine was coined by:

(a) Robert Koch (b) Zinke
(c) J. Bordet (d) L. Pasteur

Ans. (d)

Q. 4. Who first produced tobacco mosaic disease by a filterable agent?

(a) Stanley (b) Iwanowski
(c) Henle (d) Twort

Ans. (b)

Q. 5. Who first crystallized tobacco mosaic virus (TMV)?

(a) Berkefeld (b) Lindenmann
(c) Stanley (d) Kitasato

Ans. (c)

Q. 6. Fill in the blanks:

(a) Propagation of virus in embryonated eggs was first done by ....

(b) First human inoculation with antirabies vaccine was performed by ....

(c) Avian leucosis was first discovered by..............

(d) Tissue culture method was discovered by ....

Ans. (a) Goodpasture and Woodruff (b) L. Pasteur
(c) Ellerman and Bang (d) Enders, Weller and Robbins

Q. 7. (a) Interference phenomenon was discovered by ....

(b) Interferon was discovered by ....

(c) The size of virions was first determined by ....

(d) Infectious nature of saliva in rabid dog was demonstrated by ....

Ans. (a) Hoskins (b) Isaacs and Lindenmann
(c) Elford (d) Zinke

Q. 8. (a) Sarcoma tumors in fowl was discovered by ....

(b) Bacteriophages were discovered by .... and ....

(c) .... used cow pox virus for smallpox vaccination for the first time.

(d) .... of U.S. Army Commission established that yellow fever disease was caused by a virus.

Ans. (a) P. Rous (b) Twort (1915), d'Herelle (1917)
(c) Edward Jenner (d) Walter Reed

Q. 9. (a) The term viroid was coined by..............

(b) The phenomenon of phagocytosis was discovered by ....

(c) The phenomenon of anaphylaxis was first observed by .... and ....

(d) The phenomenon of haemagglutination by influenza virus was first observed by ....

Ans. (a) Diener (1971) (b) Metchnikoff (1883)
(c) Portier, Richet (1902) (d) Hirst (1941)

Q. 10. Match column A with column B

Column A	Column B
(a) Kornberg	(i) Double helix structure of DNA
(b) Watson and Crick	(ii) Synthesis of DNA
(c) Sigurdsson	(iii) One gene one enzyme hypothesis
(d) Beadle and Tatum	(iv) Slow virus infection

Ans. (a) (ii), (b) (i), (c) (iv), (d) (iii)

Q. 11.

Column A	Column B
(a) Reverse transcriptase enzyme	(i) Max Theiler
(b) Hybridoma and monoclonal antibodies	(ii) Dulbecco, Baltimore and Temin
(c) Yellow Fever vaccine	(iii) Gajdusek and Blumberg
(d) Studies or Kuru disease agent	(iv) Kohler and Milstein

Ans. (a) (ii), (b) (iv), (c) (i), (d) (iii)

Q. 12.

Column A	Column B
(a) Pillmer	(i) Role of bursa in humoral antibody
(b) Grabar and Williams	(ii) Role of thymus in immunity
(c) Good and Miller	(iii) Immuno-electrophoresis
(d) Click and Chang	(iv) Properdin

Ans. (a) (iv), (b) (iii), (c) (ii), (d) (i)

Q. 13.

Column A	Column B
(a) Barbara McClintock	(i) Nucleotide sequencing
(b) Frederick Sanger	(ii) Jumping genes
(c) Werner Arber, Hamilton Smith & Daniel Nathan	(iii) Southern blotting
(d) E.M. Southern	(iv) Restriction enzyme/restriction endonuclease

Ans. (a) (ii), (b) (i), (c) (iv), (d) (iii)

2

General Properties of Viruses

Q. 1. Briefly describe the general properties of viruses.

Ans. Viruses are submicroscopic, obligate intracellular parasites containing either deoxyribonucleic acid (DNA) or ribonucleic acid (RNA). They multiply only within living cells unlike bacteria which also multiply in artificial media. They do not multiply by binary fission but by a complex process. Viruses lack in biosynthetic enzymes and are dependent for replication on the synthetic machinery of host cells. They are not affected by bacterial antibiotics.

The extracellular infectious virus particle is called virion. Virion essentially consists of a nucleic acid core surrounded by a protein coat called capsid. The capsid with enclosed nucleic acid is known as nucleocapsid. The capsid is composed of a large number of capsomers, which form its morphological units. The capsid of some viruses is enveloped while those of other viruses is non-enveloped (naked). The chemical units of the capsid are polypeptide molecules which are arranged symmetrically. The symmetry of the capsid is either icosahedral (cubical) type or helical type and rarely of complex type. When present, the envelope is lipoprotein in nature. The protein subunits of the envelope may be seen as projecting spikes on the surface. These are known as peplomers. The genome (nucleic acid) of DNA viruses is normally double stranded but in few cases, it is single stranded. The genome of RNA viruses in most cases is single stranded and in few cases, double stranded. The nature of genome in most cases is linear type except in few viruses where it is of circular type. The genome can be segmented or non-segmented. The size and number of capsomers vary greatly in different viruses. Most animal viruses roughly are spherical and some are irregular in shape. Plant viruses are generally rod shaped.

Large number of diseases are produced by viruses in humans, animals, plants, insects and bacteria. Viruses are transmitted from infected to healthy animals directly, indirectly or through arthropod vectors. Most viruses are very heat labile. Their stability varies greatly to different pH, chemical disinfectants, sun light etc. Some viruses posses haemagglutinating property. Viruses are susceptible to interferons. Viral proteins are antigenic. Some viruses are oncogenic in nature.

Q. 2. Draw diagrams of icosahedral and helical virions and label all parts.

Ans. Virion consists of a nucleic acid (NA) surrounded by a protein coat called capsid. The capsid with nucleic acid is known as nucleocapsid. The capsid is composed of large number of capsomers which form its morphological units. Some viruses are enveloped. Other structures called peplomers may be projecting from the surface of envelope. The diagrams of icosahedral and helical viruses are shown in figure 2.1. The shape of some viruses may be of complex type. The shape of some helical RNA viruses is long, filamentous and rod shaped.

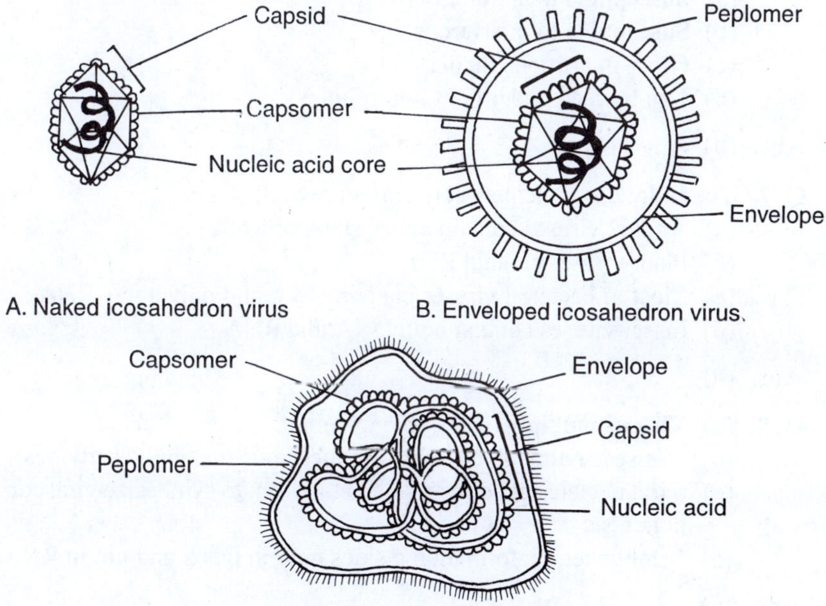

Fig. 2.1. Structure of icosahedral and helical viruses.

Select one correct answer:

Q. 3. The symmetric protein shell of the viruses which encloses viral nucleic acid is known as:

(a) Envelope (b) Capsid

(c) Capsomer (d) Nucleocapsid

Ans. (b)

Q. 4. Outside host's cell, viral nucleic acid without its coat is:

(a) Infective (b) Inert
(c) Virulent (d) Nonvirulent

Ans. (b)

Q. 5. Viruses are:

(a) Unicellular organisms (b) Haploid in nature
(c) Contain both DNA and RNA (d) Multiply by binary fission

Ans. (b)

Q. 6. The viruses are:

(a) Susceptible to antibiotics
(b) Susceptible to interferons
(c) Grow in artificial media
(d) Can be seen under light microscope

Ans. (b)

Q. 7. The following statements are correct except:

(a) Animal viruses contain either DNA or RNA
(b) Plant viruses contain RNA
(c) Most of bacterial viruses contain DNA and only a few RNA
(d) Insect viruses contain both DNA and RNA

Ans. (d)

Q. 8. (a) Viruses multiply only in living cells
(b) Viruses are not able to perform their own metabolic activities
(c) Viral nucleic acid directs cell metabolism to synthesize viral components.
(d) Viral genetic information resides only in DNA and not in RNA.

Ans. (d)

Q. 9. (a) Viruses contain proteins, carbohydrates and one of the two nucleic acids
(b) Viral proteins are antigenic in nature.
(c) Envelope is an essential component of all viruses.
(d) Most viruses lack enzymic system.

Ans. (c)

Q. 10. (a) Most viruses produce diseases and clinical symptoms in animals.
(b) Some viruses produce latent infections in animals.
(c) Some viruses are tumorogenic.
(d) Bacteria are not susceptible to viruses.

Ans. (d)

Q. 11. (a) The shapes and sizes of different viruses differ greatly.
(b) The size of viruses may be as small as 20 nm and as large as 300 nm.
(c) Viruses of the size of 200 nm and larger can be seen by light microscope.
(d) Smallest virus can not be seen even by electron microscope.

Ans. (d)

Q. 12. (a) Genetic information in RNA viruses does not exist in RNA
(b) Viral envelope confer chemical, antigenic and biological properties in viruses.
(c) Capsid is responsible for structural symmetry in viruses
(d) Peplomers are absent in non-enveloped viruses.

Ans. (a)

Q. 13. Envelope of virions has following properties except:
(a) It is lipoprotein in nature.
(b) It is sensitive to lipid solvents.
(c) It is not required for infectivity of the cells.
(d) It is antigenic in nature.

Ans. (c)

Q. 14. Name chemical composition of viruses:

Ans. (a) Structural and nonstructural proteins.
(b) Carbohydrate in the form of glycoproteins.
(c) Lipid in the form of phospholipids and cholesterols in enveloped viruses.
(d) Nucleic acid in the form of DNA or RNA.

Q. 15. Following statements are correct for peplomers except:
(a) In enveloped viruses, peplomers project from the surface of envelope.
(b) Peplomers are also called as spikes.
(c) An enveloped virus can possess only one type of peplomers.
(d) Peplomers are protein and antigenic in nature.

Ans. (c)

Q. 16. The capsid of viruses has following functions except:
(a) It protects nucleic acid from inactivation by nucleases.
(b) It is responsible for infection of susceptible cells.
(c) It participates in the attachment of virus to cells.
(d) It introduces viral genome into host cells by adsorption on cell surface.

Ans. (b)

Q. 17. The size viruses can be determined by the following except:
(a) Gradacol membrane filters (b) Ultracentrifugation
(c) Electrophoresis (d) Electron microscopy

Ans. (c)

Q. 18. Viruses can be purified and concentrated by the following except:
(a) Electron microscopy (b) Chemical precipitation
(c) Ultra centrifugation (d) Gradacol membrane filteration
(e) Haemagglutination elution

Ans. (a)

Q. 19. Following statements are correct except:
(a) Viruses produce large number of diseases in humans, animals and birds.
(b) Some viruses produce minor ailments while others produce highly fatal diseases.
(c) Some viruses produce localized infections while others produce systemic infections.
(d) Some viruses have a narrow host range while others infect a large number of animal species.
(e) Viruses do not produce intrauterine infections.

Ans. (e)

Q. 20. (a) Some viruses possess haemagglutinating activity.
(b) Some viruses produce intracytoplasmic and/or intranuclear inclusion bodies in infected cells.
(c) Viruses can be preserved for long times at–70°C or in freeze dried condition at 4°C.
(d) Viruses multiply only in the cytoplasm of infected cells.

Ans. (d)

Q. 20. (a) Most DNA viruses are double stranded and only a few are single stranded.

(b) Most RNA viruses are single stranded and only a few are double stranded.
(c) The nucleic acid of most viruses is linear in shape while it is circular in few cases.
(d) The nucleic acid in most viruses is non-segmented while in some cases it is segmented.
(e) The capsid in all viruses is icosahedral type.

Ans. (e)

Q. 22. Fill in the blanks:
(a) The isometric capsids of the viruses have .... symmetry
(b) The icosahedron has .... rotational symmetry
(c) The total number of capsomers in a virion can be calculated by the formula ....
(d) Molecular weight of nucleic acid is expressed in ....

Ans. (a) Cubic,
(b) 5 : 3 : 2,
(c) $N = 10(n - 1)^2 + 2$. N = number of capsomers and n is the number of capsomers on one edge of the equilateral triangle.
(d) Kilobase pairs (Kb)

Q. 23. (a) The number of capsomers in icosahedral viruses varies from .... to ....
(b) The shape, size, and internal structures of viruses can be determined by ....
(c) The electron dense chemicals used in negative staining by electron microscopy are .... and ....
(d) In density gradient centrifugation commonly used gradient is ....

Ans. (a) 32, 1892 (b) electron microscopy
(c) phosphotungstic acid, uranyl acetate (d) sucrose

Q. 24. (a) In centrifugation, the rate of sedimentation depends upon ...., ... and .... of particle.
(b) In electrophoresis virus proteins can be separated on the basis of .... of virus proteins and .... of buffer solution.
(c) The average pore diameter of filters will give an estimate of the .... of viruses.
(d) The negative staining compounds used in electron microscopy are .... in nature.

Ans. (a) density, size, shape (b) net electric charge, pH
(c) size (d) electron dense

Q. 25. (a) Useful magnification of an electron microscope is about .... times.
(b) Electron microscopy by shadow casting technique is used to determine ...., negative staining for .... and ultrathin sections for ....
(c) The size of viruses is measured in ....
(d) The length of 1 nanometer (nm) is equal to .... micrometer (μm).

Ans. (a) 400,000 (b) shape, fine details, internal structures
(c) nanometers (nm) (d) 0.001

Q. 26. (a) Viruses do not fall into the category of unicellular microorganisms because............................
(b) Viruses can be termed living chemicals because..............
(c) Viruses were earlier known as filterable agents because ....
(d) Viruses are called ultramicroscopic because..............

Ans. (a) they do not possess a unicellular organisation.
(b) they can be crystalized like chemicals and the extraction of nucleic acid can infect host cells.
(c) they were able to pass through filters which held back most of the bacteria.
(d) they are too small to be seen under light microscope.

Q. 27. State true or false for the following statements:
(a) High speed centrifugation can be used for the purification of viruses as well as to determine their size.
(b) Paraffin embedded tissue sections can be examined with electron microscopy.
(c) Sodium phosphotungstate can be used for negative staining of specimens by electron microscopy.
(d) Envelope is not essential for infectivity of enveloped viruses.

Ans. (a) True, (b) False, (c) True, (d) False

Q. 28. (a) Outer structure of viruses is a cell wall.
(b) Ribosomes are absent in viruses.
(c) RNA viruses are the only agents which have genetic information in RNA.
(d) Viruses have some properties of living and some of non-living, and may be termed as 'living chemicals.'

Ans. (a) False, (b) True, (c) True, (d) True

Q. 29. Briefly describe the chemical and physical agents affecting viruses:

Ans. Viruses can be inactivated within seconds at 56°C, within minutes at 37°C and within weeks and days at 4°C temperatures except few exceptions. Viruses are easily inactivated by sun light, UV rays and ionising radiations. Viruses vary greatly in resistance to acidity. They are easily disrupted under alkaline conditions. Phenolic disinfectants are weakly virucidal. Organic iodine compounds are moderately virucidal. Hydrogen peroxide, potassium permanganate and hypochlorites have antiviral activity. Formaldehyde and beta propiolactone are also virucidal and used in the preparations of killed vaccines. Enveloped viruses are sensitive to solvents like ether, alcohol, chloroform and bile salts.

Q. 30. Briefly discuss the haemagglutinating property of viruses.

Ans. Large number of viruses possess the property of haemagglutination of erythrocytes from different species of animals. The viruses of *Orthomyxoviridae* and *Paramyxoviridae* agglutinate the red blood cells from fowls at 37°C. These viruses are enveloped which have two types of peplomers on their surfaces. The specific names of these peplomers are haemagglutinin and neuraminidase. Haemagglutination of fowl RBCs takes place due to haemagglutinins present on the surface of these viruses. The neuraminidase enzyme, also present on the surface of the virus, acts on the receptors on the surface of RBCs and destroys them. This enzyme therefore is called receptor destroying enzyme (RDE). After destruction of the receptors on the surface of RBCs, there is reversal of haemagglutination and the virus is released from the surface of red cells. This phenomenon is known as elution. Different viruses agglutinate RBCs from different species and at different incubation temperatures. Surface receptors of RBCs after destruction by neuraminidase of some virus can still be agglutinated by other viruses. Some viruses possess haemagglutinin as well as neuraminidase while others, possess only haemagglutinins and no neuraminidase, most other viruses possess neither haemagglutinins nor neuraminidase.

3

Bacteriophages

Viruses infect animals, plants, insects and bacteria. Viruses infecting bacteria are known as bacteriophages. Bacteriophages are dependent on living bacterial cells for all biological activities. Phages occur widely in nature in close association of bacteria. They can be easily isolated from sewage. Phages play important role in the transmission of genetic information in bacteria by the process of transduction. They are host specific. Phage typing of bacteria helps in their identification and classification.

Q. 1. Briefly describe physico-chemical properties of bacteriophages.

Ans. Most of the bacteriophages appear to be tadpole shaped. *E.coli* T2 phage is one of the largest phages. Its hexagonal head measures about 65 × 95 nm and the tail 25 × 100 nm. The phage particle consists of a protein shell, and nucleic acid is packed tightly inside the head. Different phages differ in size, shape and structural details. In almost all cases, the nucleic acid in phages is DNA type. The phage particle attaches with tail end to bacterial host and inject DNA for multiplication. Progeny phage particles are released after lysis of bacterial cells. All phages are good antigens. Different phages are antigenically different. They are also antigenically unrelated to their hosts. Only the antibody directed against tail parts can neutralize the infectivity of phage particles. Most research work has been done on T phages of B strain of *E. coli.* The T phages of *E. coli* are T1 to T7.

Q. 2. Describe the morphology of *E. coli* T even phages with the help of a diagram.

Ans. T even phages are tadpole shaped with a hexagonal head and a cylindrical tail. The head is packed with double stranded DNA surrounded by a protein coat (capsid). The tail is composed of a hollow core, surrounded by a sheath. The tip of the tail has base plate or fibres which are protein in nature. Some other phages are spherical or filamentous. The morphology of T phages is shown in Fig. 3.1.

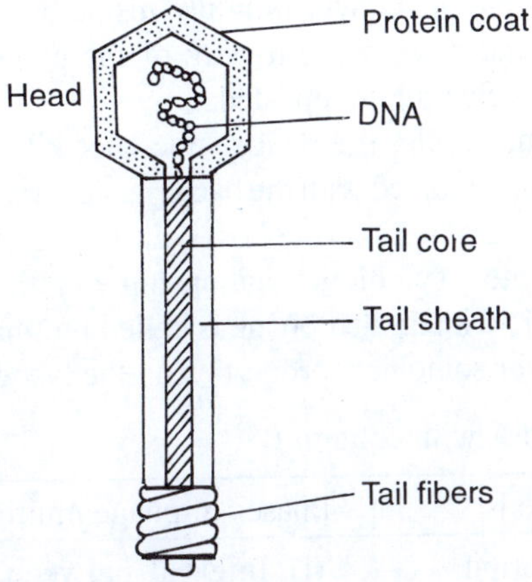

Fig. 3.1. Structure of T even phage (From Kozloff, 1959. In Zirkle, A Symposium on Molecular Biology. University of Chicago Press)

Select correct answer:

Q. 3. The term bacteriophage was first coined by:
(a) Walter Reed (b) Zinke
(c) Beijerinck (d) d'Herelle

Ans. (d)

Q. 4. Bacteriophages were first discovered by:
(a) Loeffler and Frosch (b) Pasteur
(c) Twort (d) d'Herelle

Ans. (c) and (d)

Q. 5. Bacteriophages were first detected in the year:
(a) 1898; (b) 1910; (c) 1915; (d) 1917

Ans. (c) and (d)

Q. 6. Bacteriophages are used for:
(a) Bacterial identification (b) Antibacterial agent
(c) Epidemiological studies (d) All the above

Ans. (d)

Q. 7. Briefly describe the life cycle of T phages.

Ans. The phages may have two types of life cycle:

1. Lytic cycle (virulent phage cycle)
2. Lysogenic cycle (temperate phage cycle)

In lytic cycle, the phage will multiply inside bacteria and will cause lysis of bacterial cells. The progeny of the phage will attack other cells and the cycle will be repeated.

In the lysogenic cycle, the phage does not kil! the bacteria but its DNA becomes integrated with the bacterial genome and replicate along with it, causing no harm to the host cell. In this cycle, the temperate phage enters into a symbiotic relationship with the host cells without killing them. The integrated phage is called prophage. The integrated prophage confer some new properties on the lysogenic bacteria.

Q. 8. Match column A with column B

Different periods	Phases of phage multiplication
(a) Eclipse period	(i) Interval between multiplication of bacteriophage and first release of infectious phage particle by bacterial lysis
(b) Latent period	(ii) Interval between entry of phage nucleic acid into bacteria and appearance of first intracellular phage particles
(c) Rise period	(iii) Average yield of progeny phage per infected bacterium
(d) Burst size	(iv) Period during which extra cellular number of infectious phages increase until it reached a constant titre at the end of multiplication cycle.

Ans. (a) (ii), (b) (i), (c) (iv), (d) (iii)

Q. 9. How can *E.coli* bacteriophage be isolated from a sample of sewage water?

Ans. Bacteriophages are normally present in situations where bacteria are found. They are present in intestinal tracts of man and animals, faecal samples and sewage water. For isolation of *E.coli* phage from sewage water, the sample is centrifuges at 2500 RPM for about 15 min. to sediment bacteria, dirt and other course particles. The supernatant is collected in a separate tube. In a flask containing 20 ml of nutrient broth, 1 ml of *E.coli* culture and 1 ml of supernatant fluid are added. The flask is incubated at 37°C for 8-10 hours. A portion of broth culture from the flask is centrifuged and supernatant is filtered through a glass filter. The filtrate is likely to contain *E.coli* phage. Finally add 0.1 ml of *E.coli* culture and 0.2 ml of filtrate in a tube containing 10 ml broth. The tube is incubated at 37°C and observed frequently whether or not any turbidity develops in the tube. Absence of turbidity indicates presence of *E.coli* phage in the fluid.

Q. 10. How can bacteriophages be titrated?

Ans. Ten fold dilutions of the phage is prepared in nutrient broth. Thick plates of nutrient agar are prepared and allowed to dry. The plates are marked in 4-8 equal parts. Each marked area in the plate is inoculated with a loopful of broth culture of the organism. The inoculated area should be allowed to dry, and then a loopful of diluted phage is added on cultured area. The plates are incubated at 37°C over night. The highest dilution which produces confluent lysis of bacteria is noted. This is called routine test dilution (RTD) of the phage and is generally used for bacterial typing.

Q. 11. Write short notes on bacterial phage typing.

Ans. Most bacteria are susceptible to specific phages. Some phages possess, wide host range covering many bacterial genera, while others have narrow host range limited to specific genus or species. There is a *Salmonella* genus specific bacteriophage. Gamma phage lyses all members of *B. anthracis* and Tb phage lyses all members of *Br. abortus*. TOX + phage is specific to *C. diphtheriae*. Most important application of phage typing is for intra-species typing as is the case with staphylococci. Based on International basic set of phages (1970), bovine strains of staphylococci fall into following phage groups:

Phage group	Set of phages
I	29, 52A
II	3A, 116
III	6, 42E, 53, 75, 84
IV	42D, 102, 107, 117

Another significance of bacterial phage typing is investigation of epidemic diseases. The isolation of specific phage types from epidemic areas and from the suspected source of infection will confirm the source of the disease.

Q. 13. Find out the wrong match:

Column A	Column B
(a) Bacteriophage $\phi \times 174$	(i) *E.coli*
(b) Bacteriophage P22	(ii) *Salmonella*
(c) Bacteriophage PM2	(iii) *Pseudomonas*
(d) Bacteriophage SPO 1	(iv) *Corynebacterium*
(e) Bacteriophage Lamda	(v) *E.coli*
(f) Bacteriophage T2	(vi) *E.coli*

Ans. (d) (iv)

Q. 14.

Column A	Column B
Nature of genome	Bacteriophage
(a) SS, DNA, Circular	(i) fd phage of *E.coli*
(b) DS, DNA	(ii) T1 phage of *E.coli*
(c) SS, RNA	(iii) f2 phage of *E.coli*
(d) DS, DNA, Circular	(iv) PM2 phage of *Pseudomonas*
(e) SS, RNA	(v) T7 phage of *E.coli*

Ans. (e) (v)

4

Classification and Nomenclature of Viruses

Q. 1. Why viral classification, in comparison to bacterial classification, took such a long time, to evolve when some of the viruses were discovered as early as in late 19th century?

Ans. Since viruses, are ultramicroscopic and unable to grow in artificial media, it took a long time to study most of their characteristics which were necessary for their classification. In the last decade of 19th century, Iwanowski (1892) and Loeffler and Frosch (1898) discovered filterable agents of tobacco mosaic disease and foot and mouth disease respectively. Since then, many diseases of animals and plants were discovered by demonstration of filterability of their aetiological agents. Twort (1915) and d'Herelle (1917) discovered filterable agents called bacteriophages which caused lysis of bacteria. Elford (1931) prepared gradocol membrane filters of known porosity which greatly helped to find out the size of newly isolated viruses. Few years later, Ruska and Mortom (1937) invented electron microscope which facilitated the study of shape, size and internal structures of the viruses. Another important discovery was made by Woodruff and Goodpasture (1931), who demonstrated the growth of fowl pox virus on chorioallantoic membrane of embryonated chicken eggs. Subsequently, many more viruses were grown by various other routes in embryonated eggs. Enders, Weller and Robbins (1949) propagated poliomyelitis virus in cell culture system which paved the way for growing other viruses in this system. The above discoveries facilitated the study of various properties, which were then helpful in the classification of viruses.

Q. 2. How were viruses named before their taxonomic classification?

Ans. Before taxonomic classification, viruses were known on the basis of the following systems:

(1) On the basis of their affinity to grow in certain organs or systems of the body. The examples are—dermotropic viruses (e.g. pox viruses), neurotropic viruses (e.g. rabies virus), pneumotropic viruses (e.g. influenza virus) and viscerotropic viruses (e.g. rinderpest virus, Ranikhet disease virus).

(2) Geographical location of isolation e.g. Ranikhet disease virus.

(3) By the name of the animal species affected by the virus e.g. swine fever virus.

(4) By the name of the person who first isolated the virus and studied the disease e.g. Rous Sarcoma virus, Rubarth disease virus.

(5) By clinical symptoms and organs affected e.g. foot & mouth disease virus.

(6) By the mode of transmission e.g. viruses transmitted by arthropods.

The above systems of naming were not satisfactory as in some cases, the same virus isolated from two different geographical locations was named differently which created confusion one such example is Ranikhet disease virus isolated in India and Newcastle disease virus isolated in Britain.

Q. 3. Briefly mention some early attempts to classify viruses on the basis of Linnean Binomial system.

Ans. Early attempts to classify viruses on Binomial system were made by the following microbiologists and research workers:

(1) Holmes (1948). Order Virales. In Bergey's Manual of Determinative Bacteriology, 6th edition.

(2) Casals and Reeves (1959). Arthropod borne animal viruses. In Rivers and Horsfall, Viral and Rickettsial infections of man, 3rd edition.

(3) Andrewes (1962). Classification of viruses of vertebrates. In Advances in Virus Research. 9:271-296.

(4) Andrewes (1964). Classification of viruses of vertebrates. In Taxonomic book: Viruses of vertebrates.

(5) Wilner (1964). A review: In a classification of major groups of human and lower animal viruses, 2nd edition.

(6) Cabasso (1965). Classification based on type of nucleic acid, size, symmetry, capsomers, envelope, sensitivity to ether, pH, antigenicity etc. Published by Lederle Laboratories, Pearl River, N.Y.

Q. 4. What physico-chemical and structural properties of viruses are used for their classification?

Ans. The following properties are used in the classification of viruses.

(a) DNA or RNA type of nucleic acid
(b) Size and shape of virus
(c) Type of symmetry of capsid
(d) No. of capsomers in capsid of icosahedral symmetry
(e) Presence or absence of envelope
(f) Presence or absence of transcriptase enzyme
(g) Replication in nucleus or cytoplasm
(h) Nature of genome i.e. whether nucleic acid is double stranded or single stranded, circular or linear, strands segmented or nonsegmented, size of strands, and plus or minus (–) sense in single stranded nucleic acid.

Some other useful characteristics are sensitivity to ether or chloroform and stability at pH 3.0 for 30 min. Antigenic relationship is important to subdivide closely related viruses within a recognised group.

Q. 5. What are the rules and guide lines on Taxonomy and Nomenclature of viruses at International level?

Ans. The International Committee on Taxonomy and Nomenclature of viruses has systematically established the classification of viruses into families, subfamilies and genera. The Committee has adopted binomial system of naming viruses. The suffix of virus families, subfamilies and genera are *viridae*, *virinae*, and *virus* respectively. The prefix may be another latin word. Latinized family, subfamily and generic names are written in italics. The vernacular terms derived from them are written in roman letters. For species, generally vernacular terms rather than latinized binomials are used e.g. foot and mouth disease virus.

Q. 6. Give a short description of DNA and RNA virus families with names of their genera.

Ans.

DNA Virus Families

1. Family *Papovaviridae*: These are small 45-55 nm sized, non-enveloped, double stranded DNA viruses with icosahedral capsid and 72 capsomers.

   Genera: 1. *Papilloma* 2. *Polyoma*

2. Family *Adenoviridae*: The viruses are medium sized, non-enveloped, double stranded, with icosahedral capsid and 252 capsomers. The nucleic acid in DNA type.

Genera: 1. *Mastadenovirus* (mammalian adenoviruses)
2. *Aviadenovirus* (avian adenoviruses)

3. Family *Herpesviridae*: These are 150-170 nm sized, enveloped, icosahedral capsid with 162 capsomers, double stranded DNA viruses.
   Subfamily: 1. *Alphaherpesvirinae*
   2. *Betaherpesvirinae*
   Genus: *Cytomegalovirus*
   3. *Gammaherpesvirinae*
   Genus: *Lymphocryptovirus*
4. Family *Poxviridae*: Large, enveloped double stranded DNA viruses with complex capsid.
   Subfamily 1. *Chordopoxvirinae*
   Genera: 1. *Orthopoxvirus* 2. *Capripoxvirus*
   3. *Suipoxvirus* 4. *Parapoxvirus*
   5. *Leporipoxvirus* 6. *Avipoxvirus*
   2. *Entomopoxvirinae*—Poxviruses of insects
5. *Family Iridoviridae*: These fairly large (125-300 nm), enveloped, double stranded DNA viruses with icosahedral capsid and 1892 capsomers.
   Genera: 1. *Ranavirus* 2. *Lymphocystivirus*
   3. *Iridovirus*
   African swine fever virus is unclassified.
6. Family *Parvoviridae*: These are small about 20 nm sized single stranded DNA nonenveloped viruses with icosahedral capsid and 32 capsomers.
   Genera: 1. *Parvovirus* 2. *Dependovirus*
   3. *Densovirus*
7. Family *Hepadnaviridae*: These are small about 42-45 nm sized double stranded enveloped DNA viruses with icosahedral capsid. These viruses have reverse transcriptase enzyme.
   Genus: 1. *Hepadnavirus*

RNA Virus Families

1. Family *Picornaviridae*: These are small 20-30 nm sized single stranded, nonenveloped, RNA viruses with icosahedral capsid and 60 capsomers.
   Genera: 1. *Enterovirus* 2. *Rhinovirus*
   3. *Cardiovirus* 4. *Aphthovirus*
   5. *Hepatovirus*
2. *Family Caliciviridae*: These are small viruses of 30-40 nm size,

single stranded RNA, nonenveloped with icosahedral capsid and 32 capsomers.
Genus: *Calicivirus*

3. Family *Togaviridae*: These are arthropod borne, single stranded RNA viruses, size 60-70 nm, enveloped, icosahedral capsid with 60 capsomers. Formerly these viruses were classified as group A arboviruses.
   Genera: 1. *Alphavirus* 2. *Rubivirus*
4. Family *Flaviviridae*: These are also arthropod borne, single stranded RNA viruses with a size of 40-50 nm, enveloped, icosahedral capsid. Formerly they were known as group B arboviruses.
   Genera: 1. *Flavivirus* 2. *Pestivirus*
   3. *Hepatovirus* (proposed)
5. Family *Reoviridae*: These are 60-80 nm sized double stranded RNA viruses. They are nonenveloped with icosahedral capsid and 32/92 capsomers.
   Genera: 1. *Orthoreovirus* 2. *Orbivirus*
   3. *Rotavirus*
6. Family *Birnaviridae*: These are double stranded RNA viruses of about 60 nm size, nonenveloped with icosahedral capsid and 32 capsomers.
   Genus: *Birnavirus*
7. Family *Coronaviridae*: These are 75-160 nm sized single stranded RNA viruses, enveloped with helical symmetry.
   Genus: *Coronavirus*
8. Family *Orthomyxoviridae*: These are medium 80-120 nm sized single stranded RNA viruses. They are enveloped with helical casid symmetry and haemagglutinate red blood cells.
   Genera: 1. *Influenzavirus* A and B
   2. *Influenzavirus* C
9. Family *Paramyxoviridae*: They are single stranded RNA viruses of pleomorphic shape and size varying from 150-300 nm, enveloped with helical capsid symmetry. Some of these viruses also haemogglutinate red blood cells.
   Genera: 1. *Paramyxovirus* 2. *Morbillivirus*
   3. *Pneumovirus*
10. Family *Rhabdoviridae*: They are single stranded bullet shaped RNA viruses measuring about 130 × 70 nm. They are enveloped and have helical capsid symmetry.
    Genera: 1. *Vesiculovirus* 2. *Lyssavirus*

11. Family *Arinaviridae*: These are single stranded, enveloped RNA viruses spherical and pleomorphic generally rodent parasites but capable of infecting man causing severe haemorrhagic illness.
    Genus: *Arinavirus*
12. Family *Bunyaviridae*: These are single stranded RNA viruses measuring 90-120 nm. They are enveloped and have helical capsid symmetry. These viruses are arthropod borne, some belonging to former group C arboviruses.
    Genera: 1. *Bunyavirus* 2. *Phlebovirus* 3. *Nairovirus* 4. *Hantavirus*
13. Family *Retroviridae*: These are RNA tumour viruses and related agents, single stranded with reverse transcriptase enzyme, and enveloped icosahedral capsid symmetry.
    These are RNA tumour viruses and related agents, single stranded with reverse transcriptas enzyme and enveloped icosahedral capsid symmetry.
    Subfamily: 1. *Oncovirinae*: This has RNA tumour group
    Genus: 1. *Oncovirus* type A
    2. *Oncovirus* type B
    3. *Oncovirus* type C
    4. *Oncovirus* type D
    Subfamily: 2. *Lentivirinae*
    Genus: *Lentivirus*
    Subfamily: 3. *Spumavirinae*
    Genus: *Spumavirus*

Other viruses

Filoviridae: These are single stranded RNA viruses, measuring 790-970 × 80 nm, enveloped with helical capsid.
Genus: *Filovirus*: Marburg, Ebola and Reston viruses belong to this family.

Toroviridae:These are single stranded RNA viruses, measuring 35-170 nm. They are also enveloped and have helical symmetry. The representative members of this family are Berne and Breda viruses.

Circoviridae: These are DNA viruses of 15-17 nm (porcine) and 24 nm (chicken) size. Porcine viruses are of double stranded and chicken viruses single stranded. Capsid symmetry is icosahedral type.

Astroviruses: These are single stranded RNA viruses measuring about 27-30 nm. They were isolates in the faeces of children with diarrhoea. They are not yet classified.

Arteriviruses: These are single stranded RNA viruses measuring 60-70 nm. They have icosahedral capsid. Previously they were classified under *Togaviridae* family but later on withdrawn from that family. Presently they are unclassified. Equine arteritis virus is one of these viruses and caused respiratory and generalized infection in equines.

Subacute Spongiform Encephalopathy agents: These are agents which cause degenerative neurological diseases like scrapie disease of sheep and goats, Kuru and Creutzfeldt–Jacob diseases of human beings and bovine spongiform encephalopathy. The causative agents appears to be single stranded RNA about 30-50 nm in size.

Q. 7. Give important properties of DNA and RNA virus families in a tabular form.

Ans. These have been given in Table 4.1

Table 4.1: DNA and RNA virus families showing important properties

Virus Family	Diameter (nm)	Envelope	Capsid	No. of capsomers	Trans-criptase	Nature of genome
			DNA virus families			Kb
1. *Papovaviridae*	45-55	–	Icosahedral	72	–	DS, C, NS, 5-8
2. *Adenoviridae*	70-80	–	Icosahedral	252	–	DS, L, NS, 30-37
3. *Herpesviridae*	150-170	+	Icosahedral	162	–	DS, L, NS, 120-220
4. *Poxviridae*	240-400	+	Complex	–	+	DS, L, NS, 130-230
5. *Iridoviridae*	125-300	+	Icosahedral	1892	+	DS, L, NS, 170-190
6. *Parvoviridae*	20	–	Icosahedral	32	–	SS, L, NS (–), 5.2
7. *Hepadnaviridae*	42-45	+	Icosahedral	?	+ (reverse)	DS, C, NS (–), 3-3.2
			RNA virus families			
1. *Picornaviridae*	20-30	–	Icosahedral	60	–	SS, L, NS, (+), 7-8
2. *Caliciviridae*	30-40	–	Icosahedral	32	–	SS, L, NS, (+), 7.9
3. *Togaviridae*	60-70	+	Icosahedral	60	–	SS, L, NS, (+), 12
4. *Flayiviridae*	40-50	+	Icosahedral	?	–	SS, L, NS, (+), 10
5. *Reoviridae*	60-80	–	Icosahedral	32/92	+	DS, L, S10-12,18-27
6. *Birnaviridae*	60	–	Icosahedral	32	+	DS, L, S2, 7
7. *Coronaviridae*	75-160	+	Helical		–	SS, L, NS, (+), 27-33
8. *Orthomyxoviridae*	80-120	+	Helical		+	SS, L, S-8 (–), 13.6
9. *Paramyxoviridae*	150-300	+	Helical		+	SS, L, NS, (–), 18-20
10. *Rhabdoviridae*	180 × 70	+	Helical		+	SS, L, NS, (–), 13-16
11. *Arenaviridae*	110-130	+	Helical		+	SS, L, S2, (–), 10-14
12. *Bunyaviridae*	90-120	+	Helical		+	SS, L, S3, (–), 13-21
13. *Retroviridae*	80-100	+	Icosahedral		+ (reverse)	SS, L, S3, (+), 7-10

(Contd.)

Virus Family	Diameter (nm)	Envelope	Capsid	No. of capsomers	Trans-criptase	Nature of genome
			Other Viruses			
1. *Filoviridae*	790-970 × 80	+	Helical		+	SS, L, NS, (–), 12.7
2. *Toroviridae*	35-170	+	Helical		–	SS, L, NS, (+), 20
3. *Circoviridae*	15-17 (porcine)		Icosahedral		–	DS, C, NS, 1.76
	24 – (chicken)		Icosahedral		–	SS, C, NS, 2.12
4. Astroviruses	27-30 (RNA)		?		–	SS, L, NS, (+), 7.2
5. Arteriviruses	60-70 (RNA)		Icosahedral		–	SS, L, NS, (+), 12
6. Deltavirus	35-37 (RNA)		?		–	SS, C, NS, 1.7

For genome: DS = double stranded, SS = single stranded, C = circular, L = linear, S = segmented, NS = nonsegmented, Plus (+) or minus (–) = positive or negative strands.

5

Cultivation, Purification and Concentration of Viruses

Q. 1. Name different host systems where viruses can be cultivated

Ans. Viruses can be cultivated in the following host systems:

1. Cell culture system
2. Embryonated eggs (generally chicken eggs)
3. Susceptible animals (including laboratory animals)

Q. 2. Why is it necessary to grow viruses in animals?

Ans. Even though, the viruses can be cultivated in cell cultures or embryonated eggs, some times it becomes necessary to inject viruses in animals due to following reasons:

1. To study pathogenesis and clinical symptoms of the virus.
2. To study immune response.
3. To produce hyperimmune serum.
4. To diagnose the disease.
5. Some viruses will grow only in natural hosts.

Q. 3. Why animals are not preferred for virus cultivation?

Ans. Animals are not preferred to grow viruses because:

1. They are expensive in comperison to eggs and cell cultures.
2. Limitations of space and cages to keep them.
3. Possibility of cross infection from one animal to another and man.
4. Animals may carry latent infections and antibodies.

Q. 4. Name laboratory animals which can be used for virus cultivation.

Ans. Laboratory animals in which viruses can be cultivated are: Rabbits, guinea pigs, mice, rats, hamsters, dogs, monkeys, and chickens.

Q. 5. Name different routes of virus inoculation in animals.

Ans. Different routes of inoculation are: Intramuscular (I/M), subcutaneous (S/C), intravenous (I/V), intraperitoneal (I/P), intracerebral (I/C), and intranasal (I/N).

Q. 6. What are the doses of virus inoculum by I/C route in laboratory animals?

Ans. The dose of virus inoculum in laboratory animals are: Rabbits - 0.25 ml, guinea pigs - 0.1 ml, mice suckling - 0.01 ml, adults - 0.03 ml, hamsters - 0.1 ml, chickens - day old 0.05 ml, adults 0.1 ml, monkeys-small 0.5 ml, large 1-2 ml.

Q. 7. Name animals which are generally used for antisera production

Ans. For experimental work/laboratory studies, antisera are produced in rabbits, chickens or even in mice and guinea pigs. For large scale production of antisera, generally horses are used.

Q. 8. For what type of studies large scale production of viruses are needed?

Ans. Large scale production of viruses are needed to:

(a) Study optimum conditions for growth of the viruses
(b) Find out the effects of physical and chemical agents
(c) Conduct serological tests
(d) Conduct pathogenic tests in animals
(e) Maintain stock cultures.
(f) Produce vaccines.
(g) Find out immunological properties.

Q. 9. Name different routes of virus inoculation in embryonated eggs.

Ans. Different routes of virus inoculation in eggs are:

(a) Chorioallantoic membrane (CAM) route
(b) Allantoic cavity route
(c) Yolk sac route
(d) Amniotic cavity route
(e) Intravenous route (not used frequently)

Q. 10. What is the age of embryonated chicken eggs when they are used for virus inoculation by different routes?

Ans. The age of embryonated chicken eggs by different routes of inoculation are:

(a) Yolk sac route – 7 days
(b) Allantoic cavity route – 9 to 12 days

(c) Chorioallantoic membrane route – 10 to 12 days
(d) Amniotic cavity route – 7 to 15 days
(e) Intravenous route – 10 to 15 days
(f) Intracerebral route – 8 to 14 days

Q. 11. Name doses of virus inoculum in chicken embryos by different routes.

Ans. The doses of virus inoculum in chicken embryos are:
(a) Allantoic cavity route – 0.1 to 0.2 ml
(b) Amniotic cavity route – 0.1 to 0.2 ml
(c) Chorioallantoic membrane route – 0.1 to 0.5 ml
(d) Yolk sac route – 0.2 to 1 ml
(e) Intravenous route – 0.02 to 0.05 ml
(f) Intracerebral route – 0.01 to 0.02 ml

Q. 12. What are the advantages of using cell cultures for virus cultivation?

Ans. The advantages of cultivation of viruses in cell cultures are:
(a) Economy
(b) Cells are free from latent infections.
(c) Free from antibodies
(d) Easy to handle in laboratories
(e) Majority of viruses can be grown in cell cultures
(f) Some viruses can be identified by specific cytopathic effects (CPE).
(g) Large quantity of virus can be grown in cell cultures

Q. 13. Name different cell culture types.

Ans. Cell culture types are:
(a) Primary cell cultures
(b) Diploid cell cultures
(c) Continuous cells lines

Q. 14. Select correct answer:

Primary cell cultures contain:
(a) Single cell type
(b) Several cell types
(c) Cells with diploid chromosome numbers
(d) Virus transformed cell types

Ans. (b)

Q. 15. Give examples of:
(a) Commonly used tissues for primary cell cultures
(b) Diploid cell strains
(c) Continuous cell lines

Ans. (a) The commonly used primary cell cultures are:
Calf: Kidneys, testes and thyroid.
Kid: Kidneys and testes
Lamb: Kidneys and testes
Piglet: Kidneys and testes
Dog pup: Kidneys
Young rabbit: Kidneys, testes, and embryos
Chicken: Kidneys and embryos

(b) WI-26 (Wistar strain of human embryo lung)

(c) Hela (from carcinoma of human cervix)
BHK_{21} (baby hamster kidney)
Vero cell line (African Vervet monkey kidney)
PK_{15} cell line (pig kidney)

Q. 16. Write short notes on:
(a) Primary cell cultures (b) Diploid cell cultures
(c) Continuous cell lines

Ans. (a) *Primary cell cultures:* The cells are initiated from tissues of embryos and young animals. Initially, cultures will have epithelial and fibroblastic cells but after few passages, fibroblasts will predominate. The cells can be serially transferred upto 5-10 divisions of culture.

(b) *Diploid cell cultures:* These are serially propagated primary cell cultures which retain a normal set of chromosomes. The number of serial cell transfers depends on the type of tissues and species of animals used.

(c) *Continuous cell lines:* There are capable of indefinite cell divisions. The cells have abnormal chromosome numbers and morphology.

Q. 17. Briefly describe the preparation of monolayer cell cultures.

Ans. (a) Remove the organ (generally kidneys or testes) aseptically from a freshly killed young animal in a petridish, containing sufficient balanced salt solution, (BSS).

(b) Cut the organ in small pieces and mince thoroughly with scissors.

(c) Wash the minced tissue 2 to 3 times with cold BSS to remove blood cells if any and transfer the same in an Erlenmeyer flask, containing a teflon covered magnetic bar.

(d) Add sufficient quantity of prewarmed 0.25% trypsin in BSS in a flask. Place the flask on a magnetic stirrer for about 1 hour at room temperature. This will disperse the cells into single cell suspension.

(e) Filter cells through cheese cloth and centrifuge them in a refrigerated centrifuge for about 10 min. at 1500 RPM. Wash the cells twice in cold BSS to remove traces of trypsin.

(f) Dilute the cells in lactalbumin hydrolysate growth medium in a suitable strength and dispense in tubes or prescription bottles. Incubate the tubes or bottles at 37°C in proper humidity for 3-4 days for monolayer preparations. Tubes should be incubated in an inclined position with an angle of 5-10 degrees.

Q. 18. What is meant by blind passages of a suspected virus inoculum, in embryonated eggs or cell cultures?

Ans. When an inoculum is suspected of carrying a virus, it is inoculated in chicken embryos or cell cultures and if it does not give any sign of infection in 1st or 2nd inoculation, it is given a few more successive serial blind passages before it is discarded as negative. Some viruses from a new host show signs of infection only after a few blind passages.

Q. 19. Briefly describe how virus growth in cell cultures can be detected?

Ans. The growth of viruses in cell cultures can be detected by:

(a) *Cytopathic effects (CPE):* This can be observed by low power microscopic examination.

(b) *Metabolic inhibition:* In normal cell cultures, the medium turns acidic due to cellular metabolism and detected by change of colour of the medium (the medium has phenol red indicator). when viruses grow in cell cultures, cell metabolism is inhibited and there will be no acid production and colour change in the medium.

(c) *Haemadsorption:* When haemagglutinating viruses are grown in cell cultures, they are detected by adsorption on the surface of red blood cells.

(d) *Transformation:* Tumour forming viruses induce cell transformation in susceptible cells and the growth appears in a piled up fashion which will look like microtumours under microscope.

(e) *Immunofluorescence:* Cells from virus infected cultures, can be stained by fluorescent conjugated antiserum and examined under UV microscope for presence of viral antigen.

Q. 20. What is the percentage of the following items in cell culture medium?

(a) Phenol red indicator (b) Trypsin solution

(c) Serum in growth medium (d) Serum in maintenance medium

(e) Penicillin (f) Streptomycin

(g) Mycostatin

Ans. (a) 0.5%; (b) 0.25%; (c) 10%;
(d) 2%; (e) 1000 units/ml; (f) 1000 mg/mı;
(g) 50 units/ml

Select correct answer:

Q. 21. Clear areas of CPE due to virus multiplication under agar overlay cell culture is known as:
(a) Pock (b) Plaque (c) Focal CPE

Ans. (b)

Q. 22. Ultrasonic waves release the virus from infected cells by:
(a) Dissolving the cell membrane
(b) Shrinking the cells
(c) Disrupting the cells

Ans. (c)

Q. 23. What items are required to prepare chicken embryo fibroblast cell culture?

Ans. (a) Nine to ten day old embryonated chicken eggs
(b) Hank's BSS
(c) Calf serum
(d) 0.25% trypsin
(e) Lactalbumin hydrolysate
(f) Glassware
(g) Dissecting instruments
(h) Flask containing magnetic bar and magnetic stirrer
(i) Incubator
(j) Centrifuge

Q. 24. Select true or false statements:
(a) Cell cultures and tissue explants are different systems of *invitro* cell growth.
(b) Blood serum in growth and maintenance media of cell cultures are of the same percentage.
(c) For cell culture work, blood serum from adult animals is preferred over foetus or very young animals.
(d) Tissues for cell culture work are preferred to isolate viruses infecting the animal species in question.

Ans. (a) True, (b) False, (c) False, (d) True

Q. 25. Fill in the blanks:
(a) Cell cultures can be grown in the form of .... and ....
(b) Cell lines are not generally used for virus growth for vaccine production because they are mostly derived from .... tissues.
(c) Primary purification of viruses can be made by ....

(d) Differential centrifugation is used to separate .... from viruses.

Ans. (a) monolayers, suspensions (b) malignant
(c) differential centrifugation (d) cell debris

Q. 26. Describe the methods of purification and concentration of virus.

Ans. There are several methods of purification and concentration of viruses. Methods which are commonly used are mentioned below:

(1) After propagating the viruses in eggs, cell cultures etc. the coarse material and cell debris is to be removed first by low speed centrifugation. For doing this, the tissue is first grounded in phosphate buffer solution and then centrifuged at about 4000 RPM for 15-20 min. at low temp. The course material is deposited at the bottom of the tube. The supernatant containing the virus is removed for further purification by precipitation.
The partially purified viral material obtained after low centrifugation is precipitated with salts like ammonium sulphate or ethyl or methyl alcohol. For precipitating the material with ammonium sulphate, it is mixed with equal quantity of saturated ammonium sulphate. The mixture is frequently stirred and allowed to stand for some time at room temp. The precipitate formed in the tube is centrifuged at 4000 RPM for 15 min. The precipitate containing the virus is retained and the supernatant discarded. The precipitate is again dissolved in 1/8th to 1/10th of original volume and reprecipitated with equal amount of saturated ammonium sulphate. The precipitate thus formed is again centrifuged and retained after discarding the supernatant. The precipitate is dissolved in minimum amount of phosphate buffer solution. The ammonium sulphate ions are now removed from the precipitate after keeping it in a semipermeable dialysis tube which is suspended in a beaker containing distilled water. The distilled water is changed frequently. The material thus obtained is reasonably rich and concentrated in virus.

(2) The viral suspension can also get rid of extraneous protein and impurities after digestion with suitable enzymes like trypsin and then ultracentrifuged to obtain purified virus, at low temp. For ultracentrifugation, a gravity of 50,000 to 100,000 is required to obtain a pellet of viral material.

(3) Some viruses having the property of haemagglutination and elution at suitable temp. and pH can be purified and concentrated in a small quantity.

Q. 27. Describe the methods of viral assays.

Ans. Viral assays can be done by the following methods:

1. By counting viral particles by:
   (a) *Electron microscopy:* The dispersed and diluted virus suspension in a measured quantity is mixed with known number of latex particles and examined under electron microscope. The ratio between latex particles and virus particles will give indication of virus count.
   (b) *Haemagglutination titre:* The highest dilution of virus suspension in a given volume, which produces agglutination of RBCs will give haemagglutination titre of the virus. This is not a very sensitive indicator of virus titration.
2. By measurement of infectivity. This is done by:
   (a) *Quantitative infectivity assay:* This can be done by counting pock lesions on CAM, by counting plaques on monolayer cell cultures and by counting transformation of cells in oncogenic viruses.
   (b) *Quantal assay:* This method indicates presence or absence of infectious particles and will indicate, infective dose (ID_{50}), lethal dose$_{50}$ (LD_{50}), tissue culture infective dose$_{50}$ ($TCID_{50}$) etc. The end point indicates the highest dilution of the inoculum which will produce effect in 50% animals, eggs or cell culture tubes. The 50% end point is calculated by statistical method using Reed and Muench formula.

6

Viral Genetics

Before going into the details of viral genetics and mutation, it is necessary to understand the chemical and physical structures of nucleic acids which carry genetic information in all living beings including the viruses. The nucleic acids are of two types i.e. deoxyribonucleic acid (DNA) and ribonucleic acid (RNA).

Q. 1. Briefly describe the chemical composition of deoxyribonucleic and ribonucleic acids.

Ans. There are two types of nucleic acids, one is known as deoxyribonucleic acid (DNA) and the other ribonucleic acid (RNA). Nucleic acid molecules are long chain polynucleotides composed of monomeric units called nucleotides. Each nucleotide consists of a nitrogen base, a sugar and a phosphoric acid. A nucleotide without phosphoric acid is known as nucleoside., which only has a nitrogen base and a sugar. In case of DNA the bases are adenine, guanine, cytosine and thymine. While in case of RNA the bases are adenine, guanine, cytosine and uracil. In case of DNA the sugar is deoxyribose and in RNA it is ribose. DNA is a double molecule with one chain twined around the other in helical fashion. RNA is a single stranded molecule. The chemical relationships between DNA and RNA are summarised below in Table 6.1.

Table 6.1: Showing nitrogen bases, nucleosides and nucleotides of DNA and RNA.

DNA	RNA
1. Nitrogen bases:	
Purine	
Adenine	Adenine
Guanine	Guanine

(Contd.)

DNA	RNA
Pyrimidine	
Cytosine	Cytosine
Thymine	Uracil
2. Nucleosides (Nitrogen base + sugar):	
Deoxyadenosine	Adenosine
Deoxyguanosine	Guanosine
Deoxycytidine	Cytidine
Deoxythymidine	Uridine
3. Nucleotides (Nitrogen base + sugar + phosphoric acid):	
Deoxyriboadenylic acid	Adenylic acid
Deoxyriboguanylic acid	Guanylic acid
Deoxyribocytidylic acid	Cytidylic acid
Deoxyribothymidylic acid	Uridylic acid

Q. 2. Draw structural formulae of Purines and Pyrimidines.

Ans. Purines

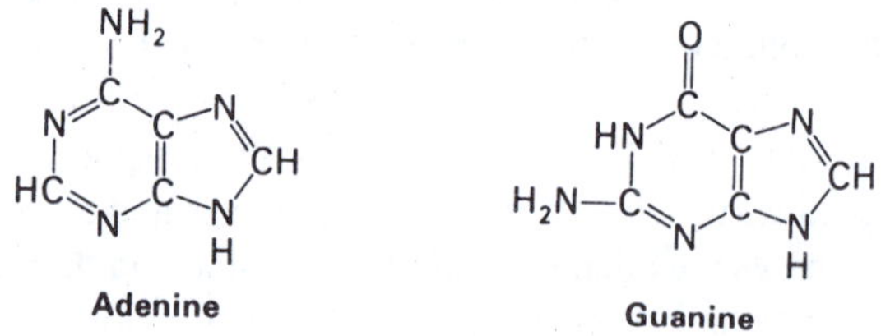

Pyrimidines

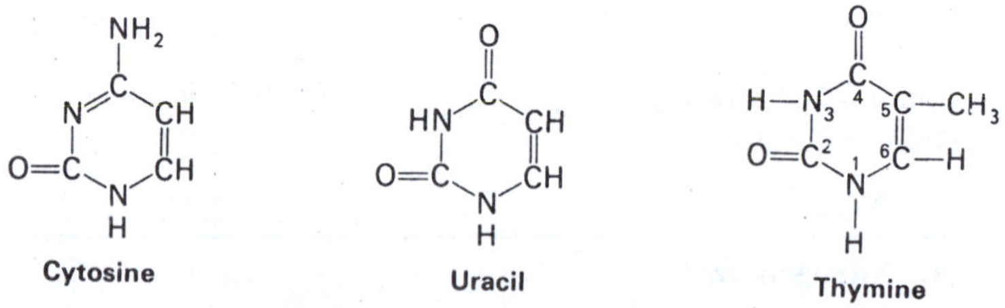

Fig. 6.1. Structures of purines and pyrimidines

Q. 3. Draw a schematic diagram of double stranded DNA and single stranded RNA.

Ans. The schematic diagrams of DNA and RNA are shown in figures 6.2 and 6.3 respectively.

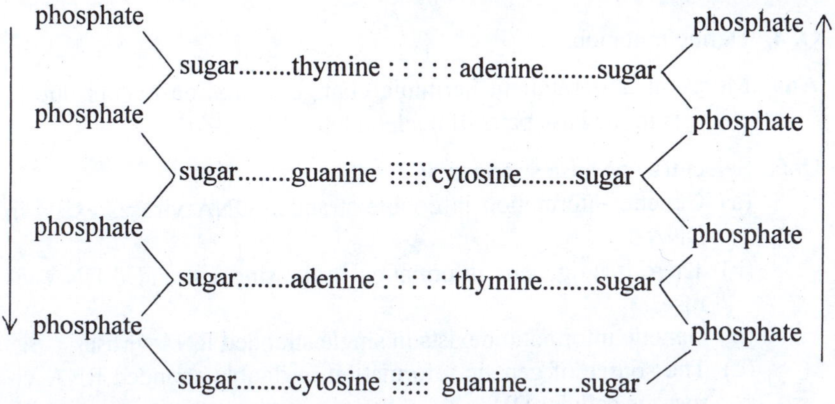

The two chains shown above are held together by hydrogen bonds. Thymine and adenine are held together by two hydrogen bonds and guanine and cytosine by three hydrogen bonds.

Fig. 6.2. Schematic diagram of DNA. (From Sagar, S. and Ryan, F.J. 1961, Cell Heredity. 1st Edition, John Wiley & Sons, Inc. New York)

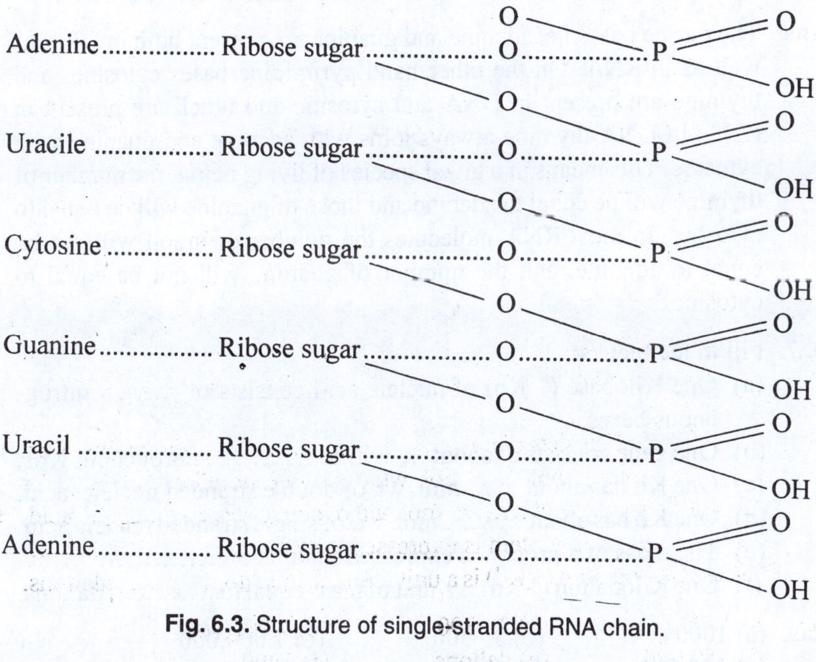

Fig. 6.3. Structure of single-stranded RNA chain.

Q. 4. Define mutation.

Ans. Mutation is permanent heritable change. Mutation occurs due to changes in the base pairs of nucleotides.

Q. 5. Select true or false statements:

(a) Genetic information in double stranded DNA viruses exists in DNA.
(b) There is no genetic information in the single stranded DNA viruses.
(c) Genetic information exists in single stranded RNA viruses.
(d) The source of genetic information in double stranded RNA viruses is cellular DNA.
(e) RNA viruses have higher rate of evolution than DNA viruses.
(f) The frequency of mutation in viruses is about 10^{-4} to 10^{-8} per nucleotide, per replication.
(g) On an average 1kd nucleic acid may constitute 1 gene and 1 gene code 1 protein.

Ans. (a) True, (b) False, (c) True, (d) False, (e) True, (f) True, (g) True.

Q. 6. What are the differences between the base pairs of DNA & RNA?

Ans. The purine bases i.e. adenine and guanine are present both in DNA as well as in RNA. On the other hand pyrimidine bases cytosine and thymine are present in DNA and cytosine and uracil are present in RNA. In DNA thymine always joins with adenine and guanine with cytosine. This means in a given species of living being, the number of thymine will be equal to adenine and those of guanine will be equal to cytosine. In most RNA molecules the number of uracil will not be equal to adenine, and the number of guanine will not be equal to cytosine..

Q. 7. Fill in the blanks:

(a) One Kilobase (1 Kb) of nucleic acid consists of .... nitrogenous bases.
(b) One gene consists of about .... to .... nitrogenous Kbs.
(c) One Kb has about ...... mol. wt. of double stranded nucleic acid.
(d) One Kb has about .... mol. wt. of single stranded nucleic acid.
(e) The mass of a protein is expressed in units of ....
(f) One Kilodalton (1 Kd) is a unit of mass equal to .... daltons.

Ans. (a) 1000 (b) 3, 300 (c) 7,000,000
(d) 350,000 (e) daltons (f) 1000

Q. 8. Name different types of mutations due to changes in the base pairs of nucleic acid.

Ans. The mutations due to changes in the base pairs of nucleic acid are of following two types.

(a) Point mutations (b) Frame shift mutations

(a) *Point mutations*: This type of mutations are due of substitution of one base or base pair by another base or base pair. This results in the change of nucleotide sequence without any change in the molecular size. Point mutations can be reverted by restoring the original sequence. Point mutation is again of two types. They are: (i) *Transition type* and (ii) *transversion type*.

(i) Transition type of point mutation occurs when there is substitution of one purine with another purine or one pyrimidine with another pyrimidine.

(ii) Transversion type of point mutation involves replacement of a purine by a pyrimidine or vice versa. As an example:

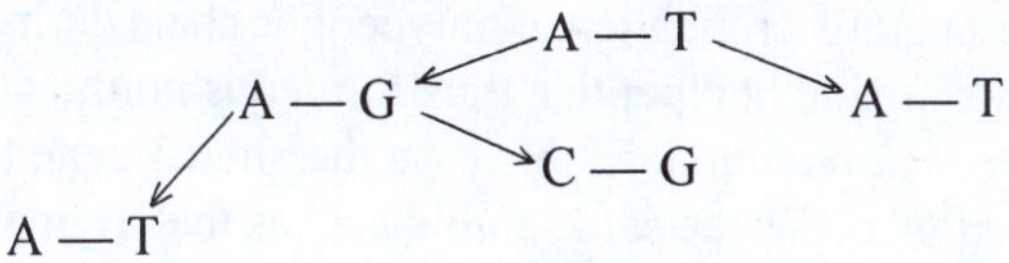

mutant

(b) *Frame shift mutations*: This type of mutation occur either by addition or deletion of one or more base pairs in a gene. This type of mutation results in changes in the base triplets (codon) of mRNA and consequently changes the coded amino acids. Frame shift mutations are again of two types. They are: (i) *Insertion type* and (ii) *Deletion type*.

(i) *Insertion type* of frame shift mutation: This type of mutation occurs when there is addition of one or more nucleotides in a gene.

(ii) *Deletion type* of frame shift mutation: In this type of mutation there is loss of one or more nucleotides in a gene. In this type of mutation, there is premature termination of amino acid sequence.

Q. 9. What is the rate of mutations in DNA and RNA viruses ?

Ans. Mutation rate in DNA viruses involving point mutations is about 10^{-8} to 10^{-11} per nucleotide (per base pair per replication) which is much less in comparison to RNA viruses. In DNA viruses, exonucleases correct errors during replication as it has proof reading activity. RNA viruses have no proof-reading mechanism in the absence of RNA exonucleases. Therefore point mutations are much higher in RNA viruses. The rate of point mutations is higher in bigger sized genomes. Most of these base substitutions are deletarious and genome containing them will be lost.

Q. 10. Describe different types of mutations based on nucleotide substitutions.

Ans. Different types of mutations based on nucleotide substitutions are:

(a) Missense mutation (b) Nonsense mutation
(c) Neutral mutation.

(a) *Missense mutation*: If this case the altered gene triplet produces codon in mRNA which codes for a different amino acids than those which are present in the normal polypeptide resulting in loss of protein function.

(b) *Nonsense mutation*: In this case the altered gene triplet produces a termination codon UAA, UAG or UGA in mRNA resulting in premature termination of polypeptide chain during translation. The incomplete polypeptide thus formed is nonfunctional.

(c) *Neutral mutation*: In this case the altered gene triplet, an mRNA codon, codes the same amino acid as the original codon due to its synonymity.

Q. 11. Name the type of interactions if a cell is infected simultaneously by two different viruses.

Ans. Infection of a cell by two different viruses may result in:

(a) Replication of both viruses independently
(b) Interference with growth of either or both viruses
(c) Complementation or enhancement of growth of one or both viruses
(d) Genetic recombination
(e) Phenotypic mixing
(f) Various combinations of above interactions

Q. 12 What are phenotypic and genotypic mixing?

Ans. *Phenotypic mixing*: When two different viruses multiply in a cell, some mixing may take place during assembly so that the genome of one virus is surrounded by the capsid of the other virus. This is a temporary variation as on subsequent passages the original capsid may be restored.

Genotypic mixing: This results from incorporation of more than one complete genome into a single virus particle. There is no recombination between different genomes of the viruses.

Q. 13. Write short notes on Genetic Recombination between two viruses.

Ans. When two different viruses simultaneously infect a cell, recombination may take place between nucleic acids of their progeny. The resulting recombination may be of the following three types:

(1) Intermolecular recombination (2) Reassortment
(3) Reactivation

(1) *Intermolecular Recombination*: This involves exchange of nucleic acid sequences between different but closely related viruses during replication. This may occur with all dsDNA viruses. Intramolecular recombination is also demonstrated in some RNA viruses. In some cases, recombination may take place between viral and cellular RNA and DNA.

(2) *Reassortment*: This type of recombination takes place in viruses that have segmented genomes irrespective of the fact whether they have ssRNA or dsRNA. In a cell infected with two related viruses, there is an exchange of segments of genome with the production of various stable reassortments. This type of recombination also occurs in nature.

(3) *Reactivation*: This type of recombination is of two types:

(a) *Multiplicity reactivation*: This term applies to the production of infectious virus by a cell, infected with two or more viruses of the same strain, each of which has suffered a lethal mutation in a different gene. UV-irradiated or chemically treated viruses used for vaccine production may lead to the production of infectious virus.

(b) *Cross reactivation*: This type of recombination occurs between an infectious virus and an inactivated virus of a related but distinguishable genotype.

Q. 14. Name different types of interactions between viral gene products:

Ans. Viral gene products are structural or enzyme proteins. The interaction between structural or enzyme proteins are:

(a) Complementation and (b) Transcaptidation

(a) *Complementation*: This means interaction between viral proteins in cells infected with two viruses which results in an increased yield of one or both viruses. In this case one or both viruses may be defective. In such cases one virus provides gene product which cannot be produced by the virus and allow the latter virus to replicate in mixed virus infected cells. This can occur between unrelated viruses also. The genotypes of one or both viruses may remain unchanged.

(b) *Transcaptidation*: Following mixed infection by two non-enveloped viruses, there is partial or complete exchange of capsids. This is known as transcaptidation. This is a phenotypic mixing. There is no involvement of genes of the viruses.

Q. 15. Define mutagens. Name important viral mutagens and their uses.

Ans. Mutagens are physical and chemical agents which act on viral nucleic acid and increase the frequency of mutations. To increase the frequency of mutations, viruses or their nucleic acids can be treated with UV or X-ray irradiation. They can also be treated with chemical agents like nitrous acid, nitrogen mustard, peroxides, hydroxylamine, nitrosoguanidine and base analogues of naturally occurring purines and pyrimidines like 5-fluorouracil or 5-bromodeoxyuridine. Base analogues can act only when virus is grown in their presence. Mutagens can be used beneficially in laboratories to study viral genetics. The mutation rate is greatly increased in their presence to select desired mutants.

Experimentally mutagenesis can be affected, at a selected site in a DNA molecule. This is done with the help of a suitable restriction endo-nuclease or exonuclease enzyme. These enzymes will expose a short single stranded region, which is mutagenized using a specific mutagen. The gap is then repaired with DNA polymerase and ligase enzymes.

Q. 16. Select correct answer:

Most efficient recombination among viruses takes place when viral genome consists of:

(a) Single molecule of single stranded RNA.
(b) Several molecules of single stranded RNA.
(c) Single molecule of double stranded RNA.
(d) Single molecule of single or double stranded DNA

Ans. (b)

Q. 17. The production of progeny virus that carries traits not found in either parents is due to:

(a) Interference
(b) Complementation
(c) Recombination

Ans. (c)

Q. 18. Write short notes on:

(a) Genetic engineering (b) Recombinant DNA technology

Ans. (a) *Genetic engineering*: Genetic engineering refers to the development of organisms with genetic structure altered by biochemical manipulations. This type of biochemical procedure is known as recombinant DNA technology. This technology involves the use of plasmids or bacterio-phages. This technology consists of isolating, purifying, and identifying genetic material from one source and then tailoring it for insertion into a new host and isolating a colony of cells with the desired new genes.

(b) *Recombinant DNA technology*: This technology employs *invitro* incorporation of segments of genetic material from one cell to another cell. This is accomplished with the help of two enzymes i.e. restriction enzyme and ligase enzyme. The restriction enzyme cuts the concerned nucleotide portion from the donor cell and the ligase enzyme joins this genetic material in the recipient cell. The genetic material from donor to recipient cell is carried through the vehicle of bacteriophage or bacterial plasmid.

Q. 19. Describe different types of mutations based on phenotypic expression.

Ans. Such types of mutants of animal viruses are:

(a) *Plaque mutants*: These plaque mutants in cell cultures are either resistant or sensitive to polysaccharide inhibitors in agar. Large size plaque mutants are produced by adeno and measles viruses. Small plaques of Western equine encephalitis (WEE) virus are dependent on bicarbonate and folic acid for growth. Small plaques of WEE virus are more thermolabile than large plaque virus. Large plaques of FMD virus are more acid stable. Some plaques are also temperature sensitive.

(b) *Cold adapted mutants*: Most attenuated strains of viruses currently in use were obtained by serial passages of wild type viruses in hosts like embryonated eggs, cell cultures etc. These strains may be adapted to grow at low temperature of incubation. Some of them are unable to grow at higher temperature.

(c) *Host dependent mutants*: Some host dependent viruses are conditional lethal mutants. They will grow in some hosts but not in others.

(d) *Host range mutants*: It has been observed in some outbreaks of FMD, that most cattle are affected severely but swine population show considerable resistance to the virus involved in the outbreak.

(e) *Temperature sensitive (ts) conditional lethal mutants*: They are produced by missense mutations which change nucleotide sequence of wild type viruses in such a way that the resulting protein is unable to perform its functional configuration correctly at the restricted temperature. In this case complete polypeptide is synthesized but its function is defective at restricted temperature and normal at permissive temperature.

Conditional lethal mutants are those which can not grow under certain determined conditions but they can grow under normal or permissive conditions. These temperature sensitive mutants, can grow at low temperature but not at higher temperature. They may be less virulent and may be used as attenuated live virus vaccines.

(f) *Defective interfering mutants*: They can be produced when large amount of inoculum is used as in case of influenza virus (Van Magnus effect). Such incomplete viruses cannot replicate alone but can replicate in presence of normal wild type viruses.

Q. 20. Define interference of viral infections.

Ans. Viral interference occurs in a mixed infection, when a virus infected cell, resists superinfection with the same or a different virus. The mediator of interference may be interferon, a soluble cellular product. Interference may also be due to destruction of cell surface receptors by previous virus.

Q. 21. The following statements may be correct regarding the interference between two viruses except:

(a) The precise mechanism of interference of all viruses is known.
(b) The first virus resists superinfection and interferes in the infection by another virus.
(c) The first virus may be inhibiting the adsorption of the second virus on the cell surface.
(d) The first virus may be preventing the action of early mRNA of second virus from being translated.

Ans. (a)

Q. 22. The phenomenon of interference has the following characteristics except:

(a) It occurs between related as well as unrelated viruses.
(b) Interference phenomenon can be produced even by attenuated virus against subsequent infection with live virulent virus.
(c) It is not necessary that interfering virus replicate to produce interference.
(d) There is no time limit for the second virus to initiate infection.

Ans. (d)

Q. 23. Interference may occur between following viruses except:

(a) Two different viruses.
(b) Two related viruses.
(c) Two strains of the same virus
(d) Interfering virus is a killed virus and the other virus is a live virus.

Ans. (d)

Q. 24. What is abortive infection? Under what circumstances abortive infection takes place and how such viruses can be made to grow normally?

Ans. Some defective viruses do not synthesize infectious particles. This is because either they do not synthesize all the components of the virion or the components do not assemble properly. Such viruses produce abortive infection. In case of influenza virus when inoculum is large and concentrated, incomplete virus is produced. The virus will lack RNA but it will still give HA test. Some parvoviruses are also defective until they are helped to grow in presence of some adenoviruses in the same cells. The transformed papillomaviruses are also defective. In this case a part of the viral genome is integrated into cellular genome and replicate with it.

7

Multiplication of Viruses

The topic will cover replication of viral nucleic acids, transcription of DNA to mRNA and translation of mRNA to enzymic and structural proteins of viruses. The role of viral enzymes will also be discussed briefly.

Q. 1. Arrange the following steps of virus multiplication in a proper sequence.

(a) Adsorption of virus on cell surface
(b) Uncoating of viral nucleic acid
(c) Translation of early mRNA into early proteins (viral enzymes)
(d) Penetration
(e) Replication of viral nucleic acid
(f) Transcription of early mRNA
(g) Assembly and maturation of virions
(h) Release of daughter virions from infected cells
(i) Translation of late proteins (structural proteins)
(j) Transcription of late mRNA

Ans. (a), (d), (b), (f), (c), (e), (j), (i), (g), (h)

Select the correct answer.

Q. 2. Virus attachment to cell surface is facilitated by:

(a) Presence of cations in the environment of negatively charged cell and viral surfaces.
(b) Specific receptors on cell surface
(c) Presence of haemagglutinins in some viruses.
(d) Presence of some co-factors
(e) Due to one or more of the above factors in different viruses

Ans. (e)

Q. 3. Viruses penetrate in the cells by:
(a) Veropexis or endocytosis methods.
(b) Fusion with plasma membrane.
(c) Direct penetration through plasma membrane.
(d) All above methods in different viruses.

Ans. (d)

Q. 4. After penetration of the virus in the cell, the uncoating takes place at:
(a) Cell membrane (b) In the cell cytoplasm
(c) In the cell nucleus (d) In any of the above sites

Ans. (d)

Q. 5. What is eclipse phase? After penetration of virus inside the cells, what steps take place during eclipse period?

Ans. From the stage of penetration of virus inside the cell, till the appearance of mature daughter viruses, they can not be demonstrated inside host cell. This period is known as eclipse phase. The steps which take place during this period are, transcription of mRNA, translation of mRNA, replication of viral nucleic acid and maturation of virion in cell cytoplasm.

Q. 6. Fill in the blanks:
(a) The interval between the disappearance of inoculated virions and release of new virions is known as.............. period.
(b) During eclipse phase .... of mRNA and .... of mRNA takes place into protein.
(c) The three main mechanisms of viral replication are .... of viral nucleic acid into mRNA, ... of mRNA into viral proteins and .... of viral nucleic acid.
(d) Attachment and penetration of the virus in cells take place within .... hours after inoculation.
(e) During viral replication, the eclipse period in DNA viruses ranges from .... to .... hours and in RNA viruses from .... to .... hours.
(f) When virus depends on cellular transcriptase, transcription takes place in the .... of cells.

Ans. (a) latent
(b) transcription, translation
(c) transcription, translation, replication
(d) 1 to 2
(e) 5 to 15, 3 to 10
(f) nucleus

Q. 7. The following statements are correct except:

(a) Non-enveloped viruses on maturation are often released late after cell lysis.

(b) After maturation, enveloped viruses are released concurrently by budding from plasma membrane of cells.

(c) Except herpesviruses, all other DNA viruses are released from cells by cytolysis.

(d) Small RNA viruses are generally released from cells by extrusion.

(e) During replication cycle, all enveloped viruses have one step growth curve.

Ans. (e)

Q. 8. (a) Cellular DNA lacks the mechanism of producing mRNA of viral genome.

(b) Cellular DNA can not transcribe viral DNA in cytoplasm.

(c) Cellular DNA transcribes only those DNA viruses which are replicated inside cell nucleus.

(d) Except DNA viruses which are replicated inside cell nucleus, all other viruses provide their own enzymes to produce mRNA.

(e) All viruses are uncoated inside cell cytoplasm.

(f) DNA synthesis can be prevented by 5′-iodo-2′-deoxy-uridine, adenine arabinoside and cytosine arabinoside thus preventing DNA virus multiplication.

Ans. (e)

Q. 9. Select correct answer:

Each infected cell yields:

(a) Less than 100 virus particles

(b) Several hundred virus particles

(c) Several thousand virus particles

(d) Several million virus particles

Ans. (b)

Q. 10. Describe virion associated enzymes and their functions.

Ans. 1. *Enzymes affecting interaction of virions on host cell surface:*

(a) *Neuraminidase:* This enzyme destroys surface receptors of RBCs. The chemical nature of surface receptors is N-acetyl muramic acid of polysaccharides. This enzyme is found in *Orthomyxoviridae* and *Paramyxoviridae* viruses.

2. *Enzymes transcribing viral genome into mRNA:*

(a) *DNA dependent RNA polymerase:* This transcriptase enzyme is found in the viruses of *Poxviridae,* and *Iridoviridae* virus families. In these viruses, mRNA is directly transcribed from one strand of viral DNA which acts as a template for its replication.

(b) *DNA dependent DNA polymerase:* This enzyme is found in the viruses of *Hepadnaviridae* family which has double stranded DNA viruses with reverse transcriptase.

(c) *RNA dependent RNA polymerase:* This transcribing enzyme is found in all RNA viruses except the RNA virus family of *Retroviridae.*

(d) *RNA dependent DNA polymerase:* This enzyme is found in RNA virus family *Retroviridae.* This family has reverse transcriptase of RNA dependent DNA polymerase.

3. *Enzymes adding specific terminal groups to mRNA:* The example of this enzyme is nucleotide phosphohydrolase.
4. *Enzymes involved in copying RNA into DNA:* The name of this enzyme is RNA dependent DNA polymerase (reverse transcriptase). This enzyme is operative in *Retroviridae* family.
5. *Enzymes for DNA replication:* The enzyme DNA polymerase, catalyses elongation of DNA chain.
6. *Deoxyribonucleases:* These enzymes function in viruses belonging to the family of *Poxviridae* and *Retroviridae.*

Q. 11. Describe the replication and elongation of DNA chain in DNA viruses.

Ans. For DNA replication and elongation of chain, following components are required:

1. Activated precursors of deoxyribonucleoside 5′ triphosphates i.e. dATP, dGTP, dTTP, and dCTP.
2. DNA polymeraseI enzyme to add deoxyribonucleotides to 3′ OH terminus of a preexisting DNA chain (primer).
3. A DNA template for chain elongation.

The step by step addition of deoxyribonucleotide units to a DNA chain is indicated as below:

$$(DNA)_n \text{ residue} + dNTP \rightleftharpoons (DNA)_{n+1} + PPi$$

DNA molecule is a double helix chain. Each chain acts as a template for synthesis of a new complementary chain, thus forming two new helices, each like the original as shown in Fig. 7.1.

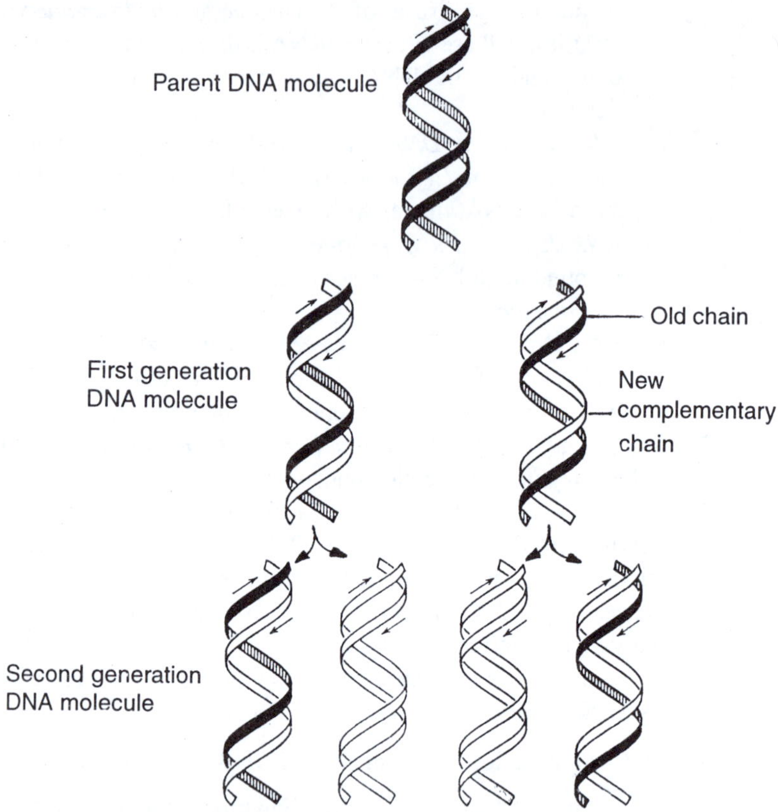

Fig. 7.1. Mechanism of DNA replication (From Meselson, M. and Stahl, F. (1958). C.S.H. Symp. Quant. Biol. 23:10)

Q. 12. Briefly describe how RNA is replicated in RNA viruses?

Ans. The phenomenon of RNA replication in RNA viruses is unique. Transcription of RNA from a RNA template requires a RNA dependent RNA polymerase, a virus coded enzyme. The replication of viral RNA requires first the synthesis of complementary RNA which then serves as a template for making more viral RNA. Where the viral RNA is of negative sense, the complementary RNA will be of positive sense and the RNA polymerase resembles virion associated transcriptase used for primary transcription of mRNAs.

Retroviruses have plus sense ssRNA. They replicate via a DNA intermediate. The virion associated reverse transcriptase, using a transfer RNA (tRNA) molecule as a primer makes a ssDNA copy. This then functioning as a ribonuclease, removes the parental RNA molecule from DNA-RNA hybrid. The free minus sense ssDNA strand is copied to form a linear ds DNA. This dsDNA then integrates into cellular DNA. Transcription of viral RNA occurs from this integrated (provirus) DNA (for details see Fig. 7.2).

Q. 13. How transcription differs in different DNA viruses?

Ans. DNA viruses fall into four different categories. Transcription in these viruses takes place as follows:

(a) *Double stranded DNA viruses with cellular transcriptase:* In this category, the viral DNA is transcribed in cell nucleus by cellular DNA dependent RNA polymeraseII. This group is represented by the DNA virus families of *Papovaviridae, Adenoviridae,* and *Herpesviridae.*

(b) *Double stranded DNA viruses with viral transcriptase:* In this group, the viruses carry their own transcriptase enzyme and the viruses are replicated in cell cytoplasm. The mRNA which is again DNA dependent RNA polymerase of the virus is directly transcribed from viral DNA. Viral DNA acts as a template for its replication. This group is represented by *Poxviridae,* and *Iridoviridae* families.

(c) *Double stranded DNA viruses with reverse transcriptase:* The DNA is first repaired by a virus associated DNA polymerase and the circular DNA of the virus is then converted into complete double stranded DNA. The minus strand of DNA is used as template for synthesis of plus strand RNA transcript. This group is represented by *Hepadnaviridae.*

(d) *Single stranded DNA viruses with cellular transcriptase:* This group represents minus (-) sense single stranded DNA viruses representing *Parvoviridae* family. These viruses require the synthesis of a complementary strand to form double stranded DNA. The virus is then transcribed in the nucleus to produce *DNA dependent RNA polymerase* which is then transferred to cytoplasm for translation.

Q. 14. *Describe the process of transcription in RNA viruses:*

Ans. (a) *Transcription in single stranded RNA viruses with plus(+) sense:* In this group, the RNA virus itself acts as mRNA (RNA dependent RNA polymerase) and is translated into protein. The single stranded parental RNA acts as a template for production of complementary strand which acts as the template for progeny virus. This group is represented by *Picornaviridae, Coronaviridae, Caliciviridae, Togaviridae* and *Flaviviridae* families.

(b) *Single stranded RNA viruses with minus(–) sense:* In this group, parental RNA produces complementary negative strands which acts both as mRNA (RNA dependent RNA polymerase) and as template for the synthesis of progeny viral RNA. This group is represented by *Orthomyxoviridae, Paramyxoviridae, Rhabdoviridae, Arenaviridae,* and *Bunyaviridae* families.

(c) *Double stranded RNA viruses with transcriptase:* This group is represented by *Reoviridae* and *Birnaviridae* families which have segmented genome. In these, each segment is transcribed separately in cytoplasm by a virion associated *RNA dependent RNA polymerase.* The mRNAs are transcribed from each segment. The RNA complex with a protein is copied to produce a double RNA, which serves as template for further mRNA transcription.

(d) *Single stranded plus (+) sense RNA viruses with reverse transcriptase: Retroviridae* family exhibits a unique cycle of virus replication. These viruses are single stranded RNA viruses. The RNA strand is first converted into an RNA:DNA hybrid by viral enzyme RNA dependent DNA polymerase (reverse transcriptase). From RNA:DNA hybrid, double stranded DNA is synthesized. The double stranded DNA form of the virus (provirus) is integrated into host cell genome. The provirus acts as the template for the synthesis of progeny viral RNA. RNA tumour viruses are known as retroviruses because their genetic information flows from RNA to DNA i.e. reverse of normal flow of DNA to RNA (Fig. 7.2).

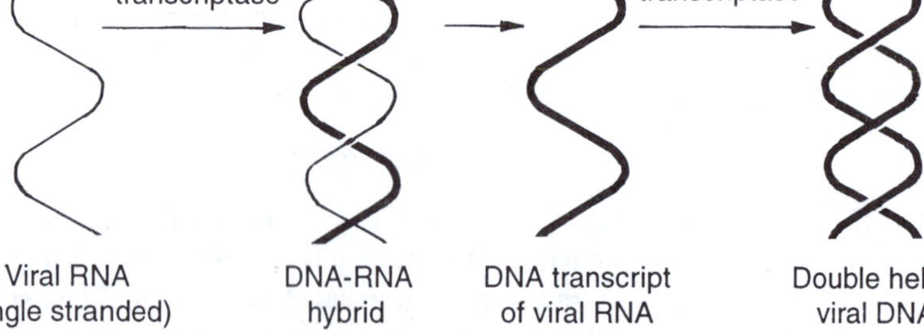

Fig. 7.2: Replication of reverse RNA transcriptase, an RNA-directed DNA polymerase of *Retroviridae* virus family. (From Stryer, L. (1989). Molecular Design of Life. W.H. Freeman & Co. New York)

Q. 15. What is the role of DNA in protein synthesis?

Ans. Amino acid sequence of proteins is genetically determined by DNA. DNA is not direct template for protein synthesis but the template for protein synthesis is RNA. The messenger RNAs (mRNA) are information carrying intermediates in protein synthesis.

$$\text{DNA} \xrightarrow{\text{transcription}} \text{RNA} \xrightarrow{\text{translation}} \text{Protein}$$

There are different types of RNAs. These are messenger RNA (mRNA), transfer RNA (tRNA), ribosomal RNA (rRNA) and small nuclear RNA (snRNA). Protein synthesis takes place on ribosomes which are complex assemblies of rRNA and more than 50 kinds of proteins.

Q. 16. How amino acids are specified in proteins by DNA?

Ans. Genetic information to code different amino acids is stored in DNA. DNA acts as a template for synthesis of mRNA. The bases in DNA and mRNA are complementary to each other. The genetic information is stored as a code (codon). The unit of code consists of a sequence of three bases. This means, the code is a triplet. Each codon specifies for a single amino acid. Some amino acids are coded by more than one codons. A segment of DNA carrying codons specifying for a particular polypeptide is called gene. A DNA molecule consists of large number of genes, each of which contains hundreds of nucleotides.

Q. 17. How does mRNA direct amino acids to join polypeptide in a correct sequence?

Ans. Amino acid is carried to the template (mRNA) by tRNA which acts like an adaptor and fits on to RNA. There are about 20 adaptors (tRNA) i.e. one for each amino acid. Each tRNA contains an amino acid attachment site and a template recognition site. tRNA molecule carries a specific amino acid in an activated form to the site of protein synthesis. The joining of amino acid to a tRNA to form an aminoacyl-tRNA is catalyzed by a specific enzyme called aminoacyl-tRNA synthetase, an activating enzyme. The esterification reaction is driven by ATP as shown below:

$$\text{Amino acid} + \text{ATP} + \text{Synthetase enz.} \rightleftharpoons \text{Amino acid-AMP-synthetase} + \text{PPi}$$

$$\text{Amino acid-AMP-synthetase enz.} + \text{tRNA} \longrightarrow \text{Amino acid-tRNA} + \text{AMP} + \text{Enz.}$$

There is at least one specific synthetase enzyme for each of the 20 amino acids. The activated amino acid binds to tRNA (Fig. 7.3). The reaction is catalyzed by the enzyme. The template recognition site on tRNA is a sequence of three bases, which recognize complementary sequence of three bases on mRNA called codon.

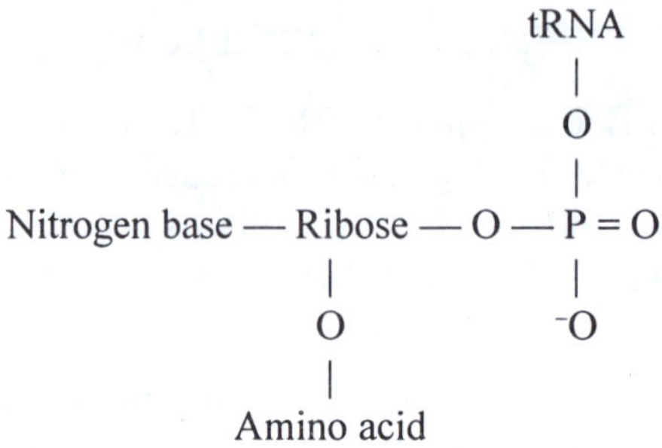

Fig. 7.3: Mode of attachment of an amino acid to tRNA molesule

Q. 18. What are important features of genetic code and how different codons specify individual amino acids for protein synthesis?

Ans. The four different nitrogen bases of nucleotides of mRNA are arranged in a sequence of three, each base triplet codes a specific amino acid. The number of sequences of 3 by 4 different bases will be $4^3 = 64$. The base triplets, each of which specifies one particular amino acid, constitute the genetic code. Out of 64 codons, 61 code for amino acids and three code for chain termination. The chain terminator codons are UAA, UGA and UAG. As 61 triplets will code only 20 amino acids, it will mean that some amino acids will be coded by more than one triplets. The genetic code for base triplets of mRNA specifying different amino acids are shown in Table 7.1.

Table 7.1: Genetic codes specifying different amino acids

1st base	2nd base				3rd base
	U	C	A	G	
U	UUU Phe	UCU Ser	UAU Tyr	UGU Cys	U
	UUC Phe	UCC Ser	UAC Tyr	UGC Cys	C
	UUA Leu	UCA Ser	UAA stop	UGA stop	A
	UUG Leu	UCG Ser	UAG stop	UGG Trp	G

(Contd.)

1st base	2nd base				3rd base
	U	C	A	G	
C	CUU Leu	CCU Pro	CAU His	CGU Arg	U
	CUC Leu	CCC Pro	CAC His	CGC Arg	C
	CUA Leu	CCA Pro	CAA Glu NH_2	CGA Arg	A
	CUG Leu	CCG Pro	CAG Glu NH_2	CGG Arg	G
A	AUU Ile	ACU Thr	AAU Asp NH_2	AGU Ser	U
	AUC Ile	ACC Thr	AAC Asp NH_2	AGC Ser	C
	AUA Ile	ACA Thr	AAA Lys	AGA Arg	A
	AUG Met	ACG Thr	AAG Lys	AGG Arg	G
G	GUU Val	GCU Ala	GAU Asp	GGU Gly	U
	GUC Val	GCC Ala	GAC Asp	GGC Gly	C
	GUA Val	GCA Ala	GAA Asp	GGA Gly	A
	GUG Val	GCG Ala	GAG Asp	GGG Gly	G

Q. 19. Give full forms of abbreviated amino acids.

Ans. The full forms of abbreviated amino acids are given below:

Ala = alanine, Arg = arginine, Asp = aspartic acid,
Asp-NH_2 = asparagine, Cys = cysteine, Glu = glutamic acid,
Glu-NH_2 = glutamine, Gly = glycine, His = histidine,
Ileu = isoleucine, Leu = leucine, Lys = lysine,
Met = methionine, Phe = phenylalanine, Pro = proline,
Ser = serine, The = threonine, Tyr = tyrosine,
Val = valine, Trp = tryptophane

Q. 20. Explain the following:
(a) Nonsense codons
(b) Degenerate code
(c) Synonym codon

Ans. (a) *Nonsense codons:* The codons which terminates protein chain synthesis are called nonsense codons. There are three such codons. They are UAA, UAG, and UGA.

(b) *Degenerate code:* There are 20 amino acids and 61 codons to specify them. This means the codes are highly degenerate as more than one codes specify some of the amino acids.

(c) *Synonym codons:* Codons which specify the same amino acid, are called synonyms. Most synonyms differ only in the last base of the triplet.

Q. 21. Translate the following genetic code into chain of amino acids. AUG, UUU, UUG, CCA, UAC, GGU, GAG and UAA.

Ans. Met–Phe–Leu–Pro–Tyr–Gly–Asp, is the chain of amino acids.

Q. 22. What are introns and exons?

Ans. In some eucaryotic cells, there are some regions in DNA which do not function as codons (between coding sequences of genes). These noncoding streches are known as introns, while those stretches of genes which code amino acids are known as exons.

8

Virus Host Cell Interactions and Pathogenesis

Virus host interaction occurs at cellular and individual levels. At cellular level, there may be many types of effects. There may not by any apparent cellular damage, or there may be rapid cell destruction. At individual level, the interaction depends upon the virulence of the virus and susceptibility of the host. The infection may be acute, subacute or chronic. The virus may be eliminated from the host or it may remain as latent infection. The interaction will also depend upon the immune status of the host and other factors like age, sex, hormonal and nutritional aspects of the host.

Q. 1. What are different routes of entry of viruses into the body?

Ans. The routes of entry of viruses into the body may be:

(a) *Skin*: Due to injury, and scratches in the skin or on account of bites by arthropod vectors, some viruses enter and multiply in the skin and produce local lesions. The examples of such viruses are pox viruses, papilloma viruses and some herpes viruses. Arboviruses enter into the body through bites by arthropod vectors either mechanically or after replication in the vectors. Rabies virus enters the body through bites by rabid animals, particularly the dogs.

(b) *Respiratory tract*: Inspite of presence of mucus and ciliiated cell linings and other protective mechanisms, respiratory tract is a very common route of entry of viruses into the body. Common viruses which enter through this route, are adenoviruses, most of the herpesviruses, rhinoviruses and apthoviruses. Other viruses which enter though respiratory tract are infectious bronchitis, infectious laryngotracheitis and Ranikhet disease viruses of poultry and influenza,canine distemper, hog cholera and lymphocytic choriomeningitis viruses.

(c) *Intestinal tract*: Some viruses may enter the body through food and water. They may infect cells of oral mucous membranes or pharynx and then carried to intestinal tract. Intestinal tract is protected from infection by mucus, acidity in stomach, bile from gall bladder and intestinal proteolytic enzymes. Viruses like coronaviruses, rotaviruses and parvoviruses enter the body through this route and are responsible for diarrhoea. Other viruses causing intestinal infection and diarrhoea are bovine virus diarrhoea, astroviruses and Breda and Berne viruses of *Toroviridae* family. There are other viruses of *Adenoviridae* and *Picornaviridae* families which produce systemic diseases after entry through intestinal tract.

(d) *Genital tract*: Viruses which enter the body through this route include herpes viruses.

(e) *Conjunctiva*: Although eyes are protected by tears, several viruses enter the body through this route and may produce systemic infections.

(f) *Congenital*: There are several infections which are received by foetus from mothers.

Q. 2. Give an account of how viruses spread in the body and cause infections?

Ans. Viruses may remain localized in cells of body surface through which they enter and produce local lesions. After replication in the epithelial cells viruses may produce spreading infections and may shed the virus outside the body. In few cases they may cause generalized infection after spreading to other parts of the body, through lymphatics and/or blood vessels, as mentioned below:

Through lymphatics: After crossing the epithelial lining and basement membrane, the virus reaches the subepithelial tissues where they are exposed to macrophages and can enter the lymphatics and then to local lymph glands. Some of the viruses may be engulfed by macrophages and inactivated. Some may be replicated in macrophages while others may pass through lymph nodes and enter the blood stream. There may be local inflammatory response.

Through blood stream: Once the virus has reached the blood stream, usually through lymphatic system, it can localize in any part of the body. On first entry of the virus in blood stream, it may cause primary viraemia. The concentration of virus increases after its replication, in vascular endothelium, spleen, liver and bone marrow, which may cause secondary viraemia. The secondary viraemia may further establish infection in other parts of the body including skin, brain and kidneys. In blood virus may be free in plasma or may be associated with various types of leucocytes and erythrocytes. Monocyte associated viraemia may be seen in diseases like blue tongue, distemper and herpes infections including Marek's disease.

The skin, respiratory and intestinal tracts are generally infected directly but they may also be infected via blood stream and cause viraemia, skin lesions, respiratory and intestinal infections. Viruses can spread from blood to central nervous system directly after localizing in blood vessels of brain and spinal cord.

Q. 3. Describe different types of interactions between viruses and the cells.

Ans. Different types of virus cell interactions are:

(a) *Cytocidal (lytic)*: In this type of infection, synthesis of RNA, DNA, and the proteins of the cells are inhibited leading to the death of cells and causing cytopathic effects. Initially some virus may be produced which ultimately stops. Examples of such viruses are herpesviruses, enteroviruses and reoviruses.

(b) *Noncytocidal*: In this category, there is no cytopathic effect on cells and there is little or no metabolic disturbance. The cells continue to metabolize and divide. The viruses produce persistent type of infection. This type of situation, is found in arenavirus, rabies virus and in some retroviruses.

(c) *Noncytocidal but nonproductive type*: There is neither any cytopathic effect, nor metabolic disturbance in this type of virus-cell interaction. The cells continue to divide, and there is no virus production. The virus may be transformed with cell nucleic acid.

(d) *Cellular transformation*: In this category cell morphology is altered, but the cells survive. The transformed cells may produce tumours. Virions may be produced by onchogenic RNA viruses.

Q. 4. How viruses cause cellular injury?

Ans. (a) Viruses after entry into the cells shut down protein and DNA synthesis of the cells.

(b) Due to viral glycoproteins, the permeability of plasma membrane is increased and cells show cloudy swelling.

(c) There may be fusion of infected cells causing cell syncytia (giant cell formation).

(d) There may be alterations on cellular surface due to viral antigens like haemagglutinins. There may also be haemadsorption in some cases.

(e) Viruses may damage chromosomes of cells.
(f) Some viruses produce inclusion bodies in cytoplasm and/or nucleus.

Q. 5. Give a brief account of viral inclusion bodies.

Ans. Inclusion bodies are certain structures inside the cell cytoplasm and/or nucleus in response to infection by some viruses. They vary in shape, size and staining properties and can be seen under the light microscope. Inclusion bodies may be crystalline aggregates of virions or made up of virus antigens at the site of virus synthesis inside the cells. Some inclusions may be degenerative changes produced by virus infection. Inclusions may be acidophilic which can be stained pink with Giemsa or eosin-methylene blue stains. Other inclusions are basophilic. Cowdry (1934) classified intranuclear inclusion bodies as Cowdry type A and Cowdry type B. Type A inclusions are of variable size and granular structures while type B inclusions are circumscribed and often multiple in numbers. The inclusions may or may not be surrounded by a membrane. In some cases they have diagnostic value as Negribodies is case of rabies.

Q. 6. What types of cytopathic effects (CPE) are produced by viruses in monolayer cell cultures?

Ans. Some viruses will produce minimum CPE in cell cultures. These viruses are parvo, retro and orthomyxo viruses. Enteroviruses will produce rapid CPE with crenation of cells, vacuolation and degeneration of entire cell sheet. The viruses of fowl pox, duck hepatitis, and African horse sickness will show rounding of cells, pyknosis, detachment and lysis of cells. The viruses of paramyxoviruses, herpesviruses and coronaviruses produce syncytia or giant cells formation due to cell fusion. They also produce discrete focal degenerations. Adenoviruses produce large granular clumps of cells. The virus of SV_{40} and some other viruses produce cytoplasmic vacuolations.

Q. 7. What type of pathological changes will be produced by the viruses of fowl pox, infectious laryngotracheitis (ILT), infectious bronchitis (IB), and Ranikhet disease (RD) in embryonated chicken eggs?

Ans. (a) Fowl pox virus will produce pock lesions on CAM and intracytoplasmic inclusion bodies in infected cells.
(b) ILT virus will produce pock lesions of CAM and intranuclear inclusion bodies in infected cells.
(c) IB virus will develop dwarfing and curling of embryos and there will be reduction in allantoic fluid.

(d) RD virus will kill the embryos and will develop haemagglutinins in allantoic fluid.

Q. 8. Briefly describe the pathogenesis of viral infections.

Ans. The viral infections may be inapparent or may show clinical symptoms.

The type of clinical infections may be:

(a) Acute (b) Chronic
(c) Latent (d) Slow

(a) *Acute infection*: This type of infection is either fatal or there is complete recovery with the elimination of the virus from the body. Some viral infections of respiratory and intestinal systems and generalised infections belong to this category.

(b) *Chronic infection*: In some chronic diseases, virus is demonstrable in the system for a long time with or without disease production. In such infections, ultimately there may be death of the animal or there may not be any symptom of the disease but the virus may be shedding for a long time intermittently. The example of this type of infection is FMD.

(c) *Latent infection*: In some viral diseases, acute infection becomes latent and may reappear from time to time causing illness till the virus is eliminated from the body. One example of this type of infection is IBR disease. Between disease episodes, the virus remains as episomal DNA in cerebral neurons. Such animals will show neutralizing antibodies.

(d) *Slow infections*: Such infections have very long incubation period and the virus produces a slowly progressive but fatal disease. The virus may be isolated during preclinical and clinical phases of the disease. The examples of such infections are scrapie disease of sheep, Visna/Maedi disease of sheep and goats, AIDS disease of humans and other lentiviral diseases affecting CNS.

Q. 9. Explain why immune response is ineffective or poor in persistent viral infections?

Ans. Some of the factors responsible for poor immune response are related to the virus, while others pertain to the host defenses. When it is related to the virus it may be non-immunogenic. Such agents may be responsible for subacute spongiform encephalopathies. In retroviruses, the proviral DNA remains integrated as part of host genome. The AIDS virus destroys the helper T lymphocytes. During latent phase of herpesvirus, the virus remains hidden in the cells of nervous system.

The viruses of visna/maedi, and equine infectious anaemia, avoid immune response of the host by antigenic drift and antigenic shift, thus facilitating persistence of the virus. Antigenic shift is abrupt and drastic variation in antigenic structure in a virus resulting in antigenically unrelated strain than predecessor strain. Antigenic drift on the other hand is due to gradual change in antigenic structure occurring regularly at frequent intervals. In this case new antigens different but related to previous antigens appear on the surface of virus.

On the part of the host, the factors responsible for persistence of the virus in the system are, absence of antibodies due to nonimmunogenic agent as seen in case of scrapie disease, presence of non neutralizing antibodies as in case of visna/maedi and AIDS, destruction of lymphocytes in case of infectious bursal disease, disturbance of macrophage functions in case of African swine fever, antigen specific suppresion in case of lymphocytic choriomeningitis and herpesvirus infections and antigenic variation of virus in case of foot and mouth disease. Some of these mechanisms also operate in non persistent infections.

Q. 10. What are different routes of shedding of virus from the body?

Ans. Shedding of virus from the body, occurs via body openings or surfaces involved in the entry. They are:

Skin: It is a major source of virus shedding in such diseases in which transmission occurs by direct contact, via abrasions e.g. papillomatosis. In other diseases like FMD, vesicular stomatitis, pox diseases, and some herpes infections, vesicular or pustular lesions are produced for direct transmission. Virus also shed via saliva in which case aerosol method plays important role in transmission. In Marek's disease, virus is shed from feather follicles.

Respiratory secretions: Many viruses, either causing localized disease in respiratory tract or generalised infections, are shed in fluid expelled from respiratory tract. Viruses from IBR, paramyxovirus and some coronavirus infections are excreted in nasal and oral secretions.

Saliva: Viruses from infected salivary glands, lungs and nasal mucosa are shed through saliva. Virus can also be shed through saliva from rabid animals.

Faeces: Viruses affecting gastro-intestinal tract are shed through faeces.

Urino-genital tract: Many viruses including herpesviruses, infectious canine hepatitis and rinderpest viruses are shed through this tract.

Milk and eggs: Some viruses pass through milk and several others through poultry eggs. Some retroviruses pass through eggs to the off-springs.

Q. 11. Select appropriate answer:

Persistent infection is commonly seen in the following virus families except:

(a) *Arenaviridae* (b) *Retroviridae*
(c) *Reoviridae* (d) *Paramyxoviridae*
(e) Some viruses of *Togaviridae*

Ans. (c)

Q. 12. Name viral diseases in which virus persists after clinical recovery.

Ans. The diseases in which virus persists after clinical recovery are: Bovine virus diarrhoea, foot and mouth disease, malignant catarrhal fever, African swine fever, hog cholera, parvovirus infections, canine distemper, infectious canine hepatitis, avian infectious bronchitis, Marek's disease, Newcastle disease, avian influenza and equine infectious anaemia.

9

Role of Viruses in Oncogenesis

Q. 1. Define the terms tumours, oncology and oncogenesis.

Ans. *Tumours*: Tumours are unrestricted growth of cells which are caused by change in one or more genes that regulate cell growth. The genetic alterations may be caused by some chemical or physical agents or certain viruses.

Oncology: It is the scientific study of tumours.

Oncogenesis: The process of development of tumours is called oncogenesis. The synonyms of oncogenesis are tumourogenesis and carcinogenesis.

Q. 2. What is the mechanism of oncogenesis due to viruses?

Ans. Oncogenic viruses are able to cause transformation of cells in cultures and induce tumours in animals under natural or experimental conditions. In case of oncogenic DNA viruses, the viral DNA or a part of it, is integrated with the host cell genome. The viral DNA becomes incomplete (defective), which is not able to produce infectious virus. However on its influence, the host cells undergo malignant transformation. In this situation the cells, are not destroyed and the viruses are also not produced.

Q. 3. Differentiate between benign and malignant tumours.

Ans. When there is abnormal cell growth which does not spread to adjacent tissues and the growth remains localized, such tumours are known as benign tumours. On the other hand, in malignant tumours, the abnormal cell growth invades adjacent tissues and may also be metastatic to other parts of the body through lymphatics and blood vessels.

Q. 4. Match the type of tumours in column A with type of origin of cells in column B.

Column A	Column B
(a) Leukaemia	(i) Malignant tumours arising from cells of mesenchymal origin
(b) Lymphoma	(ii) Malignant tumours arising from epithelial cell origin
(c) Sarcoma	(iii) Tumours of lymphoid tissues
(d) Carcinoma	(iv) Tumours of leucocytes in circulating cells

Ans. (a) (iv), (b) (iii), (c) (i), (d) (ii).

Q. 5. Match Column A with Column B.

Column A	Column B
(a) Avian leukaemia	(i) Rous
(b) Avian sarcoma	(ii) Ellerman and Bang
(c) Lymphoma	(iii) Shope
(d) Rabbit papilloma	(iv) Burkitt

Ans. (a) (ii), (b) (i), (c) (iv), (d) (iii).

Q. 6. Name important viruses which produce malignant tumours in cattle and chicken.

Ans. *Viruses producing malignant tumours in cattle are:*

(i) Bovine leukaemia virus
(ii) Bovine papilloma virus

Viruses producing malignant tumours in chicken are:

(i) Avian leukosis virus
(ii) Rous sarcoma virus
(iii) Avian erythroblastosis virus
(iv) Avian myeloblastosis virus
(v) Avian reticulo endotheliosis virus
(vi) Marek's disease virus

Leukaemia viruses of cattle and chicken do not transform cultured cells while all other viruses transform them.

Q. 7. Fill in the blanks:

(a) Rabbit fibroma is benign type of tumour and is caused by ....
(b) Myxoma tumour is a benign fibroma which occurs in ....
(c) Cutaneous papillomas in cattle are caused by .... virus.

(d) The three most important viruses causing malignant tumours in chicken are ...., ... and ....

(e) Among RNA virus families, oncogenic viruses are restricted to the family of ....

Ans. (a) laporipox virus
(b) wild rabbits
(c) papilloma
(d) avian leukosis virus, Rous sarcoma virus, Marek's disease virus
(e) *Retroviridae.*

Q. 8. Select true or false statements:

(a) Adenoviruses can cause malignant tumours in humans, cattle and chickens naturally.
(b) None of the herpesviruses cause malignant tumours.
(c) Papilloma viruses produce benign tumours in their natural hosts.
(d) Rabbit fibroma and Yaba viruses may produce fibroma of skin which are benign in nature.

Ans. (a) False, (b) False, (c) True, (d) True.

Q. 9. (a) Polyoma viruses are tumorogenic when inoculated into new born rodents.
(b) Hepadnaviruses can produce primary cellular carcinoma in liver of humans and ducks.
(c) Leukaemia tumours in cattle are transformed in cultured cells.
(d) *Oncovirinae* subfamily of *Retroviridae* is the cause of leukaemias and lymphomas of cattle and chickens.

Ans. (a) True, (b) True, (c) False, (d) True.

Q. 10. The following viruses induce tumour formation except:

(a) Retroviruses
(b) Herpesviruses
(c) Iridoviruses
(d) Papovaviruses

Ans. (c)

Q. 11. Write briefly on transformation.

Ans. Transformation is the transfer of genetic information in a cell through the agency of DNA. Any character may be transferred by transformation. Viruses can be used to bring new genes in animal cells. The most effective vectors are retroviruses. These viruses replicate through DNA intermediates. The DNA version of viral genome called proviral DNA can be expressed by host cell and replicated along with normal cellular DNA. Retroviruses do not kill host cells but induce morphological, biochemical and biological changes which may lead to tumour formation.

Q. 12. Name virus families which transform cells *in vitro* and induce tumour formation in the hosts.

Ans. Such families are:

(a) *Papovaviridae*
(b) *Adenoviridae*
(c) *Herpesviridae* (Sub. family *Gammaherpesvirinae*)
(d) *Hepadnaviridae*
(e) *Retroviridae* (Sub. Family *Oncovirinae*)

Q. 13. Fill in the blanks:

(a) Viral/proviral DNA in herpes virus transformed cells remain as …………
(b) *In vitro* cell transformation does not take place in the DNA family of ………… .
(c) Viral genome in transformed cells is either episomal or integrated into ……….. .
(d) Cells transformed by viruses may induce tumours in ……….. animals.

Ans. (a) episomal, (b) *Hepadnaviridae* (c) cellular DNA, (d) susceptible.

Q. 14. Select true or false statements:

(a) Cells transformed by DNA viruses yield infectious progeny.
(b) Cells transformed by *Onchovirinae* viruses do not yield infectious virus.
(c) Mammary tumour virus of mice is transmitted from mother to offspring through breast milk.

Ans. (a) False, (b) True, (c) True.

Q. 15. What are the characteristics of cells transformed by viruses *in vitro*?

Ans. (a) Transformed cells have greater growth potential *in vitro*, have capacity to divide indefinitely in serial cultures and have more efficiency of cloning.
(b) Have chromosomal abnormality.
(c) Have altered cell morphology, and metabolism.
(d) Are capable of producing malignant neoplasms in isologous or immunosuppressed animals.
(e) Transformed cells develop new tumour associated surface antigens and new intracellular antigens.

Q. 16. What are oncogenes and their functions?

Ans. Retroviruses have transforming ability due to specific genes carried by them. These genes are called oncogenes (*onc*). They are also known as cancer genes. Oncogenes are responsible for the induction of tumours in the infected cells. Genes with sequence similar to retroviral oncogenes exist in host cells also. Host cell genes exist not only in tumour cells but also in normal cells of man, animals and birds. Genes found in cells are known as c-*onc* and those found in viruses are known as *v-onc*. Cellular oncogenes are wide spread in vertebrates and are conserved at constant sites in their genomes. Cellular oncogenes are not reported to be of viral origin but viral oncogenes are reported to be of host cell origin. Cellular oncogenes appear to have some important controlling functions on cell growth and regulation. All oncogenic retroviruses do not contain oncogenes. Oncongenes are not essential for the replication of retroviruses. Mutants of retroviruses lack oncogenes. The mutants of retroviruses replicate normally but will not transform cells or induce tumour formation.

Q. 17. Why retroviruses having oncogene in their genomes are defective?

Ans. Normal *non-defective* retroviruses have three genes i.e. *gag, pol,* and *env.* On the other hand defective viruses have fourth *onc* gene. When oncogene is incorporated in viral RNA at a place or part of one or more normal viral genes, the genome becomes *defective* and therefore cannot grow itself without the help of non-defective helper virus. Rous sarcoma virus is exception to this, as it has all the three normal genes as well as one gene and still grows normally.

Q. 18. Match retrovirus genes in column A with encoding proteins shown in column B:

Column A	Column B
(a) gag	(i) Encoding viral polymerase and reverse transcriptase
(b) pol	(ii) Encoding envelope glycoproteins
(c) env	(iii) Encoding four core proteins

Ans. (a) (iii), (b) (i), (c) (ii).

Q. 19. Define endogenous retroviruses. Differentiate between endogenous and exogenous retroviruses.

Ans. Endogenous retroviruses are those viruses whose genome occurs as a provirus integrated into the host cell DNA thus transmitted from parent to daughter cells during cell division.

Table 9.1: Showing differences between endogenous and exogeneous retroviruses.

Properties	Endogenous	Exogenous	
		Slow transforming	Rapid transforming
Transmission	Vertical	Horizontal	Horizontal
Expression	Usually no	Yes	Yes
Genome	Complete	Complete	Defective
Replication	Productive	Productive	Requires helper Virus
Oncogene	No	No	Yes
Tumorogenicity	Nil or rare	Leukaemia after long incubation	Sarcoma, leukaemia or carcinoma after short incubation.
In vitro transformation	No	No	Yes

Q. 20. Select true or false statements:

(a) Endogenous retroviruses are transmitted from mother to offsprings.
(b) Proviral genomes are not under the control of cellular regulatory genes.
(c) Proviruses in the genomes of cells can be activated by irradiation.
(d) Exogenous retroviruses multiply and spread horizontally to contact animals.
(e) Exogenous retroviruses occur is provirus form.

Ans. (a) True, (b) False, (c)True, (d) True, (e) False.

Q. 21. Fill in the blanks:

(a) Cellular oncogenes are accidentally incorporated into the genome of ……….. viruses.
(b) Viral oncogenes originate from cellular ……….. .
(c) The number of cellular and viral oncogenes so far recognized are more than ……….. .
(d) The number of viral oncogenes is most exogenous retroviruses is/are ……….. only.
(e) Different retroviral *v-onc* closely resemble with each other but are not identical with the corresponding ……….. .
(f) Some tumour producing DNA viruses contain genes which act as …………… .

Ans. (a) retro (b) oncogenes (c) two dozens
(d) one (e) oncogene (f) oncogenes.

Q. 22. Select true or false statements:
(a) Deletion of oncogene makes the virus non-tumorogenic.
(b) Oncogenes are necessary for viral replication.
(c) The protein product of an oncogene is necessary for initiation and maintenance of transformation.
(d) Presence of an oncogene in a virus does not make it defective.
(e) The location of proteins coded by different viral oncogenes may be in plasma, cytoplasm or nucleus.

Ans. (a) True, (b) False, (c) True, (d) False, (e) True.

Q. 23. What are biological properties of cellular oncogenes?

Ans. (a) These genes are located at a particular position on the chromosome of cells similar to other cellular genes.
(b) Cellular oncogenes, contain introns (intervening sequences which are spliced out and discarded from RNA transcript).
(c) These genes are segregated.
(d) These are highly conserved genes through evolution.
(e) These are transcribed at low levels but their expression may increase in particular tissues.

The above properties of cellular oncogenes suggest that these genes are essential and play important roles in the normal cell functions.

Q. 24. Name virus families which induce malignant tumours in domestic animals.

Ans. These are *Retroviridae, Papovaviridae,* and *Herpesviridae*.

Q. 25. Name three viruses which are known for transformation of cultured cells.

Ans. Bovine papilloma virus, Rous sarcoma virus and Marek's disease virus.

Q. 26. Select correct answer:
(a) Papilloma virus produces carcinoma:
  (i) Naturally
  (ii) Experimentally
  (iii) Naturally as well as experimentally
(b) Polynoma virus produces tumours:
  (i) Naturally
  (ii) Experimentally in rodent infants
  (iii) Naturally and experimentally

(c) Adenoviruses produce tumours:
   (i) Naturally
   (ii) Experimentally in rodent infants.
   (iii) Naturally and experimentally.

Ans. (a) (iii), (b) (ii), (c) (ii)

Q. 27. Select true or false statements:

(a) Palyoma and adenomaviruses transform cultured cells of some species.
(b) Transformed cells of polyoma and adenoviruses can produce these viruses, without any manipulations.
(c) The products (proteins) transcribed by polyoma and adenoviruses in cultured cells are called T (tumour) antigens.
(d) Papilloma viruses produce warts only on skin but not on mucous membranes.
(e) Under certain conditions, benign papillomas may progress to malignant tumours.
(f) Leporipoxviruses produce localised fibromas in their natural hosts which generally disappear within weeks or months.

Ans. (a) True, (b) False, (c) True, (d) False, (e) True, (f) True.

Q. 28. (a) Proviral DNA of retroviruses remains integrated in the genome of the host cell and maintained from one generation to the next generation.
(b) Persistent provirus is associated with lentiviral infections.
(c) Visna/Maedi and equine infectious anaemia viruses avoid host's immune response by antigenic drift.
(d) Persistent infections cannot be reactivated under any physiological conditions.

Ans. (a) True, (b) False, (c) True, (d) False.

10

Laboratory Diagnosis of Viral Diseases

Proper diagnosis of viral diseases is very important to adopt suitable measures to control the diseases at the earliest and save livestock industry from mortality and other economic losses. Lack of proper facilities in most of the virological laboratories, technical facilities, difficulties in the availability of rare chemicals and equipments, length of time required for isolation and identification of viral agents have been some of the difficulties in the past in the diagnosis of viral diseases. With the development of newer and rapid techniques for diagnosis of viral infections, diagnostic virology is fast becoming a routine procedure in most of the viral laboratories. Some of these diagnostic methods are described in this chapter.

Q. 1. For diagnosis of viral diseases, what type of specimens should be made available to virological laboratory?

Ans. 1. Specimens for direct demonstration of:
   (a) Virus
   (b) Viral antigen
   (c) Nucleic acid for gene sequencing

2. (a) Specimens for isolation and identification of the virus.
   (b) Serum samples for identification and measurement of antibodies from infected and recovered animals.

Q. 2. What type of specimens should be collected for the diagnosis of viral infections and how they should be transported to viral laboratory?

Ans. For correct diagnosis of viral infections, specimens should be collected as soon as possible after the onset of clinical symptoms in the animals. It is essential to collect suitable specimens from live animals and post mortem cases. A broad guide line of the type of specimens to be collected from animals showing various types of clinical symptoms and lesions are shown in the Table 10.1.

Table 10.1: Type of specimens from clinical and post mortem cases for laboratory diagnosis:

Diseases	Live animals	Postmortem cases
Respiratory infections	Nasal and conjunctival swabs, unclotted and clotted blood	Tissues from affected organs and lymph nodes
Gastroenteritis	Faeces and blood	Tissues from infected organs, intestinal contents and lymph nodes.
Systemic diseases	Blood, urine, faeces nasal discharge, urogenital swabs	Tissues from liver, spleen, kidneys, lungs and lymph glands
Infections of central nervous system	Blood, cerebrospinal fluid, nasal swabs	Tissues from affected organs and associated lymph nodes
Urinary tract infections	Urine, blood, and urogenital swabs	Tissues from affected organs and lymph nodes
Abortion cases	Vaginal mucus and discharge, blood from mother	Tissues from placenta, blood from foetal heart, stomach contents from foetus
Infections of skin and mucous membranes	Skin scrappings, blood, swabs from affected mucous membranes	Tissues from affected sites, lymph nodes

After collection, the specimens should be properly labelled and sent to laboratory with history and suspected disease. The specimens can be collected in screw capped vials and immediately sent to laboratory in thermos flask in dry ice and preserved in deep freezer until used.

Q. 3. How can viral agents be demonstrated and identified in the laboratory directly from the specimen?

Ans. Virus isolation being more tedious and time consuming, it is preferred to identify the virus directly from the specimens. For identification of some viruses, kits are available from some manufacturers. Most of these kits are based on ELISA.

Viruses can be detected directly by electron microscopy. Detection of viruses by negative staining under electron microscope has been used for rapid viral diagnosis. For this purpose crude specimens can be clarified first by low speed centrifugation followed by high speed centrifugation. The pellet of the virus can be used for negative staining. Viruses isolated in cell cultures can also be identified rapidly by electron microscopy. The use of electron microscopy can be made to identify the virus, by immuno-electron microscopy if immune serum is available. Electron microscopy is also useful to find out the shape, size and structure of viruses.

Q. 4. What are the methods/procedures to identify the viral antigens directly from specimens?

Ans. Viral antigens in secretions, excretions and slide preparations can be directly reacted with specific antibodies which are labelled for tests like ELISA, immunofluorescence, and immunoperoxidase etc. Viral antigens can also be detected by conventional tests like precipitation and complement fixation. A brief description of ELISA, immunofluorescence and radio immunoassay tests to identify the antigens in the specimens are given below:

(a) *Detection of antigen by ELISA:* For detection of antigen by ELISA, the test requires a solid phase for coating unknown antigen, known antibody, enzyme labelled antibody (conjugate) and substrate against the enzyme. For solid phase, polystyrene microtitre plates are used. To conduct the test, the wells of the plate are coated with the antigen in optimum concentration, incubated at 37°C for 1 hour and then over night at 4°C. The wells are washed thrice with PBS containing Tween 20 detergent to remove any excess antigen. After this, specific viral primary antibody, in optimum dilution and quantity, is added in each well, mixed and allowed to incubate at 37°C for 1 hour. After washing with PBS-T, the secondary antibody conjugated with alkaline phosphatase/horse radish peroxidase enzyme is added in the wells and incubated again for 1 hour at 37°C. After washing the wells, the substrate (paranitrophenyl phosphate/ortho-phenylene diamine) is added in the wells of the plate. The plates are kept in dark at room temperature for colour development for about 30 min. The reaction is then stopped with conc. sulphuric acid, and the optical density is finally read in an ELISA reader. If the antigen coated on the plate, reacts to specific antibody, addition of conjugate and substrate will produce colour indicating the presence of antigen.

(b) *Detection of antigen by immunofluorescence:* This technique is used in many laboratories routinely on account of its specificity, sensitivity, rapidity and simplicity. The test can be conducted by direct or indirect immunofluorescence techniques. The fluorescent dye is conjugated to antibodies. The conjugated antibodies are used to identify bacterial and viral antigens (in the sections or smear preparations), when examined under flourescent microscope. The most frequently used flourescent dyes are fluorescein isothiocyanate or rhodamine B.

(c) *Detection of antigen by radioimmunoassay:* This technique is similar to ELISA except that label is not an enzyme but a radioactive isotope like ^{125}I and the reaction is measured in a gammacounter. This test is also quite reliable and sensitive. The disadvantages of the test are high cost of equipment and health hazards due to handling of radioisotopes.

In all above mentioned tests positive and negative controls should always be included.

Q. 5. What is the procedure of diagnosis of the disease with the help of viral nucleic acid present in the specimens?

Ans. The identification of viral infections on the basis of nucleic acid probe is rapid and very sensitive. This is a recent technique and may not be available in most of the viral diagnostic laboratories. Normally radioactive isotopes like ^{32}P and ^{35}S, are used to label nucleic acid or oligonucleotides as a probe for hybridization tests. Nucleic acid of a virus can be identified on the basis of following tests:

(a) *Nucleic acid finger printing:* The viral DNA is digested with restriction endonuclease and electrophoresed on agarose gel. The pattern of bands observed is characteristic of a virus. This is compared with the DNA of a known virus, after similar digestion with restriction endonuclease and gel electrophoresis on agarose in parallel lanes. If the virus is RNA type, its nucleic acid is digested with ribonuclease enzyme and then processed as above in case of DNA.

(b) *Nucleic acid hybridization:* Restriction endonucleases are used to cleave viral DNA into shorter fragments which are afterwards separated by electrophoresis on agarose or acrylamide gel. Afterwords the Southern blotting for DNA or Northern blotting for RNA is carried out to transfer the nucleic acid fragments on to a nylon membrane. The blots on nylon membrane are then hybridized with virus specific probe. If the specimen is positive for the virus, (from which DNA probe has been made), a positive signal on autoradiography is obtained. Diagnosis with this method is highly specific and sensitive.

(c) *Dot-Blot hybridization:* In this test, DNA or RNA extracted from virus or infected cells is denatured, and then spotted directly on a nylon membrane to which it binds tightly on UV cross linking. The single stranded radio labelled DNA or RNA probe is then hybridized to the target nucleic acid *in situ* on membrane. A positive signal by bound probe is detected by autoradiography.

Q. 6. The following statements are correct except:

(a) When viral DNA is labelled with ^{35}S it can be used as a DNA probe to detect related DNA.

(b) Non-radioactive hybridization is based on the incorporation of biotin conjugated nucleotides into DNA probe.

(c) DNA probe can detect viruses which are noncultivable, nonviable or dangerous to handle.

(d) Genetic probe can not detect viruses directly in specimens.

Ans. (a)

Q. 7. How would you isolate and identify the virus from specimens supplied to the laboratory?

Ans. For isolation and identification of the virus, the material can be processed in two stages i.e. isolation of the virus, and characterization and identification of the virus. For isolation of the virus, the details of preparation of viral inoculum, inoculation of suspension in suitable host systems and harvesting the materials may be seen in chapter 5. For characterization and identification of the virus following criteria are followed.

(a) *Host specificity:* Different species of animals and birds may be infected by different viruses. This information may be found out from the history and source of viral specimens received from the field.

(b) *Clinical symptoms and lesions:* Most of the viruses, will produce specific clinical symptoms and lesions in natural hosts. This information can be very useful in the identification of the virus.

(c) *Changes and symptoms in laboratory animals, embryonated eggs and cell cultures:* The type of clinical symptoms in laboratory animals, changes in embryonated eggs and cell cultures inoculated with viral specimens may give some indications of the identity of the virus.

(d) *Type of nucleic acid:* Viruses have only one type of nucleic acid i.e. either DNA or RNA. Whether the viruses have DNA or RNA can be found out by applying different techniques. One of the easiest test is to grow the viruses in presence of 5-iodo-2-deoxyuridine (IUDR). In presence of IUDR, DNA viruses will not grow but RNA viruses will grow. The type of nucleic acid can also be determined by the treatment of ribonuclease and deoxyribonuclease enzymes. RNA will be destroyed by ribonuclease and DNA by the treatment of deoxyribo-nuclease enzymes.

(e) *Morphology and other internal structures by electron microscopy:* Negative staining of purified viral specimens can be examined by electron microscopy for shape, size, type of capsid, presence or absence of envelope, and internal structures including inclusion bodies. The nature of genome including whether it is single stranded or double stranded, whether linear or circular and segmented or nonsegmented can also be found out.

(f) *Other properties:* The size of the virus can be measured by gradocol membrane filters. Presence of envelope on the virus can be found out by its sensitivity to ether and chloroform. Effect of temperature and pH stability are also helpful in the identification of some virus groups. The property of haemagglutination is used to identify the viruses of *Orthomyxoviridae,* and *Paramyxoviridae* families and some other viruses possessing this property. *Poxviridae* family viruses possess intracytoplasmic inclusion bodies. The viruses of *Herpesviridae* family possess intranuclear inclusions. Negri bodies present in the cytoplasm of neuron cells is a diagnostic test of rabies virus. The preparations of smears or sections after staining can be examined under ordinary light microscope for inclusion bodies in the infected cells. The molecular weight of viral proteins can be determined by sodium dodecyl sulphate-polyacrylamide gel electrophoresis (SDS-PAGE). The property of transmission of viruses through arthopod vectors in some viruses is also helpful in their identification.

(g) *Serological tests against known antiserum:* For definitive identification of the viral isolate(s), it is absolutely necessary to test the virus or its antigen serologically against known hyperimmune antiserum. Some of the serological tests like ELISA, radioimmunoassay and immunofluorescence have already been described earlier in this chapter. These tests are carried out against known antiserum. The other useful serological tests to identify the unknown virus are:

(i) *Virus neutralization:* In this test, the known antibody neutralizes the infectivity of the unknown virus; this inhibits the cytopathology in cell culture, protects animals or embryos in eggs and reduces the number of plaques in monolayer cell cultures.

(ii) *Haemagglutination inhibition:* Some viruses agglutinate red blood cells. If the virus is mixed with specific antibody prior to the addition of red blood cells, haemagglutination is inhibited. This test is very simple and sensitive.

(iii) *Immunodiffusion:* When soluble antigen of the viral isolate is reacted with known antiserum in a gel, they diffuse towards each other and form visible lines of precipitation.

(iv) *Complement fixation:* In this test antigen antibody complex binds complement which is not available for lysis of sensitized sheep red blood cells.

(v) *Immuoblotting (Western blot):* This test can be used for detection of several protein antigens of a virus. First the virus is denatured with sodium dodecyl sulphate (SDS) and then the disrupted proteins are separated into different bands according to their molecular weight by polyacrylmide gel electrophoresis (SDS-PAGE). The separated proteins are electrophoretically transferred (blotted) onto a nitrocellulose membrane and the known antiserum is allowed to bind with the viral proteins on the membrane. Their presence is detected by using a radiolabelled or enzyme labelled secondary antibody and appropriate substrate solution.

Measurement of serum antibodies: Serological methods can be used to identify antibodies against known antigens in individual animals or in animal population. This type of study is very useful for epidemiological point of view. For the purpose of diagnosis, it is desirable to collect paired sera to find out how much antibody titre has increased in the second serum sample. The 1st serum sample is collected during acute phase of the disease and 2nd serum in the convalescent phase after 2-4 weeks of 1st sample. A rise in antibody titre between 1st and 2nd samples is the basis for a specific viral diagnosis.

The appearance of IgM antibodies is the indication of a recent viral infection. After 2-3 months IgM antibodies will be at a low level and IgG type of antibodies will show rising trend.

Q. 8. What are the advantages of the use of monoclonal antibodies? Give details of production of monoclonal antibodies.

Ans. Monoclonal antibodies are specific antibodies produced by hybridoma cells and can be used for diagnosis of diseases. With these antibodies, one can differentiate various strains of bacteria and viruses. To produce monoclonal antibody, inbred mice of a specific strain are immunized with a specific antigen. Few days after the final infection, the spleen of the mice is removed and antibody synthesizing B lymphocytes are collected and mixed with myeloma cells of the same inbred strain of mice in presence of polyethylene glycol which acts as a fusing agent. The fusion of two types of cells results in a hybridoma.

Hybridomas are separated from mixed population of myeloma cells, B lymphocytes and hybrid cells (hybridomas) by growing in Hypoxanthine, aminoptrin, thymidine (HAT) medium. Hybridomas are then cloned to give rise to monoclonals. The hybridoma cells are used for large scale production of monoclonal antibodies by injecting the cells in mice and then purifying the antibody from ascitic fluid.

11

Epidemiology of Viral Diseases

Epidemiology is the study of the factors determining the occurrence and distribution of a disease in a population. The factors involved pertain to host, parasite and the environment.

Q. 1. Define the following terms:

(a) Incidence of the disease
(b) Prevalence of the disease
(c) Enzootic/Endemic
(d) Epizootic/Epidemic
(e) Panzootic/Pandemic
(f) Incubation period
(g) Carriers

Ans. (a) *Incidence of the disease:* It is the number of new cases of a disease within a specified period of time (generally within a year). This is generally useful for acute cases of short duration.

$$\text{Incidence rate} = \frac{\text{Number of cases} \times 10^n}{\text{population at risk}} \text{ in a specified time}$$

$10^n = 1000, 100{,}000$ or $1{,}000{,}000$

(b) *Prevalence of the disease:* It measures the frequency of all current cases of the disease (old and new) and is of following types:

(i) *Point prevalence:* It measures the frequency of all current cases of a disease (old and new) at a given point of time.

(ii) *Period prevalence:* It measures the frequency of all current cases of disease (old and new) for a prescribed period of time.

(iii) *Seroprevalence:* It relates to the proportion of animals in a population that have antibodies to a particular pathogen.

(c) *Enzootic/Endemic:* Diseases occurring regularly and continuously within a given geographical area, including possible seasonal variations.

(d) *Epizootic/Epidemic:* Usually frequent occurrence of a disease in a community or region. The cases are in excess of normal expectancy and generally derived from a common or propagated source.

(e) *Panzootic/Pandemic:* Disease outbreak of exceptional proportion spreading quickly in many countries.

(f) *Incubation period:* It is the interval between effective exposure to an infectious agent and onset of clinical symptoms of the disease.

(g) *Carriers:* Healthy person or animal harbouring and excreting an infectious agent for a long period.

Q. 2. Name different types of epidemiology

Ans. They are:

(a) *Descriptive epidemiology:* This describes health and disease patterns and trends which are the diagnostic criteria of community health.

(b) *Analytical epidemiology:* This analyses the described variables. This makes definitive diagnosis of community health.

(c) *Experimental epidemiology:* This introduces variables into study and control groups and observes trends. This is achieved by research on community health.

Q. 3. What are the agents/factors which are intimately involved in the epidemiology of diseases?

Ans. These are:

(a) *Host:* The age, sex, religion, culture, race occupation, health status etc. affect in the causation of the diseases in hosts.

(b) *Agent:* This may be physical (heat, cold etc.) chemical (pollution of water, food, milk, air), and biological (bacteria, viruses, protozoa, fungi and helminths).

(c) *Environment:* This factor may be physical e.g. climate vegetation, and topography of the land; biological including animal bite, presence or absence of arthropods, presence of certain plants causing allergy, whether the disease is zoonotic in nature, and social and economic factors.

Q. 4. What are the goals of epidemiological research

Ans. The goals of epidemiological research are:

1. Description of disease occurrence.
2. Characteristics of the causative agents.
3. Portal of entry of the agent into the body.
4. Portal of shedding the agent from the body.
5. Methods of transmission of the virus from infected to healthy animals.

6. Understanding the pathogenesis of the disease.
7. Mechanism of survival of the agent in nature.
8. Persistent infection in the body.
9. Accurate and quick diagnosis of the disease.
10. Prevention and control of the disease.

Q. 5. Name trained personnels who are involved in and supposed to practice epidemiology.

Ans. They are:

1. Nurses, compounders and livestock men.
2. Sanitary inspectors.
3. Veterinarians and medical practitioners.
4. A field epidemiologist.

Q. 6. What are different methods of epidemiological investigations?

Ans. Investigation of the causes of disease can be carried out by the following types of studies:

(i) *Cross sectional studies:* It provides data on the prevalence of a particular disease in the population. This type of investigation is relatively quick.

(ii) *Case control study (Retrospective study):* This type of investigation starts after the disease has occurred and attempts are made to find out the cause of the disease.

(iii) *Cohort study (Prospective study):* In this type of study investigation starts with a presumed cause of the disease. This requires creation of new data. This type of study takes more time and is more expensive.

Q. 7. Define molecular epidemiology and its use in the investigation of epidemiology of viral diseases.

Ans. The term molecular epidemiology has been applied to the use of molecular biological methods for epidemiological investigation of viral diseases.

The knowledge of molecular epidemiology is useful in the identification of field isolates. With DNA viruses the techniques of finger printing, and mapping of genome can be used. With many viruses, epidemiological informations can be obtained by determining complete or partial nucleotide sequence. Polymerase chain reaction can be used to detect very low copy numbers of a viral DNA in the sample. Most of molecular techniques pertaining to nucleic acids of viruses have been described in chapter 10 entitled 'Laboratory Diagnosis of Viral Diseases'.

Q. 8. What is seroepidemiology?

Ans. This type of epidemiology is very useful in veterinary public health programmes and research. Large number of sera can be made available freely from slaughter houses. The type of species of animals, their age and sex, the geographical area from which they are brought, their past history of viral infections, vaccination status, prevalence of different types of viral antibodies and their titres and many other types of information can be made available. Veterinarians practicing in the area can examine these animals before and after their slaughter. The information made available after testing the sera will be useful to evaluate disease eradication and immunization programmes including the emerging viral infections. Monoclonal antibodies provide useful information in distinguishing strains and subtypes of some viruses which is not possible with polyclonal sera. Correlation of serological data with clinical observations will make it possible to determine the ratio of clinical and subclinical infections. Serological survey may detect virus infected herds and success of immunization programmes. Rise of antibody in second sample of paired sera and presence of IgM antibody will give information of past and recent infection.

Q. 9. Name non-arthropod borne viral zoonotic diseases.

Ans. The non arthropod borne viral zoonotic diseases are:
Some pox diseases (e.g. cow pox, monkey pox, pseudopox and orf), rabies, vesicular stomatitis, influenza type A virus, lymphocytic choriomaningitis, and diseases due to Ebola and Marburg viruses.

Q. 10. Name arthropod borne viral zoonotic diseases.

Ans. **Table 11.1:** Arthropod borne viral zoonotic diseases with vertebrate hosts and arthropod vectors

Viral diseases	Principal vertebrate hosts	Arthropod vectors
Eastern equine encephalitis	Birds	Mosquitoes
Western equine encephalitis	Birds	Mosquitoes
Venezualan equine encephalitis	Mammals	Mosquitoes
Japanese encephalitis	Birds and pigs	Mosquitoes
Murray Valley encephalitis	Birds	Mosquitoes
St. Louis encephalitis	Birds	Mosquitoes
West Nile encephalitis	Birds	Mosquitoes
Russian spring-summer encephalitis	Rodents, birds, other mammals	Ticks

(Contd.)

Viral diseases	Principal vertebrate hosts	Arthropod vectors
Louping ill	Sheep, other mammals	Ticks
Kyasanur forest disease	Primates	Ticks
Rift Valley fever	Mammals	Mosquitoes
Colorado tick fever	Mammals	Ticks

Q. 11. Name arthropod vectors of the following viral diseases.

1. Blue tongue disease
2. African horse sickness
3. Equine infectious anaemia
4. African swine fever
5. Yellow fever
6. Dengue fever

Ans. Table 11.2: Arthropod borne viral diseases showing their arthropod vectors

Disease	Arthropod vector
1. Blue tongue disease	Culicoides (biting midges)
2. African horse sickness	Culicoides and mosquitoes
3. Equine infectious anaemia	Biting flies
4. African swine fever	Ticks
5. Yellow fever	Mosquitoes
6. Dengue fever	Mosquitoes

Q. 12. Give examples of the following viral diseases:

(a) Where infection occurs directly from animal to animal.

(b) Where infection involves an arthropod vector.

(c) Where infection involves an arthropod vector as well as a reservoir host.

Ans. (a) In most of the viral diseases, infection occurs directly or indirectly without involving any vector. The examples are rinderpest, Ranikhet disease etc.

(b) There are some viral diseases which involve some arthropod vector. Examples are Yellow fever, dengue and African swine fever diseases.

(c) In this category of diseases, in addition to arthropod vector, a reservoir host is also involved. Normally infection in principal vertebrate hosts spread through arthropod vectors. However, in some cases arthropod vector also infects other accidental hosts like man or some domestic animals. The examples of such diseases are zoonotic diseases like Eastern equine encephalitis in which case principal vertebrate host is a bird, but accidental hosts are horses or men (Fig. 11.1).

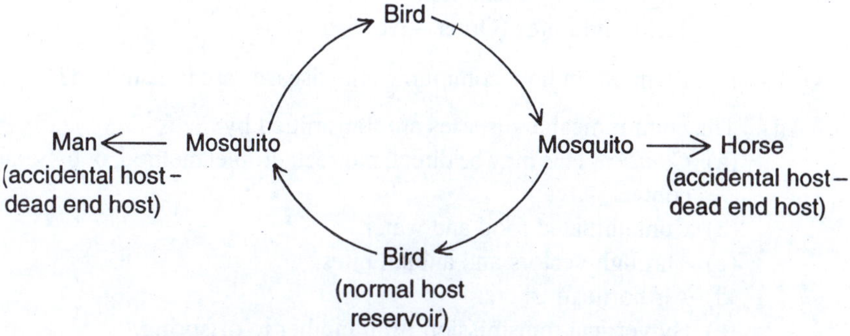

Fig. 11.1: A zoonotic disease involving a normal host, a parasite, an arthropod vector and an accidental or dead end host.

Q. 13. Name viral infections which may occur by arthropod bites mechanically.

Ans. They are:

(a) Some pox diseases (fowl pox, swine pox).

(b) Marek's disease

(c) Papillomatosis

Most other viral diseases are spread by arthropod biologically by biting, regurgitation or scratching in of infected faeces. In some arthropods there is transovarial transmission of pathogen from parent to offsprings.

Q. 14. What are different sources of reservoir of infectious agents.

Ans. The reservoirs of infections agents are:

(a) Human beings (e.g. in case of yellow fever).

(b) Arthropod vectors (e.g. ticks and mites transmit infection from mother to offsprings).

(c) Vertebrates: This is common in zoonotic diseases. The sources can be man, birds and other mammals.

Q. 15. Name arthropod vectors which transmit infectious agents in susceptible man and animals.

Ans. A vector is a living carrier of causative agent of the disease and transmit the same in susceptible animals. Different types of vectors involved in the transmission of infectious diseases are:

1. Flies and mosquitoes (Order-Diptera)
2. Fleas (Order-Siphonaptera)

3. Cockroaches (Order—Orthoptera)
4. Sucking lice (Order—Anoplura)
5. Bugs (Order—Hemiptera)
6. Ticks and mites (Order—Acarina)

Q. 16. Briefly mention how communicable diseases are transmitted?

Ans. The communicable diseases are transmitted by:

(a) *Contact:* This may be direct, indirect, droplet method, or by sexual contact.

(b) Contaminated food and water.

(c) Through vectors and animal bites.

(d) Air borne, dust etc.

(e) By vertical transmission from mother to offspring.

Q. 17. What are the routes of entry of microbial agents into host?

Ans. The routes of entry of microbial agents into the hosts are:

(a) Ingestion: By contaminated food and water.

(b) Inhalation: By droplet method.

(c) Inoculation: Through vectors or direct inoculation.

(d) Transplacental infection.

Q. 18. Select true or false statements:

(a) There is no difference between infectious and contagious diseases.

(b) The portal of entry into body and exit of causative agents from body is usually same.

(c) Inapparent infection is not infective to a susceptible host.

(d) Epidemiological surveys can be retrospective (backward) as well as prospective (forward).

(e) Epidemiology of diseases is applicable to communicable diseases only.

Ans. (a) False, (b) True, (c) False, (d) True, (e) False

Q. 19. Select true or false statements:

(a) Subclinical cases occur in Newcastle disease, and foot and mouth disease.

(b) There is no reservoir host in wild life for Newcastle disease, rinderpest and foot and mouth disease viruses.

(c) There is persistent infection in rinderpest and foot and mouth diseases.

(d) There in no infectivity during prodromal stages of canine distemper, Newcastle disease, rinderpest and foot and mouth disease.

Ans. (a) True, (b) False, (c) True, (d) False

Q. 20. Following viral infections occur via skin except.

(a) Pox diseases
(b) Diseases due to herpesviruses
(c) Tumours due to papilloma viruses
(d) Blue tongue disease

Ans. (d)

Q. 21. Name common routes of transmission of viral infections in DNA and RNA virus families.

Ans. **Table 11.3:** Showing common routes of viral transmission in different virus families.

Virus families	Common routes of viral transmission
DNA virus families:	
Papovaviridae	Contact and skin abrasions
Adenoviridae	Oral and respiratory tracts
Herpesviridae	Sexual in equine coital exanthema, respiratory in infectious bovine rhino-tracheitis, trans-placental in canine herpesvirus
African swine fever virus	Respiratory tract, orally by faecal contamina tion and by arthropod vectors
Poxviridae	Contact in cowpox, contact and respiratory tract in sheeppox, arthropod vectors in case of myxoma virus infection
Parvoviridae	Respiratory tract, contact, transplacental and orally by faecal contamination
RNA virus families:	
Picornaviridae	Respiratory routes in cases of enteroviruses and rhinoviruses and orally by faecal matter
Caliciviridae	Contact, respiratory and oral routes
Togaviridae	Arthropod vectors in alphaviruses, respiratory tract, oral tract and transplacental in case of hog cholera
Flaviviridae	Arthropod vectors
Orthomyxoviridae	Respiratory route
Rhabdoviridae	Animal bites in case of rabies, arthropod vectors, and by contact in vesicular stomatitis
Paramyxoviridae	Respiratory route and by contact
Coronaviridae	Contact, respiratory route and orally by faecal contamination

(Contd.)

Virus families	Common routes of viral transmission
Arenaviridae	Respiratory, and contact with contaminated urine
Bunyaviridae	Arthropods in Rift Valley fever
Reoviridae	Orally by faecal contamination in cases of rota and reoviruses and by arthropods in case of orbiviruses
Birnaviridae	Orally by faecal contamination
Retroviridae	Through contaminated eggs and by contact

Q. 22. Name factors which affect survival of viruses in nature.

Ans. These factors are:
Antigenic variation, subclinical and chronic infections, persistent infections, reservoir hosts, transmission from mother to offsprings, population size, and resistant viruses. Some viruses survive in arthropod vectors.

Q. 23. Name viral infections in which virus may remain persistent.

Ans. Such infections are:
Foot and mouth disease, hog cholera (virus persists in haemopoietic system), bovine virus diarrhoea (congenital infection), blue tongue disease (virus persists in mosquitoes), Visna/maedi diseases (virus persists in CNS and respiratory systems), bovine leukaemia (virus persists in haemopoietic system), African swine fever (virus persists in haemopoietic system), infectious bovine rhinotracheitis (virus persists in nerve ganglia), and pseudorabies (congenital infection).

Q. 24. Name viruses which are transmitted vertically from mother to offsprings.

Ans. Some of these viruses belong to *Retroviridae, Herpesviridae, Parvoviridae,* and *Arenaviridae* families. Some orbiviruses, togaviruses, coronaviruses and bunyaviruses are also transmitted from mother to offsprings.

Q. 25. What are the modes of vertical transmission of viruses?

Ans. The viruses are transmitted through egg or sperm in retroviruses and across placenta or through milk in some other cases.

Q. 26. Name congenital infections of domestic animals in *Togaviridae, Bunyaviridae, Retroviridae,* and *Reoviridae* families.

Ans. *Togaviridae* : Bovine virus diarrhoea, and hog cholera.

Bunyaviridae: Riftvalley fever.
Retroviridae : Bovine leukaemia, feline leukaemia, and avian leukosis (sarcoma).
Reoviridae : Blue tongue disease.

Q. 27. Name herpesviruses which may cause congenital infections in domestic animals.

Ans. These viruses are:

Cattle : Infectious bovine rhinotracheitis virus causing foetal death and abortion.
Equine : Equine herpesvirus type 1 causing abortion and foetal death.
Swine : Porcine herpes virus 1 causing foetal death and abortion.
Dog : Canine herpesvirus 1 causing perinatal death of pups.

Q. 28. Briefly mention the sequence of events in a typical systemic virual disease.

Ans. In most of the systemic viral diseases, following events take place:

1. After incubation period, the onset of the disease is gradual or abrupt. In this phase, virus circulates freely in the body. The animal will show various types of clinical symptoms, including rise of body temperature. The level of circulating antibodies will be very low. If the disease is arthropod borne, vectors may become infected by biting.
2. In the second phase, the body temperature starts declining along with increasing levels of antibody formation. Circulation of virus becomes minimal by the end of this phase. Vectors do not become infected.
3. In the phase of convalescence the animal is recovered from the disease. Protective antibodies are increased considerably.
4. In the last phase, the animal is fully recovered and develops good immunity.

Q. 29. How the chain of viral infection can be broken to control the infection?

Ans. From the source/reservoir, the causal agent is transmitted via direct or indirect contacts, through contaminated food or water, by droplet infection or through arthropod vectors and may establish infection in humans and animals. This chain of infection can be broken by adopting sanitary and hygienic measures, by isolating infected animals from healthy ones, by slaughtering animals suffering from infectious diseases, by proper disposal of contaminated articles, by breaking the link of transmission by control of vectors and by immunization of livestocks.

12

Immunization Against Viral Diseases

In spite of several limitations, immunization against viral diseases, is the best answer to control these diseases. Edward Jenner was the first to use the art of immunization against small pox disease in human beings in the year 1796. Jenner observed that milk maids milking cows with cowpox lesions on teats suffered from mild pox lesions on their hands. These maids later on did not suffer from smallpox, a much severe disease of human beings. Jenner gave a practical approach to immunization against smallpox by vaccinating an eight year old boy James Phipps, using cow pox material. About hundred year later, Louis Pasteur in July 1885 vaccinated a nine year old boy Joseph Meister against rabies by giving a course of 13 injections of infected spinal cord vaccine. The boy bitten by a rabid dog, survived after vaccination. These historic landmarks in the development of viral (and bacterial) vaccines opened gates to develop large number of human and animal vaccines against infectious diseases. On account of the efforts of WHO and virologists from various countries, the smallpox disease had been eradicated from the whole world in the year 1977. Though the conventional procedures to manufacture vaccines have greatly reduced the number of outbreaks of animal diseases like rinderpest, Ranikhet disease and Marek's disease etc., the field of vaccinology is now being advanced by the application of recombinant DNA technology.

Q. 1. Classify immunity

Ans. Immunity can be divided into two classes:

1. *Natural or innate immunity*
2. *Acquired immunity*

Acquired immunity is subdivided into natural and artificial immunity. The natural and artificial immunity are further subdivided into active and passive immunity. Divisions and subdivisions of various types of immunity are shown below:

1. *Natural or hereditary immunity:*
   (a) Species immunity e.g. equines do not suffer from rinderpest.
   (b) Race immunity e.g. Algerian sheep are reported to be more resistant to anthrax disease.
   (c) Individual immunity: Some individuals are more susceptible to some diseases than others.
2. *Acquired immunity:*
   (a) Natural immunity:
      (i) *Natural active immunity:* This type of immunity develops after infection due to some pathogen and recovery from the disease.
      (ii) *Natural passive immunity:* This type of immunity is acquired by young ones through colostrum and/or milk from mother. During pregnancy antibodies are also received through placenta.
   (b) Artificial immunity:
      (i) *Artificial active immunity:* After vaccination with attenuated, inactivated or other suitable vaccines, antibodies are developed in the system which will protect from attack by that organism.
      (ii) *Artificial passive immunity:* A short time immunity can be conferred by injecting hyperimmune serum/sera against one or more pathogen(s). This type of immunity is useful when unprotected valuable animals are exposed to contaminated and unhygienic environment.
      Active immunity develops in animal's own system in response to vaccination. Passive immunity on the other hand is conferred by injecting hyper immune serum prepared in another individual.

Q. 2. What are the merits and demerits of live and inactivated vaccines?

Ans. In general there are two types of vaccines. They are:

1. Live vaccines
2. Inactivated vaccines.

Their merits and demerits are shown in the Table 12.1.

Table 12.1: Merits and demerits of live virus and inactivated virus vaccines

Parameters	Live virus vaccine	Inactivated virus vaccine
Antigen per dose	Low	High
Cost	Low	High
Route of administration	Injection, oral, or nasal	Injection
Number of doses	One	More than one
Adjuvant	Not required	Required
Chances of reversion to virulence	Possible	No
Duration of immunity	Longer, sometimes life long	Shorter, may be months or years
Antibody response	IgG (IgA if given orally)	IgG
Cell mediated response	Good	Variable
Maintenance of cold chain	Required	Not required
Vaccination during pregnancy	Depends on type of vaccine	Usually done

Q. 3. Name different types of viral vaccines

Ans. Viral vaccines are classified as:
Live virus vaccines
In activated virus vaccines
Protein vaccines

Q. 4. Describe different types of live virus vaccines.

Ans. Live virus vaccines are:
(a) Naturally occuring virulent virus vaccines
(b) Attenuated live virus vaccines
(c) Virus vectored vaccines

(a) *Naturally occuring virulent virus vaccines:* (a) There are some examples of this type of vaccines. Virulent herpes turkey virus is used in chickens to control Marek's disease. Herpes turkey virus is antigenically similar to Marek's disease virus and is not pathogenic to chickens. Pigeon pox virus may be used as first dose in chickens against fowl pox. This is preferred especially for layers to avoid any reaction. Before goat tissue vaccine (GTV) was available to control rinderpest in cattle, vaccination was done with virulent rinderpest virus along with rinderpest hyper immune serum, to minimise reaction (serum-virus simultaneous vaccine).

To control rotavirus infection in pigs. bovine rotavirus can be used as vaccine.

In some diseases virulent virus can be given by unnatural routes. In case of infections laryngotracheitis (ILT) of chickens virulent virus is given by cloacal route. Orf live virus is injected in sheep in inguinal region. To control contagious bovine pleuropneumonia (CBPP), the injection of live organisms is given in candal fold regions of tail.

(b) *Attenuated live virus vaccines:* (a) There are some naturally available less virulent viruses of Newcastle/Ranikhet disease of poultry. These strains are F strain, (isolated in England), B-1 and Lasota strains (isolated in USA), and CDF-66 strain (isolated in India). Except CDF-66 strain, all other strains are poorly antigenic. Indian strains of infectious bronchitis virus of poultry are less pathogenic. All these strains are used in young chicks as vaccines to avoid post vaccinal reactions.

Virulent viruses can be attenuated by serial passages in embryonated chicken eggs, cell cultures, or laboratory animals. These viruses lose virulence for the original host but maintain their antigenicity. Large number of such vaccines are available. Some of the examples are: GTV and tissue culture vaccines of rinderpest, R_2B vaccine of Ranikhet disease, fowl pox and sheep pox vaccines. In some diseases temperature sensitive mutant strains are used as vaccines.

Attenuated live virus vaccines can also be obtained by employing the technique of genetic engineering. In the viral genome, the gene which is responsible for virulence, is excised, and removed. The virus without the gene responsible for virulence, can be used as attenuated live virus vaccine. Pseudorabies virus vaccine for swine has been obtained by removing the thymidine kinase (TK) gene which is responsible for its virulence.

(c) *Virus vectored vaccine:* This is a new approach of immunization in human beings and animals. In this approach, the genes of viruses responsible for protective antigens are introduced in the genome of large viruses which can be used as vectors. Viruses used as vectors may be fowl pox, vaccinia, herpes and adeno viruses. It should be ensured that the vectored vaccine replicates and does not cause any untoward reaction in the vaccinated animal. As an example, the genes of rabies virus responsible for protective antigens have successfully been incorporated into the genome of vaccinia virus which has been used as a vaccine to immunize animals against rabies.

Q. 5. Mention inactivated viral vaccines and how they are manufactured?

Ans. Under normal circumstances virulent viruses can not be used as vaccines. To make them safe for animal vaccination, the viruses are inactivated by physical or chemical agents. Physically, heat or ultra-violet rays are used to kill the viruses. These agents should inactivate the virus without denaturing the proteins acting as antigens. The pH and ionic environment of the medium also effects the rate of heat in-activation of the viruses.

Commonly used chemical agents for inactivation of viruses are formaldehyde, Beta-propiolactone and ethylamine. Formaldehyde in a proper dilution say 1: 4000, is used for inactivation of the virus at 37°C until there is no residual infectivity and maintain antigenicity and immunogenicity. Beta-propiolactone is considered a good inactivating agent as it is hydrolysed completely within hours to nontoxic products. The drawbacks of inactivated vaccines are the use of larger and repeated doses to maintain immunogenicity.

Large number of viral inactivated vaccines are used in animals and birds. The examples are IBR, FMD, sheep pox, equine influenza and hog cholera vaccines.

Q. 6. What are recent developments in the manufacture of various protein vaccines?

Ans. Some of the experimental viral protein vaccines are mentioned below:

(a) *Virus subunit vaccine:* Whole virion does not act as antigen but only the epitope portion on the protein surface of the virus acts as antigen for antibody production. It is desirable to include only the immunogenic or epitopic portion of the virus surface in the vaccine and discard the remaining portion of the virus. Such subunit vaccines have been used against human rabies, measles, FMD and hepatitis B viruses. This type of vaccines are highly specific in nature. One of the disadvantages of sub-unit vaccine is that it is of low immunogenicity and needs an adjuvant.

(b) *DNA vaccine:* Viral genes responsible for antigenic proteins are excised and cloned in procaryotic cells by recombinant DNA technology. When these genes are expressed in procaryotic cells, the resultant proteins are harvested from host cells and used as vaccine in the concerned species of animals. Experiments of this type of vaccine have been carried out with VP-1 antigenic protein of FMD virus.

(c) *Synthetic Peptide Vaccine:* The amino acid sequence of viral proteins are determined first and then antigenic sites (epitope) are located on the proteins. It is then possible to synthesize short peptides corresponding to the antigenic determinant to which neutralizing antibodies bind. Synthetic peptides used as vaccines, produced neutralizing antibodies against some viruses including the viruses of foot and mouth disease and rabies.

(d) *Anti-idiotypic vaccines:* When an antigen is administered in the body, it generates an antibody response. This antibody, in turn acts as an antigen and produces antibody which is known as idiotypic antibody and is the mirror image of antigen. These idiotypes act as antigens and elicit the production of anti-idiotypic antibodies.

Q. 7. What are adjuvants and what role do they play when mixed with vaccines?

Ans. Adjuvants are substances like aluminium hydroxide, Freund's complete adjuvant and mineral oils. These substances when mixed with vaccines enhance immune response by:

(a) Slow release of antigen and its retention for a longer period.
(b) Activation of macrophages involved in the production of humoral and cell mediated immunity.

Adjuvant vaccines need lesser antigen per dose and require fewer doses. Their immune response is for a longer duration.

Q. 8. What are the prerequisites of a good vaccine? Briefly describe the precautions to be taken at the time of vaccination.

Ans. Prerequisites of a good vaccine are:

(a) It should contain all possible antigens in good proportion.
(b) If it is inactivated vaccine, the inactivating agent should not affect its antigenicity, the inactivating agent should not harm the animal receiving the vaccine and it should preserve the vaccine well.
(c) The vaccine should be preserved and stored under ideal conditions.
(d) The vaccine should not be used after its expiry date.
(e) Vaccination should be done in adequate doses, by proper route of vaccination and proper interval of time.
(f) Each batch of vaccine should be tested for sterility, safety and potency.
(g) Do not vaccinate animals in very young age & advance pregnancy.

Q. 9. Name different types of immunoglobulins.

Ans. The different types of immunoglobulins are :

IgM They appear early in response to infection or vaccination and present in blood plasma.

IgG The are most important antibodies and appear some what late and always after IgM antibodies. They are present in plasma, tissue fluids and lymph.

IgA They are most important antibodies relevant to the prevention of infection of mucosal surfaces like respiratory, intestinal and urinogenital tracts. The immuoglobulin is locally produced in response to infection in the mucosa of these tracts and prevents infection on these sites. Some vaccines are given orally or intranasally to prevent infection affecting these sites. They are found in saliva & other secretions.

IgD It is produced in response to penicillin and insulin.

IgE It is skin sensitizing antibody in allergy and is important for parasitic immunity.

Q. 10. In a tabular form give a schedule of vaccination against important animal and bird viral diseases.

Ans. Schedule of vaccination against animal and bird viral vaccines is given in Table 12.2.

Table 12.2: The schedule of vaccination against important viral diseases of animals and birds.

Disease	Type of vaccine	Dose	Route of vaccination	Age at 1st vaccination	Revaccination
CATTLE AND BUFFALOES					
IBR	Attenuated (Herpes virus)	1ml	S/C	3-4 months	Annual
	Inactivated	2ml	S/C	3 and 4 months	Annual
FMD	Inactivated (foot & mouth disease virus) (polyvalent)	5-10 ml	S/C	4 months	6-12 months
Rinderpest	GTV & Cell culture (attenuated)	1 ml	S/C	all age group	Every 3-5 yrs.
Parainfluenza type 3 infection	Attenuated (Paramyxo virus)	1-2 ml	S/C	4 & 6 months 2 doses	Annual
SHEEP AND GOATS					
Sheep & goat pox	Inactivated with alum hydro. gel	0.3-0.5 ml	S/C	8 weeks	Annual
	Attenuated cell culture	0.1	I/D caudal fold	8 weeks	Annual
FMD	Inactivated	5 ml	S/C	3-4 months	Annual
Blue tongue	Attenuated egg adapted (Orbivirus)	1 ml	S/C	3-6 months	Annual

(Contd.)

Disease	Type of vaccine	Dose	Route of vaccination	Age at 1st vaccination	Revaccination
HORSES					
ERP	Attenuated	1 ml	S/C	1st dose at 3 months 2nd dose at 6 months	Annual
African horse sickness	Attenuated (mouse brain)	1 ml	S/C	6-8 months	2-3 yrs.
Equine influenza	Inactivated	20 μg/ml (adjuvant)	S/C	3-6 months (2 doses at 3 month interval)	Annual
SWINE					
Hog cholera	Attenuated (rabbit adapted spleen tissue)	1 ml	I/M	8 weeks	None
	Inactivated (cell culture)	1 ml	I/M or S/C	8 weeks	None
African swine fever	Attenuated	1 ml	S/C	8 weeks	None
Transmissible gastroenteritis	Inactivated with adjuvants	1 ml	S/C	Pregnant sows before 3 weeks of farrowing	None
Pseudorabies	Inactivated	1 ml	S/C	4 weeks, (2 doses at 4 week interval)	6 months
POULTRY					
Ranikhet disease	Lentogenic strain (F or B-1)	4 drops	I/N	1st week	4th week
	R_2B, (attenuated)	0.5 ml	S/C	8th-10th week	None
Fowl pox	Pigeon pox strain	Wing web method		3rd-4th week	—
	Attenuated (egg adapted)	Wing web method		—	at 8th week
Marek's disease	Herpes turkey virus vaccine	0.1-0.2 ml	I/M	1 day old	None
	Attenuated (Chicken strain)	0.1-0.2 ml	I/M	1 day old	None
Avian encephalomyelitis	Attenuated as well as inactivated	In drinking water		10 week old	None
DOGS					
Rabies	Attenuated (cell culture)	1 ml	I/M	10-12 Weeks	Annual
	Attenuated (LEP)	2 ml	I/M	10-12 Weeks	Annual

(Contd.)

Disease	Type of vaccine	Dose	Route of vaccination	Age at 1st vaccination	Revaccination
Canine distemper	Attenuated (cell culture)	1 ml	S/C or I/M	8 weeks (1st dose) 12 weeks (2nd dose)	Annual
Canine hepatitis, Parvovirus and Parainfluenza	Attenuated (cell culture) (mixed vaccine)	1 ml	S/C or I/M	8 weeks (1st dose) 16 weeks (2nd dose)	Annual

Q. 11. In a tabular form give important human viral vaccines indicating the vaccine strain, method of preparation and whether attenuated or inactivated.

Ans. Human viral vaccines indicating the vaccine strain, method of preparation, and route of vaccination are shown in Table 12.3.

Table 12.3: Human viral vaccines indicating vaccine strain, method of preparation and route of vaccination.

Disease	Vaccine strain	Cells/egg embryos used for growth	Whether killed or attenuated	Vaccination route
Small pox	Vaccinia	Grown on calf skin	Attenuated	I/D
Yellow fever	17 D	Chicken embryos	Attenuated	S/C
Polyomyelitis	Sabin strain 1, 2, 3	Grown on WI-38 cells	Attenuated	Oral
Rabies	Pitman-Moore	Grown on W/I-38 Cells	Killed (HDCS)	S/C
Mumps	?	Egg embryos by allantoic route	Killed	S/C
Measles	Schwarz strain	Chick fibroblast cells	Attenuated	S/C
Rubella	RA-27/3	WI-38 Cell line	Attenuated	S/C
Influenza	A/HK/68 (H_3N_2)	Chick embryos	Killed	S/C

13

Interferons

Interferons are glycoproteins produced by cells in response to viral or nonviral inducers. Interferons act on cells rendering them refractory to virus infection.

Q. 1. Name different types of interferons and type of cells which induce them.

Ans. The interferons are of alpha (formerly known as type I or leucocyte), beta (formerly known as type I or fibroblast) and gamma (formerly known as type II or immune) types. Alpha interferon is produced by B lymphocytes or macrophages, beta interferon by fibroblasts or epithelial cells and gamma interferon by T lymphocytes. The abbreviation of interferon is IFN.

Q. 2. Differentiate among alpha, beta and gamma interferons.

Ans. Table 13.1: Properties showing differences among alpha, beta and gamma interferons.

Property	Alpha interferon	Beta interferon	Gamma interferon
Inducing agent	Viruses	Viruses or nucleotides	Antigens or mitogens
Mol. weight	15,000-25,000	20,000	20,000-25,000
Stability at pH 2-11	Stable	Stable	Not stable
Stability at 50°C for 1 hr	Stable	Stable	Stable
No. of subtypes (in humans)	16	1	1

Q. 3. Describe various properties of interferons.

Ans. 1. Interferons are non antigenic, and do not elicit antibody production.
2. They can be produced by live or inactivated viruses. Nucleic acids (specially DS, RNA) are good IFN inducer.
3. Interferons are natural defence mechanisms against viral infections.
4. Interferons are species specific and not virus specific. They act on cells and not on viruses.
5. Different viruses differ in their capacity to produce interferons.
6. Maximum interferon production reaches within 6-12 hrs. For higher interferon production, temperature little higher than 37°C is preferred.
7. They are inactivated by proteolytic enzymes and not by nucleases.
8. They are not sedimented even at 100,000 g, for several hours.
9. They are non toxic and can be used for therapeutic purposes.
10. It appears they inhibit transcription or translation to proteins by viral mRNA.

Q. 4. Select true or false statements:

(a) Interferons are neutralized by specific antiviral antibodies.
(b) They are host species specific.
(c) Alpha and beta interferons are produced in cell cultures, and by cells of embryonated eggs and animal hosts but gamma interferon is produced *in vivo* in cells of host animals only.
(d) Most DNA viruses are better interferon producers than most RNA viruses.

Ans. (a) False, (b) True, (c) True, (d) False.

Q. 5. Fill in the blanks:

(a) Interferon was discovered by ...... and ...... in the year ....
(b) The functions of gamma interferon are chiefly ...... in addition to some antiviral and antitumour activities.
(c) Interferon is produced within .... (time) and continue to act for ....
(d) The chemical nature of all three types of interferons is ....

Ans. (a) Isaacs, Lindenmann, 1957, (b) immunoregulatory
(c) hours, several days, (d) glycoprotein

Q. 6. Select true or false statements:

(a) Interferons are not produced by ultraviolet irradiated viruses.
(b) Interferons can be produced in response to synthetic polynucleotides.

(c) By the use of recombinant DNA technology, an interferon producing gene can be inserted in a procaryotic cell to produce large quantity of interferon.
(d) The biological properties of cloned interferons are different from those of naturally occuring interferons.
(e) Human alpha, beta and gamma interferons have been cloned by genetic engineering technology.
(f) Interferon produces nonspecific antiviral proteins by the cells.

Ans. (a) False, (b) True, (c) True, (d) False, (e) True, (f) True.

PART II

PATHOGENIC VIROLOGY

14

Family *Papovaviridae* (Pa = papilloma, Po = polyoma, Va = Vacuolating)

Almost all members of the family can cause tumours. Most of the naturally occurring papovavirus tumours are however benign.

Q. 1. What are important properties of *Papilloma* and *Polyoma* genera of the family?

Ans. Table 14.1: Important physico-chemical properties of *Papovaviridae* genera:

Property	*Papillomavirus*	*Polyomavirus*
Diameter (nm)	55	45
Envelope	Absent	Absent
Capsid symmetry	Icosahedral	Icosahedral
No. of capsomers	72	72
Transcriptase	Absent	Absent
Site of multiplication	Nucleus	Nucleus
Mol wt (Daltons)	5×10^6	3×10^6
Nature of genome:		
Nucleic acid	DNA	DNA
No. of strands	Double-stranded	Double-stranded
Shape	Circular	Circular
Segments	Nonsegmented	Nonsegmented
DNA content (W/W)	10%	12.3%

Q. 2. Name different species of *Papilloma* and *Polyoma* viruses, and the diseases produced by them.

Ans. Table 14.2: Species and diseases produced by *Papilloma* and *Polyoma* viruses

Genus	Species/Type	Disease
1. *Papillomavirus*	Rabbit papilloma virus	Shop papilloma
	Papilloma viruses affecting domestic animals	Warts in young animals
2. *Polyomavirus*	Polyoma virus of mice	Tumours in mice
	Simian vacuolating Virus$_{40}$ (SV$_{40}$)	Cytoplasmic vacuolation

Genus *Papilloma*

Q. 3. Briefly describe the pathogenicity of *Papillomavirus* in different species of domestic animals.

Ans. These viruses produce warts of different sizes, around head, neck, shoulders, nostrils and eyes. Young animals are more susceptible then adults. The warts regress as the animal advances in age. The virus spreads by contact and multiplies in skin epithelium. Skin injury helps in infection. The affected parts become thick and nodular. The virus does not produce malignant tumours but transform infected cells.

Q. 4. Select true or false statements :

(a) *Papillomavirus* can be grown in chicken embryos.

(b) The virus produces cytopathic effects in cell cultures.

(c) Different serotypes have not been reported in the viruses infecting different species of animals.

(d) Viruses infecting different species of animals cross react by immunodiffusion test.

(e) Viruses can be identified serologically by virus neutralization test.

Ans. (a) True, (b) False, (c) True, (d) False, (e) True

Genus *Polyomavirus*

Q. 5. (a) *Polyomavirus* is oncogenic in rodents and transforms cells in cell cultures.

(b) *Polyomavirus* does not haemagglutinate RBCs from any species of animal.

(c) The mice are latently infected with *Polyomavirus* without any clinical symptoms.

(d) *Polymavirus* does not produce cytopathic effects in mouse embryo cell cultures.

(e) Some adenoviruses need SV$_{40}$ as helper virus for replication.

(f) SV_{40} polyomavirus does not show any clinical symptoms in monkeys.

Ans. (a) True, (b) False, (c) True, (d) False, (e) True, (f) True

Q. 6. What precautions should be taken for using monkey kidney cells to grow viruses for vaccine production?

Ans. Some monkeys are carriers of SV_{40}. The virus can contaminate the vaccine, if the cells are used for virus multiplication in primary cell cultures. SV_{40} does not show any clinical symptoms in monkeys but produces cytoplasmic vacuolation in vero cell cultures.

15

Family *Adenoviridae*

Adenoviruses are so named because originally they were isolated from human adenoid tissue. These viruses are highly species specific. They generally produce subclinical infections and occasionally upper respiratory tract infections.

Q. 1. Give important physical and chemical properties of *Adenoviridae* family viruses.

Ans. Table 15.1: Showing important properties of adenoviruses.

Diameter	70-90 nm
Envelope	Absent
Capsid symmetry	Icosahedral
Number of capsomers	252
Transcriptase	Absent
Site of multiplication	Nucleus
Mol. Wt. (Daltons)	20×10^6 to 29×10^6
Nature of genome:	
Type of nucleic acid	DNA
No. of strands	Double
Shape	Linear
Segments	Non-segmented
Genome size	30-37 kbs

The virus produces intranuclear inclusion bodies, and agglutinates RBCs. Except avian virus strains, most other serotypes from different species of animals, produce only mild upper respiratory tract infections. Some viruses are oncogenic in rodents. Virus remains latent for long periods in the host. Recovered animals produce HI, CF and VN antibodies.

Q. 2. Name the No. of serotypes of adenoviruses from different species of animals and birds and the diseases produced by them.

Ans.

Genus	Serotypes	Diseases
1. *Mastadeno virus*	Human adenovirus-41 types Bovine adenovirus-9 types Equine adenovirus-2 types Porcine adenovirus-5 types Ovine adenovirus-6 types Caprine adenovirus-2 types Monkey adenovirus-24 types	Most serotypes from domestic animals produce subclinical infections
	Canine adenovirus-2 types	One serotype produces canine hepatitis
2. *Aviadeno virus*	Fowl adenovirus-12 types Duck adenovirus-2 types Goose adenovirus-3 types Quails adenovirus	Avian types are associated with different sydromes including egg drop syndrome (EDS_{76} and CELO)

Adenoviruses are not very important from disease point of view, except infectious canine hepatitis and one serotype of fowls causing egg drop syndrome.

Genus *Mastadenovirus*

Q. 3. Briefly describe the pathogenesis of infectious canine hepatitis.

Ans. There is fever, anorexia, increased thirst, depression, leucopenia, nasal and ocular discharge and corneal opacity. The animal may stand in tucked up position. In acute cases the animal dies within a week. The virus has preference to propagate in reticulo-endothelial system and hepatic cells. The mucous membranes become congested, liver and spleen become enlarged. There is diarrhoea and vomiting. Liver cells have intranuclear inclusion bodies. Transmission of the disease occurs by droplet infection or contaminated food or water. The virus may persists in lymphoid tissues of pharyngeal region. It is also localized in kidneys and excreted in urine. Killed and modified virus vaccines are available. Combined distemper, canine hepatitis and leptospira vaccines are available.

Q. 4. How will you diagnose a case of infectious canine hepatitis?

Ans. The disease can be diagnosed by isolation and identification of the virus, clinical symptoms and histopathological findings, testing of HI, CF and SN antibodies and differences of antibody titres in paired serum samples i.e. one collected during acute phase of the disease and the second after recovery. FA test can also be employed on liver tissue sections and smears prepared from nasal and ocular discharges. Ferrets are not susceptible to the disease. They are susceptible to canine distemper. There is leucopenia.

Q. 5. Name the type of specimens to be collected for diagnosis of a canine hepatitis case and host system to be used for the isolation of the virus.

Ans. The specimens used for the isolation of the virus are affected organs like respiratory tract, lungs, intestine, liver, spleen faeces, urine and nasal discharges. For isolation of the virus cell cultures from kidneys or testicular cells from young/foetal pups for primary cell cultures are preferred.

Select the correct answer:

Q. 6. The incubation period of infectious canine hepatitis is:
(a) Less than 1 week (b) 2 to 3 weeks
(c) 4 weeks (d) 5 to 6 weeks

Ans. (a)

Q. 7. Infectious canine hepatitis virus induces:
(a) Haemagglutination inhibition (HI) antibodies
(b) Complement fixing antibodies
(c) Serum neutralizing antibodies
(d) All the three types of antibodies

Ans. (d)

Q. 8. Infectious canine hepatitis in dogs produces:
(a) Pink eye (b) Blue eye (c) Pearly eye (d) None of above

Ans. (b)

Q. 9. Infectious canine hepatitis virus is excreted from body through:
(a) Nasal discharges (b) Faeces
(c) Urine (d) Through all above

Ans. (d)

Q. 10. Select true or false statements:
(a) Adenoviruses agglutinate human 0, guinea pig, and rat RBC.
(b) Canine adenovirus can not be propagated in chicken embryos.
(c) Ferrets are very susceptible to canine hepatitis virus.

(d) Dogs recovered from canine hepatitis virus produce life long immunity.
(e) Both attenuated and inactivated vaccines are available to control canine hepatitis.

Ans. (a) true, (b) false, (c) false, (d) true, (e) true

Q. 11. Fill in the blanks:
(a) Infectious canine hepatitis was first recognised by .... in 1947. Hence the disease is also known as ....
(b) Canine adenovirus shows common ....antigens with human adenoviruses.
(c) Dogs infected with infectious canine hepatitis shed virus in urine upto about ....
(d) Canine hepatitis virus is oncogenic in .... and transforms liver cells.

Ans. (a) Rubarth, Rubarth's disease (b) complement fixing
(c) six months (d) hamester

Genus *Aviadenovirus*

Q. 12. (a) Fowl adenoviruses primarily infect ...., ... and ....
(b) Adenoviruses are generally isolated from the ...., and .... tracts of apparently normal and clinically infected chickens.
(c) Quail bronchitis virus in young quails may cause upto .... % mortality and .... % morbidity.
(d) Fowl adenovirus is vertically transmitted through ....
(e) The CELO virus was first isolated in ....as a contaminant from embryonating chicken eggs.

Ans. (a) chickens, turkeys, quails
(b) respiratory, intestinal (c) 50, 100
(d) embryonating eggs (e) 1957

Q. 13. Briefly describe general properties of the virus causing egg drop syndrome in chickens.

Ans. The virus is one of the major causes of drops is egg production in fowls. The egg drop syndrome$_{76}$ (EDS$_{76}$) strain was originally isolated by Dutch workers in the year 1976. Infection of the virus may reduce egg production in laying fowls upto 40%. The eggs produced by fowls infected by this virus, are soft shelled or shell less with irregular shapes and sizes. The virus does not grow in mammalian cells but gives optimal growth in duck cells and duck embryos by allantoic route. The virus does not grow in chicken embryos. The transmission of the virus is vertical as well as horizontal through nasal secretions and faeces etc. The virus develops intranuclear inclusion bodies in cell cultures as well as in epithelial cells of oviduct of infected birds. The virus haemagglutinates duck, chick and goose RBCs. The EDS_{76} virus has only one serotype. The seroprevalence of the disease was first reported in India by Mohanty *et al* in 1984.

Q. 14. Name diseases caused by avian adenoviruses.

Ans. In addition to CELO and egg drop syndrome in chickens, other avian adenoviruses cause bronchitis, enteritis, and egg drop in turkeys, hepatitis in ducks and bronchitis in quails.

Q. 15. What is the role of CELO virus in poultry farming?

Ans. The virus is generally endogenous contaminant from embryonating chicken eggs. The virus apparently does not cause any clinical disease in chickens. The virus however may activate other infections like mycoplasmosis and infectious bronchitis. Since the virus is a contaminant in kidney cell cultures, it may contaminate the vaccine, if such cultures are used for vaccine production. It may also interfere in the propagation of other viruses in eggs. The virus was first isolated in India in 1971 by Verma *et al.*

Q. 16. What are important clinical symptoms and pathogenesis of quail bronchitis?

Ans. (a) The virus causes an acute and fatal respiratory disease.
(b) Young quails are most susceptible.
(c) The incubation period of the disease is 2 to 7 days.
(d) The birds suffer from depression, coughing, and sneezing. There is lacrymation and conjunctivitis.
(e) The mortality may be as high as 50 per cent.
(f) The virus may produce malignant tumours in new born hamesters.
(g) Immunity in experimental quails may be upto 6 months.
(h) Virus neutralising antibodies have been demonstrated in recovered quails.

Q. 17. How will you diagnose egg drop syndrome in chickens?

Ans. The disease can be diagnosed by decrease in egg production, soft shell or shell less eggs, discolouration of coloured eggs, isolation of virus in duck embryonated eggs from disease free flocks, presence of intranuclear inclusion bodies in infected cells and HI and SN tests with known antiserum.

16

Family *Herpesviridae*

About one hundred herpesviruses have been isolated and characterized from mammals, birds, insects and reptiles. Some of them cause major diseases in domestic animals and birds.

Q. 1. Give important physico-chemical properties of herpesviruses in a tabular form.

Ans. Table 16.1: Important physico-chemical properties of herpesviruses.

Diameter	150-170 nm
Envelope	Present
Capsid symmetry	Icosahedral
No. of capsomers	162
Transcriptase	Absent
Site of multiplication	Nucleus
Nature of genome:	
Type of nucleic acid	DNA
No. of strands	Double
Shape	Linear
Segments	Non-segmented
genome size	120-220 kbs

Other properties: These viruses are sensitive to ether and chloroform, and are labile at pH 3.0. They have different types of peplomers and produce intranuclear inclusion bodies. The virus establishes latent infection with recurrent or continuous shedding of virus. The virion contains more than 30 proteins and produces humoral and cell mediated immunity.

Q. 2. Name different subfamilies of herpesviruses and differentiate them on the basis of important properties.

Ans. Herpesviruses are classified into three subfamilies. They are:

1. *Alphaherpesvirinae*, 2. *Betaherpesvirinae*, 3. *Gammaherpesvirinae*

Table 16.2: Showing differences among the three subfamilies.

Properties	*Alphaherpesvirinae*	*Betaherpesvirinae*	*Gammaherpesvirinae*
Replicative cycle	12-18 hours	More than 24 hrs	Longer
Host range	Wide	Narrow	Narrow
Tendency of latency	Yes, in ganglia of trigeminal nerve	Yes, in salivery glands & other organs	Yes, in lymphoid tissues
Cytopathic effects	Rapid, virus released from cells	Slow, virus remains cell associated	Slow, CPE in 5-10 days
Preference of cells for growth	Variety of cells	Grow best in fibroblasts	Replicates in B or T cells
Oncogenic tendency	Nil	Nil	Yes

Q. 3. Name serotypes and diseases produced by different subfamilies in different species of animals.

Ans. **Table 16.3:** Different serotypes and diseases produced in different species of animals.

Species of animals	Serotypes & diseases by *Alphaherpesvirinae*	Serotypes & diseases by *Betaherpesvirinae*	Serotypes & diseases by *Gammaherpesvirinae*
Bovines	Herpes virus-1, IBR; HV-2, skin infection & mammillitis; HV-4, respiratory syndrome	–	HV-3, malignant catarrhal fever
Equines	HV-1, abortion; HV-3, coital exanthema; HV-4, mild respiratory disease	HV-2, (CMV); mild respiratory disease	–
Swine	HV-1, pseudorabies (Aujezsky's disease)	HV-2 (CMV) mild generalized infection	–

(Contd.)

Species of animals	Serotypes & diseases by *Alpha-herpesvirinae*	Serotypes & diseases by *Beta-herpesvirinae*	Serotypes & diseases by *Gamma-herpesvirinae*
Ovines	HV-1, inapparent infection	–	–
Canines	HV-1, haemorrhagic disease in pups	–	–
Fowls	HV-1, ILT HV-2, Marek's disease	–	–
Ducks	HV-1, duck plague	–	–
Humans	HV-1 and 2, herpes simplex & vericella zoster (Chicken pox)	Human CMV, no disease	Human-HV (EBR), Burkitt's lymphoma

IBR - Infectious bovine rhinotracheitis
ILT - Infectious larygotracheitis
CMV - Cytomegalovirus
EBR - Epstein Barr virus

Bovine *herpesviruses*

Q. 4. What are other properties of bovine herpes virus-1 causing IBR?

Ans. The properties are:

(a) The virus grows in wide variety of cell cultures.
(b) The CPE produced by the virus in cell cultures is balooning, degeneration and polycaryocytosis type.
(c) Virus transforms hamester embryo cells.
(d) The virus contains more than 30 proteins.
(e) The virus causes latent infection also.

Q. 5. Give an account of the pathogenesis of infectious bovine rhinotracheitis.

Ans. There are 5 clinical forms of IBR. They are respiratory, genital, conjunctival, abortion and encephalitic forms.

Respiratory form: Sudden onset of high fever, increased rate of respiration, persistent cough, anorexia, depression, nasal discharge (mucopurulent), salivation, dyspnoea, inflammed nasal mucosa (red nose). Finally diphtheritic membrane is formed over nasal mucosa and trachea. The virus causes viraemia for a short duration and the virus is recovered from buffy-coat leucocyte cultures. The incubation period of the disease is about 4-6 days. The disease has been reported from several parts of India.

Genital form: The disease is known as infectious pustular vulvovaginitis (IPV), infectious pustular balanoposthitis (IPB) and coital vesicular exanthema. Symptoms are elevation and switching of tail, frequent urination, hyperaemia of vulvovaginal mucosa, vaginal discharge, and formation of pustules which may lead to metritis and infertility. Genital form usually causes infertility but not abortion. In males the disease is known as IPB with similar lesions on the penis and prepuce. The condition does not affect the quality of semen and reproductive ability of bulls. Incubation period varies from 1-3 days after mating.

Abortion: Foetus is infected and dead when expelled. Placenta may be retained temporarily. Metritis occurs rarely and does not cause infertility. Abortion generally occurs in the third trimester following natural infection. There are no characteristic signs and lesions in the cow and foetus. The virus can be isolated from placenta and sometimes from pleural and peritoneal fluids.

Conjunctival form: This is generally accompanied with respiratory form of IBR. There is serous to mucopurulent ocular discharge. Some animals recover and others develop corneal opacity. Conjunctivitis may give pink eye appearance.

Encephalitic form: The incidence of this form is less, and usually seen in calves. This is generally characterised by incoordination, occasional circling, recumbency and death. The course of the disease is rapid and fatal.

Q. 6. What type of materials should be collected for isolation of bovine herpes virus-1?

Ans. Affected tracheal, nasal, conjuctival and genital swabs, foetal tissues and semen from infected bulls, should be collected for isolation of the virus.

Q. 7. Briefly describe how IBR can be diagnosed?

Ans. The disease can be diagnosed by history of the herd, clinical symptoms and lesions, isolation and identification of the virus, and serological testing against known antiserum. Smears can be tested by FA test. Other useful tests are indirect HA, CF and VN. Virus grows very fast in cell cultures and characteristic CPE develops within 12 hours after infection. For serological diagnosis, paired serum samples are very useful.

Q. 8. Describe the pathogenesis of vesicular skin infection and mammillitis caused by bovine herpes virus-2 in bovines.

Ans. The virus produces vesicular skin infection and mammilitis in cattle. The virus was first isolated in South Africa in 1957 from cattle and was known as pseudo lumpyskin disease. Later on it was isolated from several other countries. The virus affects udder, teats and some times there is generalized skin infection. There may be mild fever but no viraemia. In generalized infection, nodules appear on skin of face, neck and back. In 8-10 days local swelling subsides. In Africa wild animals like buffaloes, giraffe and other ruminants may be affected. The virus may be transmitted through arthropod vectors. Antigenically the virus is related to human herpes simplex virus. For proper diagnosis, the disease should be differentiated from warts, FMD, cowpox, pseudo cowpox, and vesicular stomatitis. The incubation period of the disease is 3-7 days.

Q. 9. Give a brief account of the pathogenesis of malignant catarrahl fever due to bovine herpesvirus type-3.

Ans. The virus is classified under the subfamily *Gammaherpesvirinae,* and causes bovine catarrhal fever in cattle and buffaloes. The disease occurs in peracute form causing generalized fatal disease affecting respiratory and intestinal tracts and other organs. There is ophthalmia and corneal opacity. Infected animals show symptoms of dyspnoea, acute stomatitis, profuse salivation, pneumonia, and swelling of lymphnodes of head and neck, which also become haemorrhagic. The incubation period in experimental animals is 8-10 weeks. The disease generally terminates in death due to encephalitis within 5-10 days after the onset of fever.

Q. 10. What are suitable specimens and host systems for the isolation of bovine HV-3? How would you diagnose the disease?

Ans. The best specimens for isolation of bovine HV-3 is buffy coat leucocytes and fresh thyroid tissue. Lymph nodes are very rich in the virus. The virus grows well in calf thyroid cell cultures. The virus produces small nonprogressive CPE in 2-3 weeks. There may be multinucleated vacuolated syncytia and type A intranuclear inclusions. The disease can be diagnosed on the basis of symptoms, isolation and identification of the virus and CPE in cell cultures. Serological tests are of no help due to low infectivity titre.

Equine *herpesviruses*

Q. 11. Describe the pathogenesis of the disease caused by equine herpesvirus type-1.

Ans. The virus produces at least three following types of disease syndromes:

(a) Respiratory disease in young horses.

(b) Abortion in mares

(c) Neurological form in older horses

A brief description of these syndromes is given below:

(a) *Respiratory disease:* This is also known as equine rhino-pneumonitis (ERP). The symptoms of the disease are fever, anorexia and profuse nasal discharge which later on becomes mucopurulent. There is transient leucopaenia. In older horses there is subclinical infection. There are intranuclear inclusion bodies in infected cells of respiratory tract. Deaths are uncommon in uncomplicated cases.

(b) *Abortion:* In mares abortion may occur as a sequelae to respiratory infection. Mares usually abort in 9th and 10th months of gestation period. This virus is also responsible for still births after full gestation or birth of weak foal which die within 72 hours of birth. Before abortion, mares do not show any clinical sign and abortion occurs suddenly. Experimentally the genital disease caused by this virus is similar to equine coital exanthema caused by equine herpesvirus-3.

(c) *Neurological form:* It involves central nervous system and may be enzootically associated with respiratory disease and abortion. The clinical signs are incoordination, weakness and paralysis. The virus has been isolated from brains and spinal cords from paralytic cases.

Q. 12. What are the properties of equine herpies virus-2?

Ans. (a) The virus is wide spread in equine population and isolated from apparently normal, subclinical or having various disease syndromes. This is classified under subfamily *Betaherpesvirinae.*

(b) The virus grows slowly and only in some cell cultures. It takes 10 to 15 days before initial foci appear in cell cultures.

(c) It remains cell associated and yields small amount of free infectious virus.

(d) The virus has generally been isolated from respiratory and genital tracts.

(e) It is also termed as equine cytomegalovirus.

(f) Adult horses carry low level of serum antibodies which can be detected by VN and CF tests.

(g) The virus has not been recovered from foetal tissues, and does not cross placenta.

Q. 13. Briefly give an account of the pathogenesis of coital exanthema caused by equine herpesvirus-3.

Ans. The virus causes equine coital exanthema. The venereal disease in females and males is transmitted through coitus. The virus grows only in equine cell cultures. It is host specific and grows rapidly producing plaques of about 1 cm. diameter. The disease produced by the virus is acute. The lesions are produced on external genitalia and sometimes on upper respiratory tract. Incubation period varies from 2 to 10 days. The lesions are formation of vesicles which convert into pustules and finally cause ulceration of vaginal mucosa. In males, there are haemorrhagic erosions and ulcers on penis and prepuce. Inclusion bodies are present in the epithelial cells at the origin of ulcers.

Q. 14. What are the clinical features of equine herpesvirus type-4?

Ans. The virus causes respiratory disease in foals which is generally known as equine rhinopneumonitis (ERP). There is fever, profuse nasal discharge which later on becomes mucopurulent. Many foals develop only mild respiratory infection. The disease occurs under stress conditions caused by secondary infections. Older horses may carry the virus and become source of infection to foals. Both inactivated and attenuated herpesvirus type-1 vaccine are generally used for prevention of the disease.

Swine *herpesvirus*

Q. 15. Describe pathogenesis of Aujeszky's disease (psendorabies) due to porcine herpes virus type-1.

Ans. The disease caused by the virus is known as Aujeszky's disease, pseudorabies or maditch. The virus can infect man, cattle and several other domestic animals. Infection takes place through ingestion, skin, nasal and oral mucous membranes. In pigs, lesions are observed in respiratory, nervous and reproductive systems. There is encephalitis. The infected sows may abort. Still births or mummified foetuses and reproductive failures are also associated with the diseases. The animals rub and scratch body parts due to continuous itching. Both killed and attenuated vaccines are available.

Q. 16. Briefly describe, how pseudorabies can be diagnosed in swines?

Ans. The virus multiplies in rabbit and pig kidney and testicular cell cultures, and in chicken embryo fibroblasts. It produces pock lesions on chorioallantoic membrane of chicken embryos. Intranuclear inclusion bodies are observed in affected cells of central nervous system. The virus should be confirmed by serological tests using known antiserum.

Fowl and duck *herpesviruses*

Q. 17. Describe the properties and pathogenesis, of fowl herpesvirus-1.

Ans. The virus produces infectious laryngotracheitis (ILT) in chickens and appears to be antigenically homogeneous. However some strains, though fully antigenic, are poorly neutralized by its antiserum. Different strains of the virus vary in pathogenicity, some are highly pathogenic, others are non-pathogenic or mildly pathogenic. The virus grows in embryonated chicken eggs and produces opaque pock lesions on CAM with 4 to 5 days. The pocks have a depressed central area of necrosis. The pock lesions are of variable sizes, the larger pock's diameter may be about 4-5 mm. The virus is adapted to grow in chicken embryo cell cultures. The virus has a narrow host specificity, infecting only chickens and pheasants of all age groups. The disease can be produced experimentally by intranasal, intraocular and intratracheal inoculation and occurs naturally by droplet infection. The disease is highly contagious affecting respiratory tract. In acute form, it is characterized by respiratory gasping and nasal discharge of blood stained exudates with high mortality. The lesions are found in upper respiratory tract i.e. trachea and larynx with intra-nuclear inclusion bodies in infected cells. There is no evidence of transmission through eggs. With the virulent virus, incubation period is 2 to 6 days and the course of the disease varies from 1 to 2 weeks. With mild virus strains, the disease runs a protracted course. The disease can be diagnosed by symptoms and lesions, pock lesions on CAM, intranuclear inclusion bodies (Cowdry type A), and isolation of the virus. The virus is confirmed by serum neutralization, agar diffusion and FA tests with known antiserum. Live attenuated virus vaccines are in use to control the disease. In India the infection was reported for the first time in 1964. The disease is widely prevalent, but occurs in mild or subclinical forms and does not need vaccination.

Q. 18. Briefly describe the properties and pathogenicity of duck herpesvirus-1 causing duck plague.

Ans. Most of the properties of duck plague virus, are similar to the viruses of *Herpesviridae* family. The virus multiplies on CAM of embryonated duck eggs, and duck embryo fibroblast cells and can be easily adapted to grow on chicken embryos and chicken fibroblasts. After inoculation, duck embryos die in 4-5 days with extensive haemorrhages. The virus produces small plaques in monolayer cell cultures. Duck herpesvirus strains are similar serologically. Different strains are reported to vary in virulence. The virus produces acute, fatal contagious disease in ducks. Outbreaks of the disease is reported in geese, swans and water fowls of all ages, with an incubation period of 3 to 7 days. The affected birds have viraemia, thirst, anorexia, ruffled feathers, nasal discharge, droopiness and watery diarrhoea. There is reduction in egg production, in the infected flock. The transmission of disease is by direct and indirect contacts but not through eggs. Experimental infection is through oral, intranasal and parenteral routes. There is septicaemia, and haemorrhages in internal organs. The intranuclear inclusions appear in liver and gastrointestinal mucosa. Diagnosis of the diseases can be done by symptoms and lesions of the diseases, isolation of the virus and confirmation by VN test. A chick embryo-adapted attenuated virus vaccine has given good results. The vaccine is given in ducklings over 2 weeks of age. The vaccine virus does not spread through contacts.

Q. 19. What are the clinical features of fowl herpes virus-2 causing Marek's disease (range paralysis)?

Ans. Marek's disease was first discovered by Marek in 1907. The disease was known avian leukosis complex (ALC) before 1967, when Marek's diseases virus (a DNA virus) was separated from avian leukosis (a RNA virus). Earlier the virus was classified under subfamily *Gammaherpesvirinae* but recently on account of its genome resembling with the genomes of other members of *Alphaherpesvirinae* has been shifted under this subfamily. Marek's disease occurs in four clinical forms known as neurolymphomatosis, acute Marek's diseases, ocular lymphomatosis, and cutaneous Marek's diseases.

The disease commonly occurs in 2-4 months old chickens. Only a small percentage of infected chickens develops clinical disease. In the clinical forms of neurolymphomatosis, there is progressive paralysis of one or more limbs, incoordination, drooping of limb(s) and head. Blindness occurs in ocular lymphomatosis. There is depression in acute cases. In cutaneous forms there are nodular lesions particularly at feather follicles. There are lymphoid tumours in gonads, lungs, liver, spleen and kidneys. Affected organs are enlarged and pale due to infiltration of lymphocytes. Peripheral nerves are enlarged and infiltrated with immature mononuclear cells. The virus matures in feather follicle cells, sheds into environment and transmit the disease to healthy birds through respiratory tract. Many apparently healthy birds are lifelong carriers and shedders of virus. There is no transmission through eggs. Tumour material containing virus can also transmit the disease. As the virus is cell associated, cell free filtrate does not transmit the disease. Chickens infected with MDV, produce humoral and cell mediated immunity.

Q. 20. Explain how Marek's disease virus, behaves differently in lymphoid and non-lymphoid cells?

Ans. (a) In lymphoid cells, there is transformation of the virus resulting in proliferation of cells without cell death. No virus is produced in these cells. The infected cells contain Marek's associated tumour specific surface antigen (MATSA).

(b) In transformed cells, MATSA can be detected by immuno diffusion and immunofluorescent tests using serum prepared with transplantable tumour cells.

(c) In non lymphoid cells either there is productive infection resulting in the production of infectious virion as in case of feather follicle cells or production of non infectious virion. The non infectious virion produces intranuclear inclusions and causes cell death.

Q. 21. Select true or false statements:

(a) In a poultry flock the infection of Marek's disease and leukosis does not occur simultaneously.

(b) In infected flock, the birds may have antibody as well as virus of Marek's disease which may be released in danders from feather follicle.

(c) Different strains of the virus may vary in virulence.

(d) There is no immunosuppression due to Marek's disease virus.

(e) Marek's disease virus and turkey herpesvirus are antigenically related.

(f) Cell associated vaccine is preferred over lyophilized cell free vaccine in day old chicks.

(g) Newly hatched chicks from vaccinated flock may be protected from the disease upto 2-3 weeks by maternal antibody.

(h) Cell free virus transmit the disease from infected to non-infected birds.

(i) Non oncogenic strains of MDV do not produce clinical disease.

Ans. (a) False, (b) True, (c) True, (d) False, (e) True, (f) True, (g) True, (h) False, (i) False

Q. 22. How Marek's disease can be diagnosed?

Ans. The disease can be diagnosed by clinical symptoms, age when birds are infected, post mortem findings, histopathology, detection of viral antigens by FA test, pock lesions on CAM of embryos and intranuclear inclusion bodies.

Q. 23. Fill in the blanks:

(a) Marek's disease viral antigen is produced by.........cells, and MATSA by ....cells.

(b) Chickens develop both ....and......... immunity after infection with MDV.

(c) Resistance to MD is primarily due to......... response.

(d) About 80 to 90% of the virus genome in infected lympho-blastoid cells remain in ....form.

(e) Infectious virus of Marek's disease in chickens is produced by ....cells.

(f) There is transformation of MDV leading to cell proliferation without cell death in......... cells in chickens, but there is no transformation of these cells ....

(g) Turkey herpesvirus is non oncogenic in .... and can be used as ....

Ans. (a) non lymphoid, lymphoid
(b) humoral, cell mediated
(c) cell mediated immune
(d) non integrated
(e) feather follicle
(f) lymphoid, *in vitro*
(g) chickens, vaccine

Canine *herpesvirus* type-1

Q. 24. Bricfly describe the pathogenicity of canine herpesvirus-1

Ans. The virus produces a highly generalized haemorragic disease in pups under four weeks of age. The incubation period of the disease is 4-8 days. The symptoms of the disease are abdominal pain, anorexia, and dyspnea. In older dogs, there may be vaginal discharge. The virus may cause mild respiratory disease. There may be viraemia. Inclusion bodies may be present in liver cells. The virus can be isolated in canine cell cultures.

Human *herpesvirus* 1 and 2

Q. 25. Briefly describe herpes simplex disease in humans due to herpesvirus 1 and 2.

Ans. Herpesvirus type-1 is generally isolated from lesions in and around mouth and transmitted by direct contact. Type-2 virus is responsible for majority of genital tract infections and transmitted venereally. These two types serologically cross react with each other. The virus grows in a variety of cell cultures including CAM of chicken embryos. The infection is wide spread in humans which is evident from serological tests. Primary infection occurs in childhood. Asymptomatic carriers are important source of infection. The virus may remain latent in ganglia of trigeminal and sacral nerves and reactivated periodically. The primary infection is more severe and wide spread while recurrent infection is localized. The lesions are thin walled vesicles, which become pustules and scabs and heal without any scarification.

17

Family *Poxviridae*

Poxviridae family has largest virus particles with complex nucleo-capsid. These viruses can be seen under ordinary light microscope. They cause skin lesions in man, animals, birds and insects. There are still some pox viruses which have not been assigned to any genus namely *Molluscum contagiosum* affecting human beings.

Q. 1. What are physico-chemical properties of pox viruses?

Ans. Table 17.1: Properties of pox viruses.

Size (nm)	300 × 240 × 100 (It is brick-shaped and largest among animal viruses)
Envelope	Present
Capsid	Complex type
No. of capsomers	–
Transcriptase	Present (Some other enzymes also present)
Site of multiplication	Cytoplasm
Nature of genome:	
Nucleic acid	DNA type
No. of strands	Double
Shape	Linear
Segments	Non-segmented
Mol. Wt. (Daltons)	100 to 200 × 10^6
DNA content (W/W)	5% (130-230 kbp)
Percentage of G + C	35 to 40%

Q. 2. Name different subfamilies, genera and species of *Poxviridae*

Ans. Subfamily: 1. *Chordopoxvirinae*

Genus: 1. *Orthopoxvirus*

Species: 1. Vaccinia virus (Smallpox vaccine virus)

2. Cowpox virus

3. Buffalopox virus
4. Horsepox virus
5. Camelpox virus
6. Ectromelia virus (Mouse pox)
7. Monkeypox virus
8. Rabbitpox virus
9. Variola (Small pox)

Genus 2. *Capripoxvirus*

Species: 1. Goatpox virus
2. Sheeppox virus
3. Lumpy skin disease virus (affects bovines in Africa)

Genus 3. *Avipoxvirus*

Species: 1. Fowlpox virus
2. Canarypox virus
3. Pigeonpox virus
4. Turkeypox virus
5. Quailpox virus

Genus 4. *Leporipoxvirus* (Tumour producing poxviruses)

Species: 1. Myxoma virus (affects rabbits)
2. Rabbit fibroma (Shope)
3. Hare fibroma

Genus 5. *Parapoxvirus*

Species: 1. Orf virus (Contagious pustular dermatitis virus or contagious Ecthyma virus of Sheep)
2. Pseudocowpox virus (Milker's nodule virus)

Genus 6. *Suipoxvirus*

Species: 1. Swinepox virus

Different genera share some antigens, while they have their own specific antigens.

Genus *Capripoxvirus*

Q. 3. Describe the properties, pathogenicity and immunity of sheep pox virus.

Ans. Sheep pox virus causes a contagious and most severe pox disease. The virus is quite resistant to dessication. It is antigenically related to goat pox virus but not to the virus of contagious pustular dermatitis virus. There is no serological relationship between sheep pox and vaccinia viruses. The virus grows well in sheep and goat kidney and testes cell cultures. The virus can be adapted to grow on CAM of embryonated chicken eggs. It produces CPE in cell cultures and cytoplasmic inclusion bodies in infected cells. The incubation period of the disease in sheep is 4 to 7 days.

The affected sheep show nasal discharge, fever, eruption of pustules through out the body, which become dark red and flat. The pustules become necrosed in 6-8 days, and later on the epithelium slough off. The entire course of the disease is about 3-4 weeks. During the course of the disease, there is viraemia, when the virus can be isolated from tissues and skin lesions. Infected animals develop SN and ID antibodies. Mortality in sheep can be upto 50%. The recovered animals develop solid immunity. Both attenuated as well as killed vaccine with adjuvant are available to control the disease.

Goat poxvirus

Q. 3. What are the properties and pathogenicity of goat poxvirus? Describe its antigenic relationship with sheep and other poxviruses.

Ans. Most of the properties of goat poxvirus are similar to sheep poxvirus. The disease is more common in young animals and milking females. The virus is adapted to grow in lamb and kid kidney cell cultures with CPE similar to sheeppox virus including intracytoplasmic inclusion bodies of different shapes and sizes. On experimental inoculation goatpox is characterized by erythematous swelling on 4th day followed by pustule formation on 6th or 7th day. The pustules become necrosed on 10th to 12th day. Human beings handling goats suffering from goat pox, contract the disease. There is no serological relationship between vaccinia virus and goat pox virus. The titre of cell associated goat poxvirus is higher than cell free virus in cell cultures.

Genus *Parapox Virus*

Q. 5. Describe the pathogenesis and immunity of contagious pustular dermatitis (contagious ecthyma) virus.

Ans. The virus causing CPD is quite resistant, and in dessicated form survives for years. The virus is contagious, cause CPD in sheep and goats. It primarily affects the lips, mouth and rarely interdigital region of the feet. In adults lesions on udders & genitals may occur. The mortality in affected animals is very low, but the morbidity is high. The virus has some antigentic relationship with other parapox viruses and also with goat pox virus. The virus grows well in ovine and bovine kidney cell cultures and testicular cells with typical CPE and intracytoplasmic inclusion bodies. The course of the disease is 3-4 weeks, when thick scabs develop. Recovered animals develop cell mediated immunity, which is long lasting. Human beings are also infected with the virus. Live virus vaccine given to lambs and kids by scarification method gives satisfactory immunity which should be repeated after 2-3 months.

Genus *Orthopoxvirus*

Q. 6. Describe the pathogenicity of variola and vaccina viruses.

Ans. The variola virus is the causative agent of small pox, a severe disease of human beings. Small pox used to occur in two distinct clinical forms known as Variola major and Variola minor. Variola major caused typically highly fatal small pox disease which used to occur in India and other Asian countries. The other milder form (variola minor) was seen in Latin America. The variola major and variola minor viral strains are antigenically identical. Small pox virus enters the body through respiratory tract, then to regional lymph nodes and finally to blood stream. Lastly reticulo-endothelial system is affected which caused viraemia. Due to Viraemia mucous membranes, skin and other tissues are affected causing clinical illness. The incubation period of the disease is 9-15 days.

The prodromal (pre eruptive) stage of small pox is characterised by onset of fever and headache. After 2 or 3 days, the temperature falls and simultaneously skin rashes appear. The congested spots on skin develop into papules, which in turn gets converted to vesicles and pustules, and lastly a scab is formed which separates after 2-3 weeks leaving a depressed scar. Smallpox vaccine was prepared by growing the virus in the skin of healthy calf and sheep and also on CAM of embryonated chicken eggs. Smallpox disease was eradicated from India in the year 1975 and soon after from all countries of the world.

Q. 7. Write short notes on cow pox and buffalo pox viruses.

Ans. Cow pox virus is antigenically different from vaccinia virus. Buffalo pox virus is also distinct from cow pox and variola viruses. These viruses cause mild infection of udder and teats. The incubation period ranges from 3-7 days. There is no systematic reaction. The lesions are small, congested spots which develop into papules surrounded by red oedematous tissue. The papules become vesicles, pustules and then scabs before healing.

Genus *Suispoxvirus*

Q. 8. Briefly describe the pathogenesis and immunity of swine pox virus.

Ans. It is a benign disease of young pigs. Lesions are usually found on lower parts of abdomen and inside thighs and arms. Lesions appear as red papules which convert to vesicles, pustules and then to scabs in 10-12 days. The crust fall off within 3-4 weeks. Transmission is by direct contact and possibly through insect bites. Pigs can also be infected with vaccinia virus. The virus replicates only in cell cultures of pig origin and cannot be propagated on CAM of chicken embryos. Re-covered pigs develop life long immunity to disease. There is no cross immunity between vaccinia and swine pox viruses.

Genus *Avipoxvirus*

Q. 9. Briefly describe properties, pathogenecity and immunity of fowl pox virus.

Ans. The virus causes a serious disease in chickens. In the infected tissues, the virus remains cell associated as well as cell free. The virus grows well on CAM in chicken embryos and produces good sized pock lesions. It produces intracytoplasmic inclusion bodies in infected cells. The virus also grows in chicken embryo fibroblast cells.

Fowlpox elementary bodies are known as Borrel bodies and inclusion bodies as Bollinger bodies. The incubation period of the disease is 4-9 days. Fowlpox occurs in two forms i.e. cutaneous form in which generalized lesions are found in any part of the body. In this form pox like eruptions are found on comb, wattles, legs and feet. The other form is known as diphtheritic or wet form in which lesions are found in mouth, larynx, trachea and oesophagus. This form is generally responsible for mortality. In severe outbreaks mortality may be as high as 50%. Affected birds recover in about a month. Transmission of the disease is by direct or indirect contacts or through insect bites. Lesions involve epithelial hyperplasia of epidermis and feather follicles with warty epithelial crusts formation which terminate into scab formation. In immune or birds recovered from the disease, antibodies can be detected by VN, CF, FA and ID tests. In India, egg adapted attenuated fowl pox virus is used as vaccine in chickens of 6-8 weeks of age. The inoculation is done by wing web stick method. Pigeon pox viruses can be used in chickens of 2-4 weeks.

Genus *Leporipoxvirus*

Q. 10. Briefly describe the pathogenesis of myxoma virus in rabbits.

Ans. The myxoma virus is also classified under the family *Poxviridae*. The virus produces severe disease in rabbits. The disease is characterised by mucopurulent exudates from nose and eyes. The virus produces skin tumours, which when cut, exude mucinous exudate. The virus is also transmitted by mosquito bites and spreads through lymphnodes and blood to internal organs. It causes viraemia, skin tumours and generalized lesions. The virus can be grown on CAM of embryonated chicken eggs.

Q. 11. Briefly describe the pathogenicity of fibroma virus in rabbits.

Ans. The virus was first discovered by Shope in 1932. It produces fibroma tumours in cotton tail rabbits. The virus is non fatal and the benign tumours regress spontaneously. The virus also grows on CAM of embryonated chicken eggs.

Q. 12. Select true or false statements:

(a) All pox viruses share a common antigen which is nucleo-protein in nature.

(b) The smallpox virus remains carrier in human beings after recovery from the disease.

(c) Dogs and cats do not suffer from pox diseases. Insects however suffer from pox diseases.

(d) Poxvirus can be seen under light microscope.

(e) Poxvirus does not possess haemagglutinin antigen.

(f) Poxviruses possess heat labile and heat stable (LS) antigens.

(g) Humans are not infected with goat pox and contagious pustular dermatitis viruses.

(h) Buffalo pox virus is distinct from cow pox virus.

Ans. (a) True, (b) False, (c) True, (d) True, (e) False, (f) True, (g) False, (h) True.

Q. 13. What is variolation method of pox vaccination?

Ans. This was a method of introducing smallpox scab material from mild cases from arm to arm by scarification. This was safer. This method was originally introduced in England by lady Montagu. The disease was eradicated by using calf lymph (cow pox virus) or lyophilized chicken embryo vaccine.

Q. 14. Fill in the blanks:

(a) Small pox was eliminated from all countries of the world in the year ....

(b) Approved laboratory for diagnosis of small pox in India is ....

(c) .... used cow pox pustule for vaccination of a boy in 1796.

(d) Small pox in man is also known as ....

Ans. (a) 1977, (b) National Institute of Communicable Diseases, Delhi, (c) Jenner, (d) Variola major or Variola minor.

Q. 15. Match column A with column B.

Column A	Column B
(a) Guarnieri bodies	(i) Elementary bodies of small pox
(b) Borrel bodies	(ii) Inclusion bodies of fowlpox
(c) Paschen bodies	(iii) Elementary bodies of fowl pox
(d) Bollinger bodies	(iv) Inclusion bodies of small pox

Ans. (a) (iv), (b) (iii), (c) (i), (d) (ii)

Q. 16. Fill in the blanks:

(a) The species in the genus Parapoxvirus are .... and ....

(b) Milker's nodule virus is also known as *Pseudocowpox virus* or .... virus.

(c) Variola and vaccinia virus strains are antigenically ....

(d) Before eradication of smallpox, the virus strain used for vaccination was ....

(e) More severe form of small pox which occured in Asia was known as ....form and less severe form which occured in other continents was known as ....form.

(f) Different strains of smallpox virus are/were antigenically......... but they differed in ....

Ans. (a) Orf virus, milker's nodule virus, (b) paravaccinia, (c) similar, (d) vaccinia, (e) florid, alastrim, (f) similar, virulence

Q. 17. Write short notes on pox virus antigens.

Ans. All pox viruses share some common nucleoprotein (NP) antigens. L antigen is heat labile and S antigen is heat stable. These antigens are responsible for agglutination and haemagglutination. By immunodiffusion test more than 20 different antigens have been identified in pox viruses.

Q. 18. Name host system where pox viruses can be grown.

Ans. Most pox viruses except milker's nodule virus can be grown in embryonated chicken eggs by CAM route. They also grow in Hela, monkey kidney and chick embryo cells. Skin scarification method is used in monkeys, calves, sheep and rabbits for vaccine production.

18

Family *Iridoviridae* and African Swine Fever Virus

Q. 1 Name important physico-chemical properties of *Iridoviridae* family and African swine fever viruses.

Ans. Formerly African swine fever virus was classified under *Iridoviridae* family. Later on it was detected that there are major differences in the structure of DNA and mode of multiplication between African swine fever virus and other members classified under the family. So far African swine fever virus has not been classified anywhere. Most properties of the members of the family *Iridoviridae* and African swine fever virus are shown in Table 18.1.

Table 18.1: Showing important physico-chemical properties of *Iridoviridae* and African swine fever viruses

Size (nm)	200-250 (irregularly spherical)
Envelope	Present
Capsid	Icosahedral
No. of capsomers	1892
Transcriptase	Present
Multiplication	Cytoplasm
Mol. Wt.	$130\text{-}160 \times 10^6$
Nature of genome:	
Type of nucleic acid	DNA
No. of strands	Double
Shape	Linear
Segments	Non-segmented
DNA content	30% (W/W)
Percentage of G + C	30-58
Genome size	170-190 Kbp

Q. 2. Give names of different genera and species of *Iridoviridae* family.

Ans.

Genus	Species affected
1. *Ranavirus*	Large No. of species infecting frogs
2. *Lymphocystivirus*	Lymphocystis virus infecting fishes
3. *Iridovirus and Chloriridovirus*	Many species of insects
4. *African swine fever group*	Wild pigs and domestic swine

Q. 3. Describe the properties, pathogenicity and immunity of African swine fever virus.

Ans. It is one of the very serious diseases of swine industry in African countries, Western hemisphere and Europe. The virus is transmitted through soft ticks and is the only arbovirus of DNA nature. Incubation period of the disease is 5-15 days. The virus has DNA dependent RNA polymerase and several other enzymes similar to the poxviruses. The virus is sensitive to ether and heat but resistant to a wide range of pH. So far only one serotype has been reported. The clinical symptoms of the disease are similar to hog cholera (swine fever). There is fever, dyspnoea, vomiting, nasal and conjunctival discharge, haemorrhages from nose and anus. Pregnant sows may abort. Recovered animals become carriers and shed the virus. Infection occurs through respiratory tract. In chronic cases there is pericarditis, pleuritis, arthritis and pneumonia. Virus is found in blood, tissue fluids and internal organs. The virus is excreted through excretions and secretions. The virus is poorly antigenic. Antibodies can be detected by CF, ID and ELISA tests. Infected leucocytes haemadsorb pig RBCs.

Q. 4. What specimens should be used for virus isolation?

Ans. Uncoagulated blood at the height of temperature, spleen, visceral lymph nodes, tissue fluid, eye and nasal swabs should be collected for isolation of virus.

Q. 5. Name animal or cell culture systems where African swine fever virus can be grown.

Ans. The virus can be grown in pig, bovine and chicken kidney cell cultures, and in chicken embryos by yolk sac route. The virus can also be isolated from swine bone marrow or blood leucocyte cultures.

Q. 6. Briefly describe how African swine fever can be diagnosed?

Ans. The disease can be diagnosed by the clinical symptoms and lesions, isolation and identification of the virus, CPE in cell cultures and detection of antigen by FA and ID tests with known antserum. For immunodiffusion test, spleen and lymph gland suspension can be used as antigen.

19

Family *Parvoviridae*

The members of this family are very small and have, single-stranded DNA. The virus was first isolated in 1983 from a symptomless blood donor, reported to be associated with anaemia. Parvoviruses are responsible for infections in swine, cats and dogs.

Q. 1. What are important physico-chemical properties of parvoviruses?

Ans. **Table 19.1:** Showing important properties of parvoviruses.

Size (nm)	18-26
Envelope	Absent
Capsid	Icosahedral
No. of capsomers	32
Transcriptase	Absent
Site of replication	Nucleus
Mol. Wt.	$1.5\text{-}2.2 \times 10^6$
Nature of genome:	
Type of nucleic acid	DNA
No. of strands	Single (minus sense)
Shape	Linear
Segments	Non-segmented
Genome	5.2 kb

The virus is resistant to a wide range of pH and temperature. It produces intranuclear inclusion bodies in infected cells, and CPE in cell cultures. The virus has three structural proteins namely VP_1, VP_2 and VP_3.

Q. 2. Name different genera and species of Parvoviruses and diseases caused by them.

Ans. Table 19.2: Showing different genera, species and diseases, due to parvoviruses

Genus	Species	Disease
1. *Parvovirus*	Kilham rat virus	
	Bovine parvovirus type 1 & 2	Mild enteritis
	Porcine parvovirus	Still birth, abortion, foetal death, sterility
	Canine parvovirus type 1 & 2	Neonatal disease, enteritis, panleukopenia
	Feline parvovirus	Panleukopenia and enteritis
	Parvovirus of Mink	Encephalopathy
2. *Dependovirus*	The viruses of this genus are defective and depend on a helper virus which is usually an adenovirus. Adeno associated virus (AAV) There are bovine AAV and other animal AAV.	
3. *Densovirus*	Parvo viruses of insects	Insect diseases

Genus *Parvovirus*

Q. 3. Briefly mention the clinical symptoms of the diseases produced by various species/serotypes of parvoviruses.

Ans. *Bovine parvovirus type 1 and 2:* These viruses produce mild infections in bovines. These viruses have been isolated from faeces of calves with diarrhoea.

Porcine parvovirus: The virus causes serious reproductive disease causing embryonic and foetal death, abortion, still birth and sterility.

Canine parvovirus type 1 and 2: Type-1 causes mild diarrhoea and type-2 generalized neonatal disease, enteritis, myocarditis and panleucopaenia. Type 1 and type 2 differ antigenically. Young pups of 2-4 months of age are mostly affected. The disease is mild in adults. There can be transplacental infection during viraemic stage. Older dogs suffer from enteritis.

Feline panleucopaenia virus: The virus causes cerebellar hypoplasia, panleucopaenia and enteritis. It affects kitten at the time of their weaning. Incubation period is about 5 days. There is loss of appetite, vomiting, diarrhoea, dehydration and emaciation.

Q. 4. Name the type of specimens and host systems for the isolation of parvoriruses.

Ans. **Table 19.3:** Showing type of specimens and host systems for the isolation of parvoviruses from different species of animals.

Species of animals	Specimens	Host system for isolation
Bovines	Faecal samples from calf diarrhoea	Foetal kidney, spleen, testes and lymphnodes of bovines
Porcines	Vaginal mucus, aborted foetus, still born piglets, intestinal scrappings and boar semen	Primary cell cultures of testicles, kidneys and thyroid glands of porcines
Canines	Intestinal scrappings, lymphnodes, spleen, liver of foetus	Dog epithelial cell lines, primary cell cultures from pup kidney and lymphnodes
Feline	Intestinal scrappings, spleen, lymphnodes, faecal and vomit samples	Primary cell cultures of foetal spleen, kidney and lymph nodes

Q. 5. Describe immune response due to natural parvovirus infections and vaccination in dogs and cats.

Ans. Due to natural parvovirus infections, neutralizing antibodies develop very fast which can be detected within a week. The antibody titre becomes very high before recovery and life long immunity is maintained. Maternal antibodies in dogs and cats are transferred to foetus and after birth through colustrum. The antibody protects the kittens and pups for few weeks after birth. For prophylactic use, formaline killed vaccine with adjuvants are available.

Q. 6. How will you diagnose parvovirus disease?

Ans. The disease can be diagnosed by clinical symptoms and by isolation and identification of the virus by serological tests using known antiserum. The virus haemagglutinates RBCs from different species of animals at 4°C. This can be confirmed by HI test. Other tests used, are VN, FA and ELISA. Virus can also be seen by electron microscopy. Bovine parvovirus haemagglutinates guinea pig and human O, RBCs, and porcine strains, haemagglutinate guinea pig, human and monkey RBCs.

Genus *Dependovirus*

Q. 7. What are adeno associated parvoviruses?

Ans. The *Dependovirus* is defective and depends on a helper virus for replication. The helper virus is generally an adenovirus. The *Dependovirus* contains either positive or negative DNA strand. Adeno associated parvoviruses are 'satellite' viruses and multiply only in presence of helper adenoviruses.

20

Family *Hepadnaviridae*

The members of this family have limited importance from veterinary point of view. Some viruses resembling hepadnaviruses, have been isolated from ducks and few other birds. The most important virus of this family is hepatitis B virus causing acute and chronic diseases in human beings.

Q. 1. What are important physico-chemical properties of *Hepadnaviridae* family viruses?

Ans. **Table 20.1:** Showing properties of the genus *Hepadnavirus*

Size (nm)	40-48
Envelope	Present
Capsid	Icosahedral
Transcriptase	Reverse transcriptase present
Site of multiplication	Nucleus
Nature of genome:	
Type of nucleic acid	DNA
No. of strands	Double
Shape	Circular
Segments	Non-segmented
Sense	Negative
Size of genome	3.0-3.2 Kb

Genus *Hepadnavirus*

Q. 2. Briefly describe pathogenicity of hepadna B virus in human beings.

Ans. This virus is reported to be much more infectious than AIDS virus. Large number of human beings world over are reported to be infected with this virus. About two lakh babies are supposed to be infected with this virus each year. Recently, great emphasis has been given for vaccination against this disease in India. The virus is quite resistant and difficult to propagate. It may remain symptomless for a long time in human beings. Blood transfusion, unsafe sex, transmission from mother to child at the time of birth are some of the methods of transmission. The symptoms of the disease are loss of appetite, fatigue, pain in the body, mild fever, jaundice, pale faeces and dark urine. In chronic cases there is cirrhosis and failure of liver functions. Large number of liver cancers are reported to be due to hepatitis B virus in humans.

Q. 3. What are the antigens of Hepatitis B virus?

Ans. The envelope of the virus is composed of three proteins. The material is formed of noninfectious spherical or filamentous particles called hepatitis B surface antigen (HBs Ag) particles. These particles express 5 antigenic specificities. Each of these antigenic specifities, is used in diagnostic tests and also for persistent virus carrier status. In chronic carriers, the virus is accompanied by a large amount of noninfectious HBs Ag particles used for diagnosis and also to prepare vaccine. Blood samples of individuals can be tested by using Australia antigen.

Q. 4. What are preventive measures of the disease?

Ans. The disease can be prevented by adopting all preventive measures recommended for AIDS disease. All children upto 5 years of age are recommended 3 injections of the vaccine, the first two injections are given at one month interval and the third after 6 months of second injection. At present a recombinant DNA vaccine expressed in yeast cells is also available.

21

Family *Picornaviridae*

The family has five genera and large number of species affecting domestic animals. Historically it is important as Loeffler and Frosch (1897) for the first time discovered that foot and mouth disease (FMD) was caused by a filtrable agent. FMD virus which is one of the smallest viruses belongs to this family.

Q.1. In a tabular form, mention the properties of *Picornaviridae* family viruses.

Ans. Table 21.1: Showing properties of *Picornaviridae* family viruses.

Size (nm)	20-30
Envelope	Absent
Capsid symmetry	Icosahedral
No. of capsomers	60
Transcriptase	Absent
Site of multiplication	Cytoplasm
Nature of genome:	
Type of nucleic acid	RNA
No. of strands	Single, positive strand
Shape	Linear
Segments	Non segmented
Mol. Wt. (dalton)	2.5×10^6 (7.5-8.5 kb)
RNA content (% W/W)	30

Q. 2. Name different genera and species of picornaviruses and the diseases caused by them.

Ans. Table 21.2: Showing different genera, species and diseases caused by them.

Genus	Species	Disease
1. Enterovirus	Human poliovirus types 1 to 3	Poliomyetritis
	Coxsackie Virus A several types	Coxsackie disease
	Coxsackie virus B several types	Coxsackie disease
	Bovine enteroviruses types 1 to 7	Mostly subclinical infection
	Porcine enteroviruses types 1 to 11	Mostly subclinical but type 1 causes polioencephalo-myelitis (Teschen disease) and type 9 causes swine vesicular disease.
	Avian enterovirus Serotype 1	Avian encephalomyelitis
	Duck enterovirus Serotype 1	Duck hepatitis
	Turkey enterovirus	Turkey hepatitis
2. *Rhinovirus*	Human rhinovirus types 1 and 2 (There are many other types)	Cause common cold
	Bovine rhinovirus types 1 to 3	Bovine rhinitis
	Equine rhinovirus types 1 to 3	Not assigned to any genus
3. *Cardiovirus*	Encephalomyocarditis virus	Mammals affected in contact with rodents
4. *Aphthovirus*	FMD types O, A, C, Asia 1, SAT 1, SAT2 and SAT3.	Foot and mouth disease in cattle, buffaloes, pigs, sheep, goats, and wild ruminants.
5. *Hepatovirus*	Simian hepatitis A virus	Hepatitis in monkeys

Genus *Enterovirus*

Q. 3. Describe the properties and pathogenecity of poliovirus.

Ans. The virus produces paralytic disease (poliomyelitis) in children. In most cases there is inapparent infection. Experimentally monkeys, chimpanzees and cotton rats can be infected. The virus has serologically 3 distinct types known as type 1, type 2 and type 3. The three types are antigenically distinct. The immunity is type specific but there is some cross protection. Disease due to Type 1 is most common. The polioviruses are strictly neurotropic and multiply only in neural tissues. Enders, Weller and Robins in 1949 were successful in multiplying the virus in nonneural cells from human embryos, which also produced CPE. The virus is quite resistant and is stable at pH 3.0. It enters the body by ingestion and rarely by inhalation. The virus multiplies in lymphatic tissues of alimentary canal and then enters in regional lymphatics and then via blood to spinal cord and brain. The incubation period of the disease is about 10 days. The disease is controlled by vaccination of the children. Earlier killed vaccine developed by Salk in 1953 was used. Presently live attenuated vaccine (developed by Sabin) is used commonly. Killed vaccine was given by injection, however the live attenuated vaccine is administered orally. Live attenuated vaccine is prepared by growing attenuated strain in monkey kidney cells. Children vaccinated with Salk's vaccine develop immunity to CNS, but on exposure develop intestinal infection. The Sabin vaccine produces mild intestinal infection and does not produce viraemia to spread the disease to CNS.

Q. 4. Describe the pathogenesis of Teschen disease caused by porcine enterovirus type-1.

Ans. The virus causes Teschen disease in swine. The disease is also known as polioencephalomyelitis. Young pigs are more susceptible. The disease may be mild, acute or chronic. The incubation period may be 1 to 4 weeks. Transmission of infection may be direct or indirect including ingestion and inhalation. Pathogenesis of the disease consists of multiplication of virus in alimentary canal and associated lymph nodes. The virus then goes to blood causing viraemia and finally affects CNS. There is fever, anorexia, depression, incoordination and stiffness of extremities. In severe cases there is convulsions, prostration and death. Mortality may be upto 50 to 60 percent. The virus multiplies in primary pig kidney cells, PK cell line, monkey kidney and BHK-21 cells.

Q. 5. Describe the pathogenesis of swine vesicular disease.

Ans. The disease is caused by porcine enterovirus type-9. The virus is serologically related to *Coxsakie* B-5 virus of man. It is very resistant to temperature and pH. The incubation period of the disease is 2-14 days. The transmission of infection is by direct or indirect contacts. The symptoms of the disease are fever, lameness, vesicles on snout, coronary bands and interdigital space. Vesicles may also be on teats, buccal cavity and tongue. The animal may recover after few days. The disease is indistinguishable from FMD, vesicular exanthema and vesicular stomatitis on the basis of clinical symptoms. Man is also susceptible to the disease. The virus grows in primary pig kidney cell cultures and PK_{15} cell line. No vaccine is available for control of the disease.

Q. 6. Give an account of the pathogenesis of avian encephalomyelitis caused by enterovirus-1.

Ans. The virus is neurotropic and infects central nervous system of chickens. It has only one antigenic type. However various strains differ in virulence. Incubation period of the disease is 1-7 days. The virus is transmitted by direct or indirect contacts including food and water and through eggs during viraemia. Primarily the virus infects chicks upto 3 weeks of age. The disease is characterised by dullness, loss of condition, paralysis, prostration and death. Mortality is 25-50 percent. The disease can be diagnosed by FA test. Recovered birds develop immunity. The virus is shed in droppings and other discharges. It can be propagated in baby chicks, in chicken embryos (by yolk sac route), and in chicken embryo kidney, brain and fibroblast cells. Brain and spinal cord specimens are most suitable for isolation of the virus. The virus produces relatively mild encephalomyelitis in turkeys, pheasants and quails. Attenuated and killed vaccines are available.

Q. 7. Describe the pathogenesis, mode of transmission, clinical symptoms and diagnosis of duck hepatitis caused be serotype-1.

Ans. There is only one serotype of the virus. The virus is quite resistant to temperature and pH. It can be cultivated in chicken embryos (by allantoic or yolk sac route) and chicken embryo cell cultures. The disease occurs in ducklings upto three weeks of age. The incubation period is 1-3 days. The disease takes a rapid course, killing ducklings within 3 to 4 days. Ducklings suffering from the disease close their eyes partially, fall on sides, suffer from spasms and die showing greenish diarrhoea. The mortality can be upto 100%. On postmortem, liver is found enlarged, haemorrhagic and mottled. Spleen and kidneys become swollen. Recovered birds are solidly immune.

Transmission of infection takes place by direct or indirect contacts, and by ingestion. There is no transmission through eggs. Chickens are not susceptible to experimental infection.

Diagnosis of the disease can be made by history, clinical symptoms and postmortem findings. Histopathologically there is hepatic necrosis, inflammatory cell infiltration and proliferation of bile duct epithelium. Virus may be isolated and identified, by FA test. The disease should be differentiated from duck plague and Ranikhet disease.

For control attenuated egg adapted live virus vaccine is available.

Genus *Rhinovirus*

Q. 8. Briefly describe the properties and pathogenicity of rhinoviruses.

Ans. In size, structures and many other properties *Rhinovirus* resemble other picornaviruses. They are more acid labile but more heat stable. More than 150 serotypes have been isolated from human beings. On the other hand only 3 serotypes of bovines and 3 serotypes of equines have been reported so far. Human rhinoviruses can be grown in tissue cultures of human and monkey origin showing cytopathic changes. They need more oxygen and little lower temperature (33°) for growth. The human, bovine and equine serotypes are antigenically unrelated. Human types cause common cold, bronchitis and sometimes bronchopneumonia. The disease is transmitted by droplets. Incubation period in man is about 2 days and in bovines 2 to 4 days. The infection in bovines may be inapparent, or mild. Pneumonia may sometimes develop in calves. Viruses produce very weak serum antibody and immunity.

Genus *Aphthovirus*

Q. 9. What are the properties of *Aphthovirus*?

Ans. The filterability of the agent of foot and mouth disease (FMD) was first reported by Loeffeler and Frosch in 1897. FMD is enzootic in Asia, Africa, South America and Europe. Australia, Newzealand and Central America are free from the disease. The last report of FMD in Canada was in 1952, and in USA in 1929. UK was free from FMD since 1968 but the disease again occurred in outbreak form in 2001 with heavy losses. The disease occurs in all cloven footed animals. Human beings are also susceptible to the disease. The virus has seven serotypes. They are designated as 'O', A, C, Asia 1, SAT 1, SAT 2 and SAT 3. Each serotype has several subtypes. The virus is quite resistant to common chemical disinfectants. Formaline, potassium permanganate, lactic acid and ethylene oxide are effective disinfectants. The best disinfectant is 1-2% sod. hydroxide which destroys the virus within 1-2 min. Pasteurization of milk may not destroy the virus. The virus replicates in cell cultures of bovine origin. It growth well in lamb and kid kidney cell cultures, BHK_{21} cell line, 6-8 days old suckling mice and on guineapig foot pad.

Q. 10. Describe the pathogenesis of foot and mouth disease.

Ans. The disease is highly contagious. All cloven footed animals including cattle, buffaloes, pigs, sheep, goats, camels, and wild ruminants are infected. FMD was also reported in an elephant in India. Horses are resistant to the disease. It has been reported that when cattle suffer from the disease, pigs in the vicinity do not show any symptoms of the disease. Vice versa has also been reported. The incubation period of the disease is 2-5 days. Indian breeds are more resistant than exotic breeds and cross bred animals. In more susceptible breeds, there is high fever, viraemia, anorexia, and drop in milk yield. Vesicles appear on tongue, lips, cheeks, gums, dental pads, muzzle, inter digital spaces and coronary band of feet. Vesicles also appear on udder and teats of cows and buffaloes and on snout of pigs. There is profuse salivation and lameness. The vesicles rupture in 2-3 days leaving raw and red ulcerative lesions. Secondary bacterial infection also takes place complicating the healing process. There is high morbidity but low mortality. The disease is more severe in calves, lambs and other young animals. Man is also susceptible to the disease, the lesions appear on hands and in mouth. Myocarditis has been reported in young calves particularly those of exotic breeds. Adult animals may act as carriers after recovery.

Q. 11. What are the symptoms of FMD in pigs?

Ans. Foot lesions in pigs are quite severe. The animals become lame and are not able to stand properly. Large vesicles develop on snout which may rupture quickly. Vesicles in mouth are less prominant than in cattle. Due to secondary bacterial infections between the claws, there may be suppuration and loss of claw.

Q. 12. How FMD disease can be diagnosed in cattle?

Ans. The disease can be diagnosed in cattle by clinical symptoms, vesicles on tongue, gums, lips and interdigital spaces. Vesicular fluid can be used for complement fixation test and animal inoculation for isolation of the virus. The virus multiplies in 5-7 days old suckling mice, on foot pad of guinea pigs and on bovine kidney, swine embryo kidney and BHK_{21} cell cultures. FMD should be differentiated from vesicular stomatitis, vesicular exanthema, swine vesicular disease and rinderpest. Virus can be titrated on tongue of cattle, foot pad of guinea pigs, in suckling mice (5-7 day) and by complement fixation and virus neutralization tests. Other serological tests like ELISA, FA and ID tests can also be used.

Select the correct answer:

Q. 15. Which of the following laboratory animals is most suitable for typing of FMD virus?

(a) Guinea pig
(b) Hamester
(c) Rat
(d) adult mice
(e) unweaned mice

Ans. (e)

Q. 14. How FMD virus is transmitted from infected to healthy animals?

Ans. The virus is transmitted via respiratory route by inhalation of droplets from infected animals. The animals are also infected by contaminated food and water, insemination with contaminated semen, contact or use of contaminated instruments, clothings and other objects.

Q. 15. How FMD virus is excreted from infected animals?

Ans. The virus is excreted from infected animals about 24 hours before the appearance of clinical symptoms. It is excreted by saliva, nasal discharges, droplets and milk. The virus is excreted from the pharynx for a long time after recovery in cattle but not in pigs.

Q. 16. Write short notes on structural and nonstructural proteins of FMD virus.

Ans. The RNA of the virus acting as mRNA is translated into proteins into three regions known as P_1, P_2 and P_3. P_1 region is further cleaved to yield four structural proteins known as VP_1, VP_2, VP_3 and VP_4. P_2 region codes for three nonstructural proteins and P_3 for four proteins including RNA dependent RNA polymerase.

Q. 17. Fill in the blanks:

(a) FMD virus has .... types and about .... subtypes.
(b) The virus has .... major proteins in the capsid which are antigenic.
(c) Experimental FMD vaccine has been prepared by splicing the gene responsible for VP_3 protein from the virus and recombining it in .... of *E. coli*
(d) Commonly used inactivating agents for FMD vaccine are .... and ....
(e) FMD virus type 0 stands for .... and A for ....

Ans. (a) 7, 80 (b) four (VP_1, VP_2, VP_3 and VP_4), (c) plasmid (d) formalin, betapropiolactone, (e) Oise, Allemagne

Q. 18. Select correct answer:
Typing of *Apthovirus* is done by:
(a) Enzyme linked immunosorbent assay (ELISA)
(b) Virus neutralization test (VN test)
(c) Complement fixation test (CF test)
(d) By all above tests

Ans. (d)

Q. 19. After natural infection with a type/subtype of FMD virus, the immunity produced against that type/subtype is:
(a) Life long (b) About 5 years
(c) Not more than 2 years (d) Not more than 12 months

Ans. (d)

Q. 20. The most effective chemical disinfectant to kill FMD virus is:
(a) 2% formaline (b) 70% alcohol
(c) 2% sod. hydroxide (d) 4% sod. carbonate

Ans. (c) and (d)

Q. 21. An animal may become infected by more than one type of *Aphthovirus* due to:
(a) Poor immunity (b) Antigenic diversity
(c) Antigenic drift (d) Cross reaction with each other
(e) Serological variation (f) Due to all above factors

Ans. (f)

Q. 22. In order of preferences arrange the following morbid materials from FMD cases for the isolation and typing of the virus:
(a) Blood (b) Vesicular fluid
(c) Oral scrapings (d) Vesicular epithelium
(e) Foot lesions

Ans. (b) Vesicular fluid (d) Vesicular epithelium
(c) Oral scrapings (e) Foot lesions
(a) Blood

Q. 23. Match continents of column A with the occurrence of FMD virus types in column B:

A	B
(a) Asia	(i) O, A, C
(b) Africa	(ii) O, A, C, Asia 1
(c) Europe and South America	(iii) O, A, C, SAT1, SAT2 and SAT3

Ans. (a) (ii), (b) (iii), (c) (i).

Q. 24. Name probable number of subtypes so far known, among FMD virus types.

Ans. **Table 21.3:** FMD virus types showing probable number of subtypes.

Types	Subtypes
A	1 to 29
O	1 to 10
C	1 to 5
Asia 1	1 to 3
SAT1	1 to 7
SAT2	1 to 3
SAT3	1 to 4

The above list is not complete. The actual number of subtypes has gone up.

Q. 25. What are the most frequently encountered virus subtypes in FMD outbreaks in India?

Ans. The most frequently encountered subtypes are:
A 5 and 22
O 5 and 6
C 1
Asia 1_1 and Asia 1_3

Q. 26. Name the year when different FMD virus types were first isolated.

Ans.

Types	Year of isolation
O & A	1922
C	1926
Asia 1	1957
SAT 1, SAT 2, SAT 3	1952 to 1958

SAT stands for South African Territory

Q. 27. Fill in the blanks:

(a) The FMD virus used in the preparation of vaccine is cultivated in ....and ....

(b) The frequency of various FMD virus types in India are ...., ..., ..., and .... in the order of their mentioning.

(c) All India coordinated research project on FMD was launched in the year.........

Ans. (a) bovine calf kidney, BHK_{21} cells

(b) 0, Asia 1, A and C

(c) 1966

Q. 28. Name International Foot and Mouth Disease Diagnostic Laboratories.

Ans. (a) Institute for Animal Health. Pirbright, England.

(b) Plum Island, Animal Disease Laboratory, New York.

(c) El Centre Panamericano de Fiebre Aftosa, Rio de Janeiro.

(d) Project Directorate, I.V.R.I. Mukteshwar, Dist. Nainital (U.K.) India.

Q. 29. On the basis of animal susceptibility test, differentiate foot and mouth disease, vesicular exanthema and vesicular stomatitis.

Ans. Table 21.4: Differentiation of FMD, Vesicular exanthema and Vesicular stomatitis on the basis of animal suspectibility.

Animal	Foot and Mouth disease	Vesicular exanthema	Vesicular stomatitis
Cattle	+	–	+
Swine	+	+	+
Horse	–	±	+
Guineapig	+	–	+

22

Family *Caliciviridae*

Q. 1. Describe the properties of caliciviruses.

Ans. **Table 22.1:** Showing physico chemical properties of the viruses of family *Caliciviridae.*

Size (nm)	30-40 (spherical)
Envelope	Absent
Capsid symmetry	Icosahedral (with cup-shaped depression on surface)
No. of capsomers	32
Transcriptase	Absent
Site of multiplication	Cytoplasm
Nature of genome:	
Type of nucleic acid	RNA
No. of strands	Single (Positive strand)
Shape	Linear
Segments	Non-segmented
Mol. Wt. of genome (dalton)	2.8×10^6
RNA content (% W/W)	22 (7.4 to 8.2 kbp)

Genus *Calicivirus*

The family has only one genus named *Calicivirus* which affects swines. The genus has 1-13 serotypes which are isolated from swines, cats and rabbits. Swine vesicular exanthema caused by the virus is important disease.

Q. 2. Describe the pathogenesis of swine vesicular exanthema caused by *Calicivirus.*

Ans. The disease was first reported from California, USA in 1932 and was eradicated in 1956. Since then it is not reported from any other country. Swine of all age groups suffer from the disease. Horses may also be infected but they are quite resistant. The incubation period of disease is 1-3 days. The disease occurs in acute form. Initially there is fever and anorexia which are followed by vesicles in mouth, on snout, teats, udder, coronary band and feet. Later on the vesicles rupture, animal becomes lame and recover in about two weeks. The mortality is low but the morbidity is very high. The disease resembles FMD, vesicular stomatitis and swine vesicular disease. These diseases can be differentiated on the basis of relative susceptibility to cattle, swine, horses and guinea pigs. Immunity against the disease is about 6 months against the same serotype. Different serotypes affecting swines are distinct antigenically. The virus is resistant to heat and pH. The virus grows in embryonated chicken eggs, Vero and PK cell lines and pig kidney primary cell cultures which produces rapid CPE.

Some other viruses resembling caliciviruses have been isolated from other animals. A virus named Norwalk virus causes gastroenteritis and food and water borne hepatitis E in human beings.

23

Family *Togaviridae*

The family include a large group of viruses transmitted by arthropod vectors. These viruses were originally called group A and group B arboviruses. Later on when more information was available on these viruses, group A arboviruses are classified in genus *Alphavirus of Togaviridae* family. Group B arboviruses are classified in genus *Flavivirus* of the family *Flaviviridae.* Later on Rubella virus which is not transmitted by arthropod vectors but has some properties similar to the viruses of *Togaviridae* family, has been placed in the genus *Rubivirus* under this family.

Q. 1. What are the properties of the viruses of *Togaviridae* family?

Ans. **Table 23.1:** Properties of *Togaviridae* family viruses.

Size (nm)	60-70 (Spherical)
Envelope	Present, with three glycoprotein peplomers
Capsid	Icosahedral
No. of capsomers	?
Transcriptase	Absent
Site of multiplication	Cytoplasm
Nature of genome:	
Type of nucleic acid	RNA
No. of strands	Single (positive strand)
Shape	Linear
Segments	Non-segmented
Mol. Wt. of genome	4×10^6

Q. 2. Name different genera and species of *Togaviridae* family and diseases produced by them.

Ans. **Table 23.2:** showing different genera and species of *Togaviridae* family and diseases produced by different viruses.

Genus	Virus/serotype	Disease
1. *Alphavirus*	Eastern equine encephalitis virus (EEE)	Encephalitis in equines
	Western equine encephalitis virus (WEE)	As above
	Venezualan equine encephalitis virus (VEE)	As above
	Getah virus	Febrile disease in equines in S.E. Asia
	Semliki forest virus	Symptoms as above in Africa
	Human Sindbis virus	Causes fever in man in Asia and Africa.
2. *Rubivirus* (non arthropod borne)	Rubella virus or German measles virus	Rubella in humans

N.B.– Arteriviruses have been removed from this family and classified separately.

Genus *Alphavirus*

Q. 3. Describe the properties and pathogenicity of Eastern equine encephalomyelitis (EEE), Western equine encephalomyelitis (WEE) and Venezualan equine encephalomyelitis (VEE) viruses.

Ans. These viruses have wide host range and infect equines, human beings, mice, guinea pigs and rabbits. Primarily these viruses cause neurological infections in equines, but they may also cause encephalitis in human beings. These viruses are not very resistant and are easily inactivated by disinfectants. The EEE and WEE viruses occur only in USA. All three viruses are antigenically different. VEE virus has 4 serotypes which vary in pathogenicity for equines. The incubation period of all three diseases varies from 2-6 days. The virus enters the host through arthropod bites, multiplies in cells in the neighborhood of the bite and then in regional lymph nodes. There may be viraemia. The symptoms of the diseases are fever, anorexia, depression and neurological signs. Clinically the three diseases are not differentiated easily. The VN and HI tests are helpful in differentiation. EEE is also known as sleeping sickness and is characterized by fever, leucopenia and paralysis of lips and legs. Mortality may be upto 90% in EEE, 20-25% in WEE and 40-80% in VEE. Death may occur within a week from on set of symptoms.

The cycle of infection is from wild animals or birds (chief reservoirs) to mosquitoes. The virus propagates in gut of mosquitoes and persists through out their life. The horses are dead end hosts.

The virus grows in embryonated chicken eggs and in a wide variety of cell cultures including Vero and BHK_{21} cells and primary chicken embryo fibroblasts. These viruses produce clear CPE in cell cultures. Antibodies appear within a week and can be detected by VN, HI, CF and ID tests. The antibodies in the recovered horses persist for many months.

For prophylactic use formalin inactivated vaccines are available.

Q. 4. Name arthropod vectors, animal hosts and type of diseases produced, by Getah, Semliki forest and Sindbis viruses.

Ans. **Table 23.2:** Arthropod vectors, animal hosts and diseases produced by Getah, Sindbis and Semliki forest viruses:

Virus	Arthropod vector	Animal host	Disease	Geographical area
Getah virus	Mosquito	Horse	Febrile disease	S.E. Asia
Semliki forest virus	Mosquito	Horse	Febrile disease	Africa
Sindbis virus	Mosquito	Humans	Fever and arthritis	Africa, and Asia

Genus *Rubivirus*

Q. 5. Briefly describe the pathogenicity of rubella virus.

Ans. This virus (also known as German measles) is characterised by transient macular rash and lymphadenopathy in humans. The virus is not transmitted by arthropods. It does not cause any serious disease but infection in pregnant woman may lead to congenital malformations in infants and babies including cataract, deafness and cardiac defects. The physico-chemical properties of the virus are similar to other viruses of the *Togaviridae* family. The growth of the virus is not detected in cell cultures but by interference. In humans, after 2-3 weeks of incubation period, rash appears on face, neck, trunk and extremities. The rashes are generally discrete and ordinarily disappear on 3rd day. Generally the disease occurs in children. Infection occurs by inhalation.

24

Family *Flaviviridae*

The former Group B arboviruses have been placed in *Flavivirus* genus of *Flaviviridae* family. Some non-arthropod borne viruses having physico-chemical and biological properties similar to flaviviruses have been placed within this family under the genus *Pestivirus*. A third genus *Hepatovirus* has been proposed for human hepatitis C virus.

Q. 1. Describe the properties of *Flaviviridae* family members.

Ans. Table 24.1: showing properties of *Flaviviridae* family viruses.

Size (nm)	40-50, spherical
Envelope	Present with peplomers
Capsid	Icosahedral
No. of capsomers	?
Site of multiplication	Cytoplasm
Nature of genome: (11-12 kb)	
Type of nucleic and	RNA
No. of strands	Single, plus sense
Shape	Linear
Segments	Non-segmented

Flaviviruses contain three structural proteins namely E (glycoprotein envelope), M (non-glycoprotein envelope) and C (nucleocapsid protein). Flavi and Pesti viruses are not very stable and are easily inactivated by heat and disinfectants. Hog cholera virus is comparatively more stable and is composed of four structural proteins.

Q. 2. Name genera and species of *Flaviviridae* family and diseases produced by these viruses.

Ans. **Table 24.2:** Genera and species of *Flaviviridae* family and diseases produced by them.

Genus	Virus/Serotype	Disease
Flavivirus	Japanese B encephalitis, Russian Spring-Summer encephalitis, St. Louis encephalitis, and Murray Valley encephalitis viruses	Mostly human and swine suffer from these viruses. Cattle, sheep and horses may not show any clinical symptoms.
	Louping ill virus	Encephalitis in sheep
	Yellow fever virus	Yellow fever in man
	Dengue fever virus, types 1-4	Fever in man
	Kyasanur Forest disease virus	Fever in man
Pestivirus	Bovine virus diarrhoea	Diarrhoea in cattle
	Hog cholera virus	Hog cholera in pigs
	Border Disease virus	Border disease in sheep
Hepatovirus (proposed)	Human hepatitis C virus	Hepatitis in man

Genus *Flavivirus*

Q. 3. Briefly describe the pathogenesis of Japanese B encephalitis?

Ans. The disease is widely spread is South Eastern countries including Japan, Korea, Malaysia, India, Nepal and Sri Lanka. The infection is maintained in mosquitoes. Mosquitoes feed on swine, birds, and humans. Swine suffer from infection and spreads the virus. Mosquito-swine-mosquito transmission cycle maintains the mode of virus multiplication. Humans and equines are dead end hosts. The disease causes high rate of abortion in swines with neonatal mortality. Adult cattle, horses and even swines generally do not show clinical symptoms of the disease but maintains the infection. In mild forms, there may be mild fever. In severe forms there is fever, Jaundice, haemorrhages and incoordination. Encephalitic lesions occur in brain. Incubation period of the disease in swine is about 8-10 days. The disease can be controlled in pigs and horses by inactivated mice brain vaccine. Japanese B encephalitis virus also causes disease in humans.

Three other viruses namely West Nile virus, St Louis encephalitis virus and Murray Valley encephalitis virus cause similar disease in human beings. In all these diseases mosquitoes act as vectors.

Q. 4. What are the clinical symptoms of Japanese encephalitis in human beings?

Ans. The symptoms are sudden fever, headache and vomiting. After few days there are symptoms of encephalitis with convulsions and coma. The fever remain high and continuous. Mortality may be upto 50%. Recovery may take several weeks. Large number of cases remain inapparent. In India most of these cases have been reported from North-Eastern states and South Indian states of Tamil Nadu and Andhra Pradesh.

Q. 5. How would you diagnose Japanese encephalitis? Name suitable host system for growth of the virus.

Ans. The disease can be diagnosed by clinical symptoms and testing serum samples from infected animals by SN, CF, and HI tests. Serum antibodies develop in infected animals within 1-2 weeks after the appearance of clinical symptoms and last for several years. The virus grows intracerebrally in mice, in embryonating eggs, chicken fibroblasts and pig kidney cell cultures.

Q. 6. Write short notes on:

(a) St. Louis encephalitis
(b) West Nile encephalitis
(c) Murray Valley encephalitis
(d) Russian Spring-Summer encephalitis

Ans. (a) *St. Louis encephalitis:* The virus causes mild fever to encephalitis in human beings. The disease occurs in North and Central Americas. In some outbreaks deaths may be upto 20%. The disease is transmitted by Culex mosquitoes. Wild birds act as reservoirs of the virus.

(b) *West Nile encephalitis:* The virus causing the disease was originally isolated in 1937 from West Nile province of Uganda. It has also been isolated from many other African countries and also from India. The virus causes dengue like illness in human beings and encephalitis in equines. The virus is maintained in nature in wild birds and Culex mosquitoes.

(c) *Murray Valley encephalitis:* The causative agent was isolated in 1951 in Murray river Valley from human epidemics of encephalitis. Since then it is confined to Australia and New Guinea. The virus cycle involves birds and mosquitoes.

(d) *Russian Spring-Summer Encephalitis (RSSE):* There are a number of viruses causing a complex of RSSE. The disease is found in several countries of Northern Europe and Russia. Depending upon the variations in clinical symptoms, the disease is known by different names in different countries. In Scotland the disease primarily occurs in sheep and is known as louping ill. It causes meningitis in human beings. In Russia it is known as RSSE, which is most serious causing high mortality and paralysis in survivors. The infection is transmitted by ticks, by transovarian transmission. Ticks also act as reservoir host for control of the disease. Other reservoirs are rodents and birds. A formalin killed vaccine is available.

Q. 7. Describe the pathogenesis of louping ill.

Ans. Louping ill virus is a member of serocomplex of 14 related tick borne viruses of RSSE. The disease has been reported in Scotland and some parts of Europe. The virus causes encephalitis in sheep and cattle. Horses may also be infected. The disease occurs in spring and summer months. Transmission takes place through ticks. In nature the virus is maintained in wild animals, birds and rodents. It causes prolonged viraemia, biphasic fever leading to encephalitis, incoordination and paralysis in sheep. Some animals may survive showing neurological symptoms of the disease. Looping ill is a zoonotic disease. Incubation period of the disease is 6-15 days. Infected sheep develops CF, HI, and SN antibodies. The virus can be propagated in mammalian and avian cell cultures. It also grows I/C in young mice and in embryonated eggs. Control of the disease can be done by use of inactivated adjuvant vaccine in lambs. The animals should be dipped in water with anti-tick disinfectants.

Q. 8. Describe the epidemiology and pathogenesis of yellow fever, dengue fever and Kyasanur Forest disease.

Ans. *Yellow fever:* Presently the disease is confined to Africa and South and Central Americas. The virus is transmitted by Aedes aegypti mosquitoes. The incubation period of the disease is about 3-6 days. Out side mosquito-man cycle, the virus is maintained in the forest (sylvatic cycle). In sylvatic cycle, the cycle is maintained from monkey to mosquito to monkey. The urban cycle is maintained as man to mosquito to man. Man gets infected from forest mosquitoes as well. The disease starts with fever, chill, headache, nausea, vomiting, jaundice, albuminuria. The patient dies of hepatic or renal failure. Most cases are less severe. Strain 17 D, (chicken embryo modified virus) vaccine is used to control the disease. The vaccine was developed by Theiler in 1937.

Dengue fever: The virus occurs in 4 sero-types i.e. type 1,2,3, and 4. All 4 types are reported in India. The disease is transmitted in man through mosquitoes. There is fever, headache, pain in back and limbs, lymphadenopathy and rash. Fever is biphasic and recovery takes place in 5-7 days. More severe form occurs with haemorrhagic manifestations. Virus is also maintained by sylvatic cycle. There is no vaccine. Disease can be controlled by the control of *Aedes aegypti* mosquitoes.

Kyasanur Forest disease: the virus causes tick borne haemorrhagic fever in man. In India the disease has been reported from Karnataka state, around Kyasanur forest. The disease was first reported in 1957 when several dead monkeys were noticed. Simultaneously a prostrating illness was observed in villagers in the area. The research workers to National Institute of Virology, Pune isolated a virus from patients which was antigenically related to Russian Spring Summer Encephalitis virus. In humans there is sudden onset of fever, headache, conjunctivitis, prostration and some times haemorrhages into the skin. Mortality is about 5%. Main vector to maintain the virus is tick but forest birds and small mammals are also believed to act as reservoir hosts, in addition to the monkeys.

Select correct answer:

Q. 9. Following statements are true for Dengue virus except:
(a) The virus is transmitted by *Aedes aegypti* mosquitoes
(b) The virus is maintained by sylvian cycle.
(c) The virus has only 1 serotype.
(d) Man is the only vertebrate host.

Ans. (c)

Q. 10. Among *Flavivirus* group, name the viruses which are transmitted by ticks.

Ans. These viruses are:
(a) Russian Spring-Summer encephalitis virus
(b) Louping ill virus
(c) Kyasanur Forest Disease virus

Genus *Pestivirus*

Q. 11. Describe the pathogenesis and diagnosis of bovine virus diarrhoea (BVD).

Ans. Bovine virus diarrhoea (BVD) and mucosal disease are clinically similar and caused by one and the same virus. The virus is known as bovine virus diarrhoea virus. The disease was first reported in 1946 and the virus was isolated in bovine kidney cell cultures in 1957. The virus has only one serotype. It is antigenically related to hog cholera virus. The virus grows well in cell cultures of bovine and ovine origin with little or no CPE. CPE can be enhanced by NDV in bovine testicular cell culture. Transmission of the virus takes place by contact, and ingestion of faecal contaminated feed or water. The virus is transmitted vertically to offsprings through mother. The disease occurs in acute, mild or chronic forms. The symptoms of BVD are high to mild fever, cough, nasal discharge, depression, respiratory distress, salivation, leucopenia, oral and muzzle erosion and diarrhoea. Some lesions in respiratory and alimentary tracts may be similar to those observed in rinderpest. If the introduction of infection in a herd, is recent higher number of newly born calves are infected with higher mortality. In pregnant cows, there is higher transplacental spread of virus to foetus. Mucosal disease in a herd is recognised clinically by fever, anorexia, watery diarrhoea and stomatitis. There is corneal opacity in few cases, laminitis, overgrowth of hoof, abortion and fetal damage.

The virus produces high SN antibodies which persist for a long period. Virus may also persist without circulating antibodies.

Diagnosis of the disease can be made on the basis of clinical symptoms, isolation and identification of the virus, and by FA test. Serum conjugates against hog cholera virus have been used in FA test for BVD. The disease should be differentiated from rinderpest.

Q. 12. Write short notes on Border Disease of sheep.

Ans. The virus belongs to *Pestivirus* genus of *Flaviviridae* family. This disease was first described on sheep farms in border areas between England and Wales. Hence it is known as Border Disease. On the basis of its clinical symptoms, it is also known as 'hairy shaker disease'. The disease is quite mild and does not cause much economic losses. In adult pregnant sheep, it may cause malformation of foetus or delivery of dead lamb. New lambs may have excessive hairs, poor growth and neurological symptoms. There may be immunosuppression and the lambs may act as carriers of the virus. The mode of transmission of virus is by contact and congenitally.

Q. 13. Describe the properties and pathogenicity of hog cholera virus.

Ans. Hog cholera is also known as European swine fever or swine fever. The disease occurs all over the world and causes heavy economical losses. The virus is quite resistant to pH and temperature. It does not haemagglutinate RBCs. Antigenically, it is related to the virus of bovine virus diarrhoea. The virus has only one serotype. Different strains vary in virulence. Transmission is not through vectors but by direct or indirect contacts. Wild hogs may act as carriers. The disease occurs in acute, subacute and peracute forms. In peracute form, pigs may be found dead even without showing any symptoms. In acute form, there is high fever, depression, anorexia, and coughing. There may be vomiting, diarrhoea, incoordination of movements, convulsions and leucopenia. Most animals on the farm become infected in about a week. In subacute and chronic forms, deaths may occur upto a month. In peracute and acute cases, there are petichial haemorrhages in submucosa, congestion and infarction in internal organs and button ulcers in colon. There is haemorrhagic lymphadenitis (strawberry lymph nodes) and haemorrhages in kidneys (turkey egg kidney). There is no congenital infection in piglets. At present attenuated and crystal violet inactivated vaccines are available. Rabbit and tissue culture modified vaccines are used.

Q. 14. Name the type of specimens to be used and sensitive host system for the isolation of hog cholera virus.

Ans. The specimens for the isolation of virus are citrated blood, brain tissue, tonsils, spleen, lymph nodes, nasal and eye swabs, and faecal samples. The virus multiplies in pig kidney, spleen, bone marrow, testicular and lymph node cell cultures and PK_{15} cell line. There is very little or no CPE in cell cultures.

Q. 15. How would you diagnose hog cholera disease?

Ans. The disease can be diagnosed by history of the disease on the farm, clinical symptoms, postmortem lesions, and isolation and identification of the virus. The virus/antigen should be tested by FA test against known antiserum or by ELISA test. There is antigenic relationship with bovine virus diarrhoea virus.

25

Family *Reoviridae*

The family derives its name from respiratory enteric orphan viruses. Theses viruses are frequently isolated from respiratory and intestinal tracts.

Q. 1. What are the properties of the *Reoviridae* virus family?

Ans. Table 25.1: Properties of *Reoviridae* virus family.

Size (nm)	60-80
Envelope	Absent
Capsid	Incosahedral (two layered)
No. of capsomers	Inner shell has 32 ring shaped capsomers in Genus *Orbivirus*.
Transcriptase	Present
Site of multiplication	Cytoplasm
Nature of genome:	
Type of nucleic acid	RNA (18-27 kb)
No. of strands	Double (minus strand)
Shape	Linear
Segments	Segmented in 10-12 pieces
Mol. Wt.	$10\text{-}16 \times 10^6$
G + C content (% W/W)	42-44

Q. 2. Name genera, species and diseases caused by *Reoviridae* virus family.

Ans. Table 25.2: Genera, species and diseases produced by *Reoviridae* viruses.

Genus	Virus/serotype	Disease
Orthoreovirus	Human type-1 Bovine type 1-3 Ovine type 1-3	Most of these viruses are non pathogenic

(Contd.)

Genus	Virus/serotype	Disease
	Avian type 1-11	The avian serotypes produce arthritis and myocarditis in fowls and turkeys
Orbivirus	Blue tongue diseases virus types 1-24	Blue tongue disease in sheep and cattle
	African horse sickness virus types 1-9	African horse sickness in horses and donkeys
	Ibaraki virus	Acute febrile disease in cattle, clinically similar to blue tongue disease
	Equine encephalosis virus types 1-5	Abortion and encephalitis in equines
Rotavirus	Rotaviruses of calves, piglets, foals and other young animals and children	Causes diarrhoea in young animals and children

Genus *Orbivirus*

Q. 3. Describe the pathogenesis of blue tongue disease.

Ans. The virus belongs to *Orbivirus* genus and has 24 serotypes. It is quite resistant to pH and temperature and haemagglutinates and haemadsorbes sheep RBCs. The disease is arthropod borne and primarily infects sheep but cattle and goats may also be infected and may act as virus carriers. The disease has been reported from several countries including Africa, Middle East, parts of Europe, USA, Australia and India. The incubation period of the disease is about a week. The virus spreads by *Culicoides* mosquitoes and replicates in haemopoitic and endothelial cells of blood vessels. The adult sheep may remain viraemic for weeks. Depending upon the virulence of the virus, the disease in sheep may be mild to severe. There is fever which may last for several days. In addition to fever, there will be depression, anorexia, salivation, discharge from eyes and nose and diarrhoea. There may be ulcers on tongue, dental pads and lips. Tongue becomes swollen, cynotic and purple blue in colour. The discharge from nose may turn to mucopurulent and blood tinged. There is marked loss of condition and the sheep may die. The morbidity rate is very high and mortility may be upto 50%. Transplacental infection may take place. Affected lambs and calves may become blind, may have other congenital defects and under developed.

In cattle the disease is similar to mucosal disease showing stiffness, lameness and ulcers in mouth with salivation.

To control the disease, a live attenuated chicken embryo vaccine is available which induces high virus neutralizing and complement fixing antibody titres.

Q. 4. Name the type of specimens and sensitive host system for the isolation of blue tongue disease virus.

Ans. The specimens should be citrated blood (which is collected at the height of temperature), saliva, swabs from eyes and nasal discharges, faecal swabs, lung and spleen tissues, and paired serum samples. Bovine and ovine kidney and testes cell cultures, chicken embryos (by yolk sac route), BHK_{21}, and Hela cell lines are suitable host systems for propagation of the virus.

Q. 5. How would you diagnose blue tongue disease in sheep and cattle?

Ans. The disease can be diagnosed in sheep by clinical symptoms. In cattle it can be confused with BVD, rinderpest, vesicular diseases, IBR and malignant catarrhal fever. Virus can be isolated using buffy coat of blood at the height of temperature in chicken embryos. Paired sera should be tested serologically against known virus.

Q. 6. Describe the, pathogenesis and immunological response of African horse sickness virus.

Ans. The disease occurs in horses, mules and donkeys. Donkeys are resistant, and mules and zebras are refractory. The disease has been recognized in South Africa since 18th century. Major epidemics occured in middle East and Indian subcontinent in 1959-61. During these years, the disease spread to Iran, Afghanistan, Pakistan and India and caused extensive disease in army horses and mules. In India the disease was controlled and eradicated in 1961. It is considered endemic in subsaharan Africa. It has never occured in Western hemisphere and Australia. The virus gives HA test with horse RBCs at 37°C. The virus has 9 serotypes. All serotypes have group specific CF antibodies. Some serotypes have cross reaction with blue tongue disease virus. Different strains differ in virulence. Transmission of virus takes place through mosquitoes and other blood sucking insects. There is no contact transmission. The virus produces disease in four clinical forms, which are:

(a) *Peracute or pulmonary form:* In this form, the incubation period is 3-5 days. There is high fever, severe respiratory involvement and increased breathing rate. Animal stands with forelegs apart, head extended and nostrils dialated with discharge. There is profuse sweating. Death occurs within few hours.

(b) *Cardiac or subacute form:* In this form incubation period is 7-14 days. There is fever, oedematous subcutaneous swelling of eyes, lips, cheeks, tongue and chest. Death occurs in 3-5 days after the appearance of symptoms.

(c) *Mixed form:* The disease occurs in mixed form of above two forms.

(d) *Horse sickness form:* This is a mild form of the disease. In this form incubation period is 5-14 days. There is intermittent fever and various other symptoms.

Recovered animals develop SN, CF, HI and ID antibodies. Such animals possess durable immunity to homologous strains.

Polyvalent formaline inactivated spleen tissue vaccine gives immunity for one year. Mouse brain live attenuated vaccine is also available.

Q. 7. Name specimens and host systems for the isolation of African horse sickness virus.

Ans. Specimens for isolation of the virus should be lymph nodes, spleen, lungs and brain. Citrated blood should be collected at the height of temperature. Virus can be propagated in suckling mice by I/C route, in embryonated eggs and cell cultures. In vero cells and monkey kidney cells there is plaque formation.

Q. 8. Write short notes on Ibaraki virus.

Ans. Ibraki virus has been isolated from cattle and is closely related to bluetongue virus. Clinically the disease is not distinguishable from bluetongue disease. The disease was first reported from cattle in Japan in 1959 and since then from many parts of South East Asia. It causes acute febrile disease in cattle.

Genus *Rotaviruses*

Q. 9. Briefly describe the properties of rotavirus and its pathogenesis in different species of domestic animals.

Ans. Rotaviruses infecting different animals share a common antigen. These viruses invariably infect young animals including human infants and babies. Virus specific antibodies are wide spread among adults of different species. The infectivity of the virus is associated with outer shell. The virus has 11 segmented genome. Rota virus strains from different species can be distinguished by VN test. The infection is by direct contacts and not through arthropod vectors.

Bovine rota virus has been adapted to grow in bovine kidney cell cultures. It causes diarrhoea in calves. Infection may also occur in adults. Cross infection may occur from one species to another including human babies. The diarrhoea generally occurs during winter months. The incubation period for onset of diarrhoea is 1 to 4 days. The faeces are watery, brown to light green and may contain blood and mucus. Death may occur due to dehydration, acidosis and shock. Virus induces SN antibodies in infected animals. Intestinal antibodies against rota virus Infection are more protective than circulating antibodies. Virus and antibodies can be demonstrated by ELISA. An attenuated oral vaccine is available for calves.

Rota virus from foals is not easily adapted to grow. It is also difficult to distinguish foal rota virus from rota viruses of other species. During 1st 2 weeks the foal may suffer from watery diarrhoea, depression, weakness and leucopenia. Death may occur within 2 to 4 days. There is no vaccine to control infection in foals.

In piglets the diarrhoea is observed when they are about 1 to 4 weeks of age. The disease is generally subclinical and the mortality is low. The virus has been propagated in pig kidney cells. Treatment of faecal samples with trypsin can make the virus to adapt to grow in cell cultures easily.

Rota virus of lambs is antigenically related to rota viruses of other animals. The virus causes gastroenteritis in 1 to 2 week old lambs. Colostral antibodies are transferred from immune ewes to their lambs.

Q. 10. How would you diagnose *Rotavirus* infection under laboratory conditions?

Ans. The disease can be diagnosed by demonstration of virus in faeces by negative staining with electron microscope. It needs high concentration of virus. It can also be diagnosed by ELISA and immunofluorescent tests.

26

Family *Birnaviridae*

Infectious bursal disease (IBD) in chickens was recognised in 1957. The virus causing the disease was isolated in 1962. Another virus with similar morphology and other properties causing infectious pancreatic necrosis in fishes was discovered in 1960. These two viruses were officially classified in the family *Birnaviridae* within genus *Birnavirus* in the year 1984.

Q. 1. Describe important properties of the family *Birnaviridae.*

Ans. Table 26.1: Important properties of the viruses of *Birnaviridae* family.

Size (nm)	60
Envelope	Absent
Capsid	Incosahedral
No. of capsomers	32
Transcriptase	Present (there are 4 structural proteins)
Site of multiplication	Cytoplasm
Nature of genome:	
Type of nucleic acid	RNA
No. of strands	Double
Shape	Linear
Segments	Two Segments: Segment A and segment B. Segment A is represented by N-VP_2-VP_5- VP_4-VP_3-C, proteins. VP_2 is responsible for antibody production.

The virus is quite stable and survives at 60°C for 1 hour and is stable at pH 3-9. The virus has two serotypes.

Genus *Birnavirus*

Q. 2. Give a brief account of the pathogenesis and immunity of infectious bursal disease.

Ans. The disease occurs in almost all countries including India. Chickens, 3-6 weeks old, are most susceptible. Older birds may also be affected. Chicks upto 2 weeks are not susceptible because, they do not have fully developed bursa of Fabricius. At this age they may also be protected by maternal antibodies. In infected birds, bursa is first enlarged, then return to normal size and finally become atrophied. Incubation period of the disease is 2-3 days. Transmission is by direct or indirect contacts. Affected chicks, become depressed, show ruffled feathers, anorexia, trembling, watery diarrhoea, and prostration. The virus replicates in gut associated macrophages and lymphoid cells and then goes to bursa via blood. There is primary and secondary viraemia affecting other lymphoid tissues. The changes are generally confined to bursa, spleen, kidneys and thymus. There is severe depletion of B lymphocytes from bursa and lymph glands. In bursectomised chicks, there are no clinical symptoms but such chickens produce high neutralizing antibodies. The virus acts as immunosuppressent and leads to infection by a variety of other pathogens and reduced immune response by vaccine. Killed and attenuated vaccines are available for control.

Q. 3. Name type of specimens and host system for the isolation of infectious bursal disease virus.

Ans. Specimens used are whole bird, hypertrophied bursa, spleen, lymph glands and thymus gland.

The host system for the virus isolation is embryonated chicken eggs (by CAM route). Egg adapted virus grows in cell cultures of chicken embryo fibroblasts, chicken kidney, and chicken bursal B lymphocytes.

Q. 4. How IBD can be diagnosed?

Ans. The impression smears from infected bursa of Fabricius will give positive FA test. Hypertrophied bursa of infected birds is very rich in virus and will give positive gel diffusion test. Viral particles in specimens can be confirmed by electron microscopy. The virus can be isolated in sensitive cell cultures and confirmed by neutralization test using known serum. The disease can also be diagnosed by clinical symptoms.

Q. 5. Write short notes on infectious pancreatic necrosis disease of fishes.

Ans. The virus infects fish fingerlings in hatcheries. The disease occurs in many countries, and is detected in fingerlings when they start feeding. With increasing age, the virus becomes subclinical. Affected fishes become dark, swollen, restless and then lie at the bottom of the tank before death. The death percentage can be variable and may be as high as 80-90%. Survivors remain lifelong carriers of the virus. There is no effective vaccine except hygienic measures.

27

Family *Coronaviridae*

Q. 1. What are important properties of the viruses of *Coronaviridae* family?

Ans. Table 27.1: Showing properties of coronaviruses.

Size of virus (nm)	75-160
Envelope	Present, (club shaped peplomers)
Capsid	Helical
Transcriptase	Absent
Site of multiplication	Cytoplasm, (mature by budding)
Nature of genome:	
Type of nucleic acid	RNA, plus sense
No. of strands	Single (27-33 kb)
Shape of genome	Linear
Segments	Non segmented
Mol. Wt.	9×10^6

Q. 2. Name the species of the genus *Coronavirus* and the diseases produced.

Ans. Table 27.2: Species of *Coronavirus* and diseases produced.

Genus	Virus/serotype	Disease
Coronavirus	Human coronavirus	Upper tract respiratory infection
	Bovine coronavirus	Calf neonatal diarrhoea
	Porcine coronavirus	Transmissible gastroenteritis
	Dog coronavirus	Diarrhoea in dogs
	Avian Coronavirus 1-12 types	Infectious bronchitis
	Turkey coronavirus	Turkey enteritis (bluecomb)

Genus *Coronavirus*

Q. 3. Describe general properties and pathogenicity of Infectious bronchitis virus (IBV) of poultry.

Ans. The disease was first identified in India in the year 1964. The virus has more than a dozen serotypes. It is quite fragile and is sensitive to common disinfectants. It grows well in 9-12 day old embryonating chicken eggs via allantoic route. The embryo becomes dwarf and curl like a ball. On serial passages in chicken embryos, the virus decrease pathogenicity for chickens and increased virulence for embryos. It is easily propagated in various cell cultures including chicken embryo kidney cell cultures. The virus produces an acute contagious respiratory disease in chickens. The baby chicks are more susceptible. The uncomplicated disease is accompanied by depression, coughing, and gasping with nasal discharge. In laying flock, there is reduction in egg production and the eggs are of poor quality, misshaped and soft shelled. The mortality may be 20-25% in chicks but negligible in adults. The incubation period of the disease is 1-2 days and the disease lasts for 1-3 weeks. Transmission of virus is by droplets. There is no vertical transmission. The recovered birds may act as carriers upto a month. The virus induces SN, CF, and ID antibodies. Local antibodies (Ig A) are also demonstrated. Diagnosis of the disease can be made by clinical symptoms, by isolating the virus using bronchial specimens and nasal discharges in embryonating chicken eggs. The embryos show curling and dwarfing. The virus can be identified serologically against known antibodies. Recovered birds are immune for at least a year. An attenuated live vaccine has been used widely. The presence of several serotypes poses difficulty in vaccine production.

Q. 4. Write short notes on neonatal diarrhoea in calves due to bovine coronavirus.

Ans. The virus causes most severe diarrhoea in new born calves. It is stable at pH 3.0 and gives HA test with mice and rat RBCs. It is difficult to grow some strains in cell cultures. The virus is adapted to grow in bovine embryo kidney cell culture and vero cell line. The diarrhoea causes destruction of absorptive power of intestinal epithelium and villi. The damage due to this virus is more severe than rotavirus. Death occurs due to dehydration and loss of electrolytes. Incubation period of the disease is as low as 24 hours. The affected calves become depressed, and pass on yellowish liquid diarrhoea. Later it contains mucus. An attenuated rota-corona mixed vaccine is available commercially for new born calves.

Q. 5. Describe the properties and pathogenicity of porcine coronavirus causing transmissible gastroenteritis (TGE) in piglets.

Ans. The virus produces severe diarrhoea especially in young pigs. The virus is stable at pH 3.0 and does not haemagglutinate RBCs. It can be propagated in PK and pig thyroid and testis cell cultures. Different strains show variable virulence. The disease TGE is more prevalent in winter. The incubation period of the disease is 1-3 days. The symptoms of the disease are profuse yellowish watery diarrhoea. There is vomiting and loss of weight and dehydration causing high mortality. The faeces has offensive odour and has undigested curdled milk. Death occurs within 2-7 days of onset of symptoms. The recovered piglets have stunted growth. The disease in older pigs runs a chronic course. Transmission of infection is by ingestion and perhaps by respiratory route. Intestinal lesions are similar to bovine coronavirus. Infected pigs develop SN and ID antibodies. Recovered animals are not solidly immune. Live vaccine given to pregnant sows orally is a logical approach to control the disease. Recovered swine may act as carriers of the virus.

Q. 6. Give a brief account of the pathogenesis of turkey enteritis, caused by turkey coronavirus.

Ans. The disease is also known as blue comb disease in turkeys. The causative agent was recognised in 1957. The disease occurs in USA, Canada and Australia. Incubation period of the disease is 1-5 days. Turkeys of all ages are susceptible but younger poults of 2-6 weeks old are most susceptible. The virus is not easily propagated in cell cultures, however it can be propagated in 2 week old turkeys and chicken embryos by amniotic route. Transmission of infection is by direct or indirect contacts. There is no transmission through eggs. Ciinical symptoms of the disease are anorexia, depression, frothy and watery droppings, dehydration and loss of weight. Droppings may contain mucus. There is darkening of head and comb. The duration of disease is about 12-15 days. Mortality may be upto 50% but morbidity is very high. Intestine and bursa of Fabricius contain very high amount of virus which sheds in faeces for several months. Recovered birds have a life long immunity.

Q. 7. Write short notes on canine coronavirus.

Ans. The canine coronavirus was isolated in 1971 in USA. It causes gastroenteritis with diarrhoea in neonatal puppies. The virus is found in faeces for about a week. It grows well in canine cell lines. Other properties and pathogenicity, of the virus are similar to the coronaviruses of other species.

28

Family *Orthomyxoviridae*

In the early literature enveloped RNA viruses, characterized by their ability to adsorb on to mucoprotein receptors of RBCs and causing haemagglutination, were known as myxoviruses. These viruses included, Newcastle (N) disease, mumps (M) and influenza (I) viruses. They were collectively known as NMI group of viruses. Subsequently parainfluenza viruses were also included in this group. However these viruses differed considerably from one another. Accordingly later on they were classified into two separate families known as *Orthomyxoviridae* and *Paramyxoviridae*.

Q. 1. What are the distinguishing properties of *Orthomyxoviridae* and *Paramyxoviridae* families?

Ans. Table 28.1: Showing differences between *Orthomyxoviridae* and *Paramyxoviridae* families.

Property	*Orthomyxoviridae*	*Paramyxoviridae*
Size of virion (nm)	80-120 spherical or elongated	100-150 spherical or filamentous upto 300 nm
Genome	Segmented (8 pieces)	Non segmented
Multiplication	Nucleus	Cytoplasm
Genetic recombination	Common	Absent
Effect of actiomycin D	Inhibit multiplication	Does not inhibit
Antigenic stability	Variable	Stable
Haemolysin	Absent	Present

The properties and diseases caused by Orthomyxo viruses are described in this chapter.

Q. 2. Describe important properties of *Orthomyxoviridae* viruses.

Ans. Table 28.2: Showing properties of *Orthomyxoviridae* viruses.

Size of virion (nm)	80-120 (spherical or elongated)
Envelope	Present (glycoprotein peplomers)
Capsid	Helical
Transcriptase	Present
Site of multiplication	Nucleus (maturation in plasma)
Nature of genome:	
Type of nucleic acid	RNA (13.6 kb)
No. of strands	Single (negative strand)
Shape of genome	Linear
Segments	8 pieces (code 5 structural & non-structural proteins)
Mol. Wt. (dalton)	5×10^6

Q. 3. Name genus and species of *Orthomyxoviridae* family.

Ans. Genus 1 : *Influenzavirus A and B.*
Species : Human influenza virus type A and B'
Equine influenza virus type A (subtypes 1 and 2)
Swine influenza virus type A
Avian influenza virus type A
Genus 2 : *Influenzavirus type C*
Species : Human influenza virus type C

Genus *Influenzavirus*

Q. 4. Mention four historical developments in relation to influenza virus.

Ans. These are:

(a) Shope for the first time isolated swine influenza virus in 1931,
(b) Smith, Andrews and Laidlaw isolated human influenza virus in 1933.
(c) Burnet developed chicken embryo technique for propagation of influenza virus in 1935,
(d) Hirst discovered the property of haemagglutination of influenza virus in 1941.

Q. 5. Name the discoverers of human influenza type A, type B, and type C.

Ans. Human influenza type A virus was isolated by Smith, Andrews and Laidlaw in the year 1933, type B by Francis and Magill in 1940 and type C by Taylor in 1949,

Q. 6. Describe the antigenic structure of influenza virus.

Ans. The antigens of influenza virus are:

(a) Internal antigens and (b) Surface antigens

(a) *Internal antigen:* This antigen is ribonucleoprotein (RNP). RNP antigen is found free in infected tissues. This antigen is also called soluble (S) antigen and can be demonstrated by complement fixation and immuno precipitation tests. It is type specific and on the basis of this antigen influenza viruses are classified into types A, B, and C. RNP antigen is stable and does not show any significant antigenic variation. This antigen is not protective. Antibody against RNP may develop due to natural infection but not due to killed vaccines.

(b) *Surface antigen:* The surface antigen of influenza virus is called viral (V) antigen. V antigen is composed of two virus coded proteins i.e. (i) haemagglutinin (H) and (ii) neuraminidase (N).

(i) *Haemagglutinin* is glycoprotein in nature and has two polypeptides i.e. HA1 and HA2. It is responsible for haemagglutination (HA) and haemadsorption. This antigen produces antihaemagglutinin antibodies following infection and immunization. These antibodies are protective. Haemagglutinin is a strain specific antigen and is capable of great variation.

(ii) *Neuraminidase* is glycoprotein enzyme (antigen) and destroys cell receptors. The antineuraminidase antibody develops following infection and immunization. It is not very protective but inhibit the release of progeny virions and can limit the infection. Neuraminidase is strain specific antigen and may show variation.

Both H and N glycoproteins carry subtype specific antigenic determinants. The NP and M1 proteins determine species specificity i.e. they differentiate between A and B type viruses. A, B, and C types do not share antigens. Type A is divided into subtypes 1 and 2 on the basis of H and N antigens.

Select correct answer:

Q. 7. Haemagglutinins are:

(a) Polysaccharides (b) Proteins

(c) Glycoproteins (d) Lypoproteins

Ans. (c)

Q. 8. Haemagglutination test is given by:

(a) Live viruses (b) Killed viruses

(c) Live as well as killed viruses.

Ans. (c)

Q. 9. Haemagglutinins on virus surface function as:
(a) An enzyme (b) A receptor (c) An antigen

Ans. (a) and (c)

Q. 10. How haemagglutination can be put to different uses?

Ans. Haemagglutination phenomenon was first discovered by Hirst in 1941. Haemagglutination can be used for:
1. Detecting viruses
2. Titrating viruses and antibodies
3. Purifying viruses
4. Studying host-virus interaction

Q. 11. What is the system of nomenclature of influenza virus type A?

Ans. As per WHO system, the designation of different strains of human influenza virus type A will include the following:
Type/Place of origin/Serial number/Year of isolation/Antigenic subtypes of haemagglutinin and neuraminidase in paranthesis. Accordingly strains isolated in different years will be designated as follows in Table 28.3.

Table 28.3: Old and new designations of different strains of human influenza virus type A.

Old designation	Current designation	Antigenic type	Year of isolation
A0	A/PR/8/34	(HO N1)	1918-19
A1	A/FM/1/47	(H1 N1)	1946
A2	A/Singapore/1/57	(H2 N2)	1957
A2	A/HongKong/1/68	(H3 N2)	1968

The scheme of classification is equally applicable to influenza viruses of animals and birds. The suffix of sw, eq and av after H and N are referred to their origin from swines, equines and avians respectively.

Q. 12. Fill in the blanks:
(a) The types of influenza virus are determined on the basis of .... antigens by......... test.
(b) The subtypes of influenza virus are determined on the basis of .... and ....antigens by......... or......... tests.
(c) So far the total number of haemagglutinin and neuraminidase antigens in subtypes of influenza virus type A are ....and ....respectively.
(d) On the basis of ribonucleoprotein internal antigens, influenza virus is classified into........., ... and .... types.

Ans. (a) ribonucleoprotein, complement fixation

(b) haemagglutinin, neuraminidase, haemagglutination inhibition, immunoprecipitation
(c) 16, 10
(d) A,B,C

Q. 13. Select true or false statements:
(a) Swine influenza virus can cause infection in human beings.
(b) Swine influenza virus type A is classified into subtypes.
(c) Swine influenza virus was isolated earlier than human influenza virus.
(d) Swine influenza virus does not exhibit frequent antigenic drift.

Ans. (a) True (b) False (c) True (d) False

Q. 14. Write short notes on the types and subtypes of equine influenza virus.

Ans. Equine influenza virus belongs to type A on the basis of their type specific internal antigen (S antigen) by CF test. The subtype and strain specific antigens are associated with haemagglutinin (viral or V antigen) detected by HI test. There are 2 subtypes of equine influenza virus A. They are A/equi/1 and A/equi/2. Subtype 1 has one known strain, i.e. A/equi/1/Prague. Subtype 2 has three known strains which are A/equi/2/Miami, A/equi/2/Switzerland and A/equi/2/New York. Subtype 2 is antigenically weaker than subtype 1. Each subtype virus has a different neuraminidase. Subtype 1 is without a variant, but subtype 2 has few minor variants.

Q. 15. What are antigenic relationship of equine A/equi/1 and A/equi/2 with avian and human influenza viruses?

Ans. **Table 28.4:** Equine influenza virus subtypes A/equi/ 1 and A/equi/2 showing antigenic relationship with human and avian influenza viruses.

Subtypes of equine influenza virus A	Antigens	Relationship with human and avian influenza viruses
A/equi/1 (A/eq Prague/1/56) (H eq1 N eq1)	Haemagglutinins	Avian influenza type A
	Neuraminidase	–
A/equi/2 (A/Miami/2/63) (Heq2 Neq2)	Haemagglutinins	Avian influenza type A HumanA2/Hongkong/1/68 (H3N2)
	Neuraminidase	Avian influenza type A

Q. 16. Describe the pathogenesis of equine influenza.

Ans. The virus causes an acute disease in equines of all ages, affecting primarily the lower respiratory tract. Subtype A/equi/2 is reported to be more virulent than Subtype A/equi/1. The virus affects horses, mules and donkeys causing considerable economic losses. The characteristics of the disease are nasal discharge, pyrexia, dry cough, high morbidity but low mortality in uncomplicated cases. Pneumonia develops in foals. Incubation period is 1-3 days. The course of the disease may last upto 2-3 weeks. Virus is shed from infected horses for several days through respiratory tract. CF antibody may develop against type specific S antigen after about a week of appearance of symptoms, which reaches to a peak within 2-3 weeks and then gradually declines within next 2-3 weeks. The disease has been reported in India. The Indian isolate has been typed as subtype A/equi/2/Ludhiana/1/87. The prevalence rate based on serological tests from different states is negligible. NRCE Hisar has developed an inactivated aluminium hydroxide gel vaccine using Indian isolate.

Q. 17. Describe the properties and pathogenicity of swine influenza virus?

Ans. Swine influenza virus was first isolated in 1931 by Shope. Human and swine influenza viruses have similar antigenic properties. Swine influenza was observed, simultaneously along with human influenza epidemic in USA in 1918-19. In Europe, the disease in swine was observed in 1950s and subsequently in several countries of South America, Asia and Africa. Swine mostly suffer from H1N1 and H3N2 subtypes. H1N1 subtype also infects turkeys and humans. As per WHO recommendations, swine influenza virus is designated as A/swine/Wisc/5/76 (Hsw1 N1). Due to insufficient antigenic differences among swine influenza strains, no subtypes have been designated. The virus gives HA test with RBCs of several species of animals. It is easily propagated in chicken embryo fibroblasts. Incubation period of the disease is 3-7 days. Transmission of infection is by droplets. The virus causes mild disease in upper respiratory tract. The disease is more severe in association with *Haemophilus suis* or other secondary bacterial infections. There is fever, anorexia, nasal discharge, sneezing, cough and conjuntivitis. Animals generally recover in about a week. Recovered animals have HI, SN, CF, and precipitating antibodies. Inactivated vaccine is available. In all three vaccinations are recommended, the first two at 8 weeks apart and the third after 6 months of the second vaccination.

Q. 18. What is the inter-epidemic cycle of swine influenza?

Ans. Swine influenza type A virus infects swine lungs. In case swine suffers from lung worm infection, the worm ingests the virus. The virus is passed on to the lungworm eggs and then to lung worm larvae. The infected lungworm larvae are eaten by earthworms and infected earthworm are eaten by healthy swines. Virus infected swine in presence of *Haemophilus suis* aggravate the disease causing swine flue/pneumonia.

Q. 19. Give a brief account of pathogenesis of Avian influenza.

Ans. Most of the properties of avian influenza virus are similar to the properties of swine and equine influenza viruses. Based on surface antigens, 14H and 9N subtypes of avian influenza virus type A have been identified. The virus multiplies in chicken embryos and chicken embryo fibroblast cell cultures. The clinical symptoms of the disease are, respiratory illness, sinusitis, oedema of face and head and diarrhoea. There is decreased egg production. The morbidity and mortality is variable. Avian influenza virus also causes intestinal infection leading to a generalized infection known as fowl plague. Transmission of the virus is by direct or indirect contacts Virus has been isolated from faeces and eggs. There being several H and N antigens in different strains, it is difficult to prepare a satisfactory vaccine.

Q. 20. Influenza virus mutates very fast. Discuss with examples.

Ans. Influenza viruses mutates due to antigenic shifts and antigenic drifts. The examples of mutation of human influenza virus A and B after same intervals are given below.

Type A subtype	Duration
A	1933-1947
A_1	1947-1957
A_2 (Asian)	1957-1964

Type B subtype	Duration
B	1940-1945
B_1	1945-1955
B_2	1956-1964
B_3 (Taiwan)	1962

Q. 21. Name viruses which will show haemadsorption and haemolysis in presence of red blood cells.

Ans. *Haemadsorption:* All the members of myxo viruses will show haemadsorption in presence of RBCs. Haemadsorption can be specifically inhibited by antiserum. Haemadsorption can detect early viral growth and those viruses which give low level of HA and do not produce CPE. Myxoviruses are influenza, ND, mumps and parainfluenza viruses.

Haemolysis: Haemolysis is associated with the viruses of parainfluenza 1, 2, 3, mumps, NDV and measles. Influenza virus does not show haemolysis.

29

Family *Paramyxoviridae*

Under *Paramyxoviridae* family viruses causing several diseases of veterinary importance such as para-influenza infecting several domestic animals, Newcastle disease (Ranikhet disease) infecting chickens, canine distemper infecting dogs and rinderpest infecting cattle, buffaloes and other bovines are described.

Q. 1. What are important properties of the viruses of *Paramyxoviridae* family.

Ans. The properties of paramyxoviruses are shown in Table 29.1.

Table 29.1: Important physico-chemical properties of *Paramyxoviridae* viruses.

Size of virion (nm)	Spherical particles about 150, filamentous forms upto 300
Envelope	Present
Capsid	Helical type
Transcriptase	Present
Site of multiplication	Cytoplasm
Nature of genome:	
Type of nucleic acid	RNA (15-16 kb)
No. of strands	Single (negative strand)
Shape of genome	Linear
Segments	Non-segmented

The genome of the virus codes 10-12 polypeptides including NP or N (nucleoprotein), P (phosphoprotein), L (large polymerase protein), F (protein mediated fusion), HN or H or G (haemagglutinin and neuraminidase) and M (matrix protein).

The family has three genera, namely *Paramyxovirus, Morbillivirus* and *Pneumovirus. Paramyxovirus* produces both haemagglutinins and neuraminidase antigens, *Morbillivirus* produces only haemagglutinins and *Pneumovirus* produces none of the two antigens.

Q. 2. Describe different serotypes of *Paramyxovirus, Morbillivirus* and *Pneumovirus* and diseases produced by them.

Ans. Table 29.2: Showing different serotypes of genera *Paramyxovirus, Morbillivirus* and *Pneumovirus* and diseases produced by them.

Genus	Virus/Serotypes	Diseases produced
Paramyxovirus	Mumps virus	Causes contagious disease of children with nonsuppurative infection of parotid glands
	Parainfluenzavirus 1	This virus is called Sendai virus and causes respiratory disease in mouse, rat, rabbit, and man.
	Parainfluenzavirus 2 (SV5)	Respiratory infection in dogs and monkeys (also in humans)
	Parainfluenzavirus 3	Respiratory infection in cattle, sheep and pigs
	Newcastle disease virus (avian para-influenzavirus 1)	Generalized disease with CNS symptoms, in chickens.
Morbillivirus	Rinderpest virus	Generalized disease in bovines
	Peste des petits ruminants virus	Disease resembling rinderpest
	Canine distemper virus	Severe generalized disease in dogs
	Measles virus	Measles in human beings
Pneumovirus	Bovine respiratory syncytial virus	Respiratory disease in cattle and sheep
	Turkey rhinotracheitis virus	Respiratory disease in turkeys and swollen head syndrome in chickens

Genus *Paramyxovirus*

Q. 3. What are clinical symptoms of parainfluenzavirus 2 in dogs?

Ans. In dogs the disease is generally mild but under poor hygienic conditions, they may suffer from severe cough with nasal discharge. The fever may continue for 8-10 days. There may be anorexia and conjuntivitis. The virus may infect man and monkeys.

Q. 4. Briefly describe the pathogenesis of parainfluenza virus 3 in bovines and pigs.

Ans. In bovines the clinical symptoms due to parainfluenza virus-3 are mild fever, nasal discharge, lacrymation, depression and coughing. Gross lesions are generally confined to epical and cardiac lobes of lungs in calves. The animals may suffer from secondary bacterial infections particularly with *Past.haemolytica* causing shipping fever. The virus produces HI and SN antibodies and cell mediated immunity. The virus can be isolated from respiratory tract, blood at the height of temperature and aborted foetus. It multiplies in calf, kid and pig kidney cell cultures and in embryonated chicken eggs. Virus also grows in HeLa and Vero cell lines. For diagnosis paired sera should be tested by HI test. Various clinical symptoms, are helpful in diagnosis.

In pigs there is mild respiratory disease, if there is no secondary bacterial infection, the animal recovers within a week. In complicated cases, there may be fever, cough and nasal discharge. The disease may be severe in piglets. There may be reproductive failure and encephalomyelitis. Older pigs may suffer from corneal opacity (blue eye disease).

Q. 5. When was Newcastle disease first reported? Describe various properties of the virus including strain differences based on their virulence.

Ans. The disease was first reported from Newcastle in England in 1926, from Jawa and Korea in the same year and from Ranikhet in India in 1927. The disease is also known as Doyle's disease or Ranikhet disease. The virus varies greatly in virulence. Highly virulent strains are known as velogenic, with medium virulence as mesogenic, and with least virulence as lentogenic. Virulence of the strains is tested on the basis of mean death time (MDT) in embryonated eggs, intracerebral pathogenicity index (ICPI) in one-day old chicks and by plaque formation (PF) test in chick embryo cells. The virus has only one serotype but minor antigenic variations are detected in different strains by monoclonal antibodies. The virus is relatively more heat stable. It survives for months in infected eggs at room temperature and more than a year at 4°C. The virus gives HA and HI tests.

Q. 6. Describe the pathogenesis and clinical symptoms of Newcastle disease.

Ans. The disease is highly contagious and occurs in several species of birds. The incubation period of the disease is 2-5 days. Transmission of infection takes place by direct, indirect and droplet methods. The virus replicates in respiratory and intestinal tracts and then it spreads to other organs like spleen, liver and bone marrow. Viraemia will spread infection to all other organs of the body including central nervous system. The disease generally occurs in the following four forms:

(a) *Doyle form (Asiatic form):* This is acute, most severe and fatal disease, produced by velogenic-viscerotropic strains.

(b) *Beach's form (pneumo-encephalitic form):* In this form, central nervous system and respiratory tracts are affected. This form occurs due to velogenic-neurotropic strains.

(c) *Beaudatte form:* This is caused by mesogenic strains and generally affects respiratory system and rarely central nervous system.

(d) *Hitchner form:* This is a mild inapparent respiratory infection and caused by lentogenic strains.

In acute cases there is a systemic reaction, showing anorexia, high fever, ruffled feathers, dullness, diarrhoea, respiratory distress and haemorrhages on combs. There is a drop in egg production. Some birds will show torticollis and tremors. Surviving birds may develop nervous symptoms, paralysis of limbs and circling movements. Similar symptoms will be seen in turkeys and other birds. Mortality rate is very high.

The virus is excreted from infected birds in all secretions and excretions and they may continue to do so upto 3-4 weeks after recovery. Specimens for isolation of the virus, should be tissues from spleen, liver, lungs, brain and intestines.

Q. 7. What will happen if NDV is inoculated in embryonated chicken eggs?

Ans. New castle disease virus will produce following changes when inoculated in embryonated chicken eggs.

(a) Death of embryos within 2-3 days after inoculation by allantoic route.

(b) Development of haemagglutinins and infective virus in allantoic fluid.

(c) Development of haemorrhages on the skin of embryos.

Q. 8. Select correct answer:

Newcastle disease virus infection in human beings can cause:

(a) Generalized infection

(b) Contagious respiratory infection

(c) Contagious conjuctivitis and mild influenza like symptoms

(d) Encephalitis

Ans. (c)

Q. 9. How would you diagnose Newcastle disease in a chicken flock?

Ans. New castle disease can be diagnosed by:

(a) Clinical symptoms and post mortem lesions.
(b) Death of chicken embryos after inoculation with specimens.
(c) Presence of haemorrhages on the skin of dead chicken embryos.
(d) Allantoic fluid will give positive HA test with chicken RBCs.
(e) HA test will be prevented by specific hyperimmune serum.

Q. 10. Name different lentogenic and mesogenic strains of Newcastle disease virus, used as live virus vaccines.

Ans. (a) *Lentogenic strains:* Most commonly used lentogenic strains of NDV are:

Strain F: The strain was originally isolated by Asplin (1952) from a fowl in England. This strain has lowest virulence among all available lentogenic strains of NDV. It also has least antigenicity among such strains.

Strain B-1: This strain was isolated by Hitchner and Johnson (1948) at Blacksburg, Virginia in USA. It is slightly more virulent than F strain, and is reported to be more immunogenic than F strain.

Strain La Sota: The strain was isolated by Beaudatte (1949) in the year 1946 in New Jersey, USA. This is more pathogenic than the other two strains mentioned above.

Strain CDF-66: This is another lentogenic strain of NDV isolated from the respiratory tract of a pig in 1966 by Malik *et al* in India. This strain has good antigenicity in addition to its lentogenic nature and is tolerated well even by very young chicks.

(b) *Mesogenic strains:* Three well known mesogenic strains are:

Mukteswar strain: This strain is also known as R_2B strain and was evolved by Iyre and Hashmi at IVRI Mukteswar in the year 1945 by serial passages in embryonated chicken eggs. It is extensively used as a vaccine strain in South East Asia and had been quite effective to control Newcastle disease. This strain is more invasive but provides most durable immunity. It is not tolerated well by young chicks.

Komarov strain: This strain was evolved by Komarov in late forties by passaging a virus intracerebrally in ducklings. This is less pathogenic than Mukteswar strain.

Raokin strain: This strain is a naturally occuring isolate with sufficient attenuation. It is mostly used in USA as a vaccine strain.

Q. 11. Name the vaccine(s) and a schedule of vaccination to control Newcastle disease?

Ans. In Asian countries Newcastle disease is more severe, and the vaccination programme recommended is shown in Table 29.3.

Table 29.3: Recommendation of vaccines and schedule of vaccination for Newcastle disease.

Age of birds	Type of vaccine	Route of vaccination
1 week	F or B-1 strain	Nostril drop
4 weeks	B-1 strain	Drinking water or aerosol method
8-9 weeks	R_2B strain	Intramuscular injection
Before egg laying stage	R_2B strain	Intramuscular injection

Q. 12. Write short notes on (a) Mumps and (b) Measles.

(a) *Mumps:* Mumps virus causes a common contagious disease in children which is characterised by non suppurative infection of parotid glands (parotitis). The envelope of the virus carries haemagglutinin, neuraminidase and haemolysin antigens. Infection of the disease takes place by inhalation. The incubation period of the disease is 10-20 days. Mumps may cause abortion in first trimester of pregnancy in woman.

(b) *Measles:* Measles is commonest and most infectious exanthematous disease of children. The virus is a member of *Morbillivirus* genus. It does not possess neuraminidase enzyme, and does not grow in eggs. It grows well in human embryonic kidney cells. The infected cells show numerous acidophilic nuclear and cytoplasmic inclusions. The virus shares antigens with rinderpest and distemper viruses. It has only 1 serotype.Incubation period of the disease is 10-12 days. Initially there is fever and infection in upper respiratory tract. These symptoms subside, and within next 2-4 days rashes appear on the skin. The rashes subside, if there are no complications. In some cases there may be neurological sequelae. The disease is most common in children aged 1-5 years. One attack of the disease confers solid immunity.

A combined measles, mumps and rubella vaccine is available which may be given as early as 9 months of age.

Q. 13. Give a sequence of destruction of receptors of red blood cells by neuraminidase enzymes of mumps, New castle disease and influenza viruses.

Ans. There are different types of receptors (mucopolysaccharide) on the surface of RBCs for action by neuraminidase enzymes of different myxo viruses. RBCs after HA test and elution with mumps virus, will give HA test with ND virus. The same RBCs after HA test and elution with ND virus, will give HA test with influenza virus. The above statement indicates that destruction of cell surface receptors after HA test and elution are, in the order of mumps, ND and influenza viruses and not vice-versa. RBCs after HA test and elution with influenza virus will not haemagglutinate ND and mumps viruses.

Genus *Morbillivirus*

Q. 14. Describe the properties of rinderpest virus.

Ans. The virus belongs to the *Morbillivirus* genus of the family. Most of the properties of the virus are similar to those described for the family. The virus shares antigens with measles and canine distemper viruses. It has 7 major and two minor proteins in the capsid. All rinderpest virus strains including the strains of 'Kabete O' and 'Nakamura III' are antigenically similar. The structural proteins are large polymerase (L), phosphoprotein (P), and nucleoprotein (N). These are located inside the virus. Other 3 proteins are haemagglutinin (HA), fusion (F), and matrix (M). These 3 proteins are located in the envelope. The virus is quite labile. It shows interference with distemper and measles viruses. The virus adapted to goats, rabbits and chicken embryos for vaccine production are known as caprinised, lapinized and avianized viruses respectively.

Q. 15. Give details of pathogenesis of rinderpest virus.

Ans. The virulence of the virus varies from place to place and in different species and breeds of animals. In India hill cattle, buffaloes, exotic and cross bred cattle are more susceptible. The incubation period of the disease is 4-8 days. The prodromal stage of the disease is marked with high fever for 2-3 days. In this stage, the animal is restless, depressed, lose appetite and there is constipation. Next comes the mucosal stage, in which mouth lesions appear on inside of lower lips and adjacent gums and alimentary tract. Mucosa becomes reddened and inflammed. Discreate, small necrotic lesions develop in mouth and sometimes in nasal and vaginal mucosae. There is salivation. Temperature drops with onset of shooting diarrhoea after 1-2 days of mouth lesions. There is dehydration and ematiation. Death may occur within 6-15 days after onset of symptoms. The mortality is upto 90-100%.

Q. 16. Name different stages of rinderpest.

Ans. The stages of rinderpest are:

(a) Incubation stage
(b) Prodromal stage
(c) Mucosal stage
(d) Convalescent stage

Q. 17. What type of specimens should be collected for the isolation of rinderpest virus?

Ans. The specimens should include nasal secretions, faeces, lymph nodes from intestinal tract and spleen. During height of temperature citrated blood can also be collected.

Q. 18. What are sensitive host systems for isolation of rinderpest virus?

Ans. The virus grows well in cattle & buffalo calf and lamb kidney cell cultures, and also in Vero cell line. In cell cultures, the virus produces syncytial type of CPE with cytoplasmic and intranuclear inclusion bodies.

Q. 19. How would you diagnose rinderpest cases?

Ans. The disease can be diagnosed by clinical symptoms, demonstration of virus/antigen in specimens, and specific antibodies in serum samples during convalescent stage. CPE in calf kidney cells is neutralized by rinderpest antiserum. Serological tests including SN/VN, HI, CF, FA and ELISA will help in the diagnosis. Immunodiffusion test using intestinal lymph nodes against known antiserum is a good and sensitive test. Recently molecular techniques like cDNA probe and reverse transcriptase polymerase chain reaction (RT-PCR) have been found sensitive, rapid and reliable.

Q. 20. Name different types of vaccines used for the control of rinderpest.

Ans. In the past virulent virus, was attenuated by serial passages in rabbits (lapinized vaccine), in chicken embryos (avianized vaccine) and in goats (caprinized vaccine i.e. goat tissue vaccine). In India most states used GTV for a number of years which controlled the disease to a great extent. This vaccine was not tolerated well by hill cattle, cross bred and exotic breeds of cattle. This vaccine also could not be used in sheep and goats. Since, 1980s tissue culture vaccine is used for all types of cattle, sheep and goats. The disease has more or less been controlled and no outbreaks of the disease are now reported from most parts of India.

Q. 21. Write short notes on Peste des Petits ruminants.

Ans. Peste des petits ruminants (PPR) virus is another member of *Morbillivirus* group. The virus has caused a distinct disease in small ruminants (sheep and goats) since 1960s. The clinico-pathological features of PPR are similar to rinderpest and was 1st detected in equatorial region of west Africa. Subsequently the disease was introduced in Middle East. In Indian state of Tamil Nadu, the disease was detected in 1988. The mortality was high in both sheep and goats. The incubation period of the disease is 5-6 days.

Symptoms of PPR in sheep and goats are quite similar to rinderpest. Primary pneumonitis is a significant feature due to PPR which is not so distinct in case of rinderpest. Other symptoms of the disease are fever, anorexia, necrotic stomatitis and diarrhoea. There seems to be no skin eruptions in PPR. Diagnosis for PPR is quite difficult in these animals. Virus identification in cell cultures require differential neutralization tests using anti-rinderpest and anti-PPR reference sera. There is little genetic homology between the genomes of rinderpest and PPR on the basis of nucleic acid probe of N genes of two agents. A difference in the position of N proteins of the two viruses in SDS-PAGE test is also regarded as a differential feature. PPR and rinderpest viruses cross immunise each other. Because of close antigen relationship rinderpest vaccines can be used to protect sheep and goats.

Q. 22. Describe the properties and pathogenicity of canine distemper virus.

Ans. The virus has only one antigenic type which is related to rinderpest and measles viruses. The virus grows in chicken embryos and in primary and continuous dog kidney and ferret kidney cell cultures. It produces grayish-white lesions on the CAM of chicken embryos. In dog kidney cell cultures, it produces syncytia and intracytoplasmic inclusion bodies. Under natural conditions, the virus infects dogs, wolves, foxes and other canines. The virus primarily affects puppies. Susceptible age of puppies depends whether they have received maternal antibodies or not. Older dogs are rarely affected.

Incubation period of the disease is 3-7 days. The virus is transmitted by direct contact or by droplet infection. The virus causes a generalized infection after initial multiplication in oesophagial lymphoid tissues. After this cell associated viraemia occurs and the virus is distributed to other parts of the body. The disease is characterized by coryza, diphasic fever, conjunctivitis and leucopenia. There is respiratory distress and gastroenteritis followed by cough, vomiting and diarrhoea. Older dogs may suffer from nervous symptoms, hardened foot pads and vesicular and pustular dermatitis. Recovered animals develop SN, CF and ID antibodies and good immunity.

Attenuated live vaccine is given to puppies when they are 6-8 weeks old. Ferret and egg adapted live vaccines are also available. Combined distemper, hepatitis and *Leptospira canicola* vaccine is available.

Q. 23. Describe laboratory diagnosis of canine distemper.

Ans. First of all one should eliminate other diseases like canine hepatitis, parvovirus infection and leptospirosis. Tissues from internal organs like lungs, urinary bladder, liver and brain, should be used by FA, ID and ELISA tests. Lesions on CAM of chicken embryos, intracytoplasmic inclusions in infected cells hardened footpad and vesicular dermatitis are also helpful in the diagnosis. Ferrers are very susceptible to the virus.

Genus *Pneumovirus*

Q. 24. What are *Pneumovirus* infections in bovines, turkeys and chickens?

Ans. Bovine respiratory syncytial virus produces respiratory infections causing interestitial pneumonia, pulmonary oedema and emphysema in weaned calves and young cattle. There is also, cough, fever, and rhinitis. The virus produces high morbidity but low mortality. the virus produces syncytia and intracytoplasmic inclusion bodies in bovine cell culture.

Turkey rhinotracheitis virus produces respiratory infection in turkeys and swollen head disease in chickens.

30

Family *Rhabdoviridae*

The family contains more than 150 viruses infecting vertebrates, invertebrates and plants. The virus is bullet shaped. Some viruses of the family multiply in vertebrates and arthropods.

Q. 1. Describe the properties of *Rhabdoviridae* viruses.

Ans. **Table 30.1:** Showing physico-chemical properties of rhabdoviruses

Size of virion (nm)	70 × 180
Shape	Bullet shaped
Envelope	Present (bilayer) with glycoprotein peplomers
Capsid	Helical symmetry
Transcriptase	Present (transcribes 5 sub-genomic mRNA)
Site of multiplication	Cytoplasm
Nature of genome:	
Type of nucleic acid	RNA (13-16 kb)
No. of strands	Single (negative sense)
Shape	Linear
Segments	Nonsegmented

The 5 subgenomic mRNA translate 5 proteins namely transcriptase (L), nucleoprotein (N), matrix protein (M), glycoprotein peplomer (G) and nonstructural protein (NS).

Q. 2. Name the genera and species of the family *Rhabdoviridae* and the diseases produced by them.

Ans. Table 30.2: Genera and species of *Rhabdoviridae* family and the diseases produced.

Genus	Virus/serotype	Disease
Vesiculovirus	Vesicular stomatitis virus	Vesicular stomatitis in cattle horses and swine
	Ephemeral fever virus	Ephemeral fever in cattle and buffaloes
	Chandipura virus	Affects humans (in India)
Lyssavirus	Rabies virus	Affects all warm blooded animals
	Rabies like viruses:	
	Mokola virus	Rabies like disease in Central Africa
	Lagos bat virus	Rabies like disease in Central and South Africa
	Duvenhage virus	Rabies like disease in South Africa and Europe

Genus *Vesiculovirus*

Q. 3. Describe the properties and pathogenicity of vesicular stomatitis virus.

Ans. The virus is reported to have two different strains known as Indiana strain and New Jersey strain. There is no cross serological reaction between the two strains. The virus is quite resistant and agglutinates goose RBCs at 4°C. There are several antigenic types.

The virus infects equines, bovines and swines. The disease is generally found in Americas. Transmission of the virus is by contact, discharges and arthropod vectors. Incubation period of the disease is 3-8 days. After entry of the virus in the body through mucosa or arthropod bites, there is local injury and cell damage. In bovines vesicles develop on tongue, dental pad and buccal mucosa. There is salivation, and anorexia. The vesicles rupture leading to raw bleeding surfaces. In milking cows, vesicles develop on teats and udder. There is some morbidity but no mortality. In horses, tongue lesions are more pronounced. In swine vesicles are seen on snout and in some cases lameness occurs. Humans are susceptible to the virus.

For isolation of the virus, suitable specimens are, vesicular fluid and tissues from the margins of the lesions. Saliva is also quite rich in virus.

The virus grows well in most cell culture systems where CPE is quite pronounced. It also multiplies on CAM of chicken embryos and shows pock lesions. The disease should be differentiated from vesicular exanthema and foot and mouth disease.

For control, both attenuated and inactivated vaccines are available.

Q. 4. Give a brief account of the pathogenesis of bovine ephemeral fever.

Ans. The virus affects cattle and buffaloes generally during rainy season. The disease is common in parts of Africa, most of Asia, Australia and East India. In India the disease is also known as three day fever. The disease spreads by bites of arthropod vectors. Incubation period of the disease is 2-7 days. The onset of the disease is sudden. The disease is benign and marked by biphasic fever with drop in milk production, depression, dry muzzle, drooping ears, stiffness of muscle and joints, lameness, incumbency, nasal discharge, cessation of rumination and constipation. Recovery is sudden within 3-4 days. Virus grows in bovine kidney, BHK_{21} and Vero cell lines. It also grows in brain of unweaned mice and hamesters. In some countries attenuated and inactivated vaccines are used. The vaccines however are not very potent.

Genus *Lyssavirus*

Q. 5. What are the properties of rabies virus?

Ans. Most of the properties of virus are those of the viruses of *Rhabdoviridae* family. Rabies virus consists of a single antigenic type. Three other rabies like viruses are recognized. They are: Lagos bat, Mokola and Duvenhage types. These serotypes can be distinguished from each other by monoclonal antibodies prepared against glycoprotein and nucleocapsid determinants. The disinfectants of choice for the virus are formalin and mercuric chloride. The virus gives positive HA test with goose RBCs at 4°C. It has 67% protein 26% lipid, 4% RNA and 3% carbohydrate. The 5 polypeptides of the virus are nucleoproteins (N and NS) 2, glycoprotein (G) 1, and membrane proteins (M1 and M2) 2. The virus infects all warm blooded animals including man, dogs, cats, domestic animals, wild carnivores, mongoose and bats. Fowls are infected experimentally. There is a report of infection in elephant. More deaths in cattle are reported in Central and South Americas. Rabies is present through out the world. Most cases of rabies in animals are due to bites by rabid dogs.

The virus can be propagated in chicken and duck embryos, day old chicks, young mice and hamesters, BHK-21, Vero cell lines human diploid cells and chicken embryo fibroblasts.

Q. 6. Describe the pathogenesis and clinical features of rabies.

Ans. The virus is present in the saliva of rabid animal which happens to be a dog in most cases. When rabid dog bites a man or animal, the virus from saliva is deposited in the wound. The virus multiplies in muscles, connective tissues and nerves at the site of animal bite. It penetrates the nerve endings and travels centripetally along the axons of peripheral nerves towards the spinal cord and the brain. The virus multiplies fast in the brain. It then spreads outwards along the nerve trunks to various parts of the body including salivary glands. It also multiplies in salivary glands and is shed in the saliva. The virus may also be present in milk and urine.

The disease occurs in two forms i.e. furious form or dumb form. In furious form, the rabid animal becomes restless, alert, snaps at imaginary objects. After this prodromal stage, the dog runs aimlessly here and there, bites without provocation, also bites objects like stone, wood etc. The lower jaw droops and saliva drools from mouth, tail hangs towards ground, eyes becomes wild and red. The animal can not eat and drink, howls and bark persistently. There is incoordination, paralysis and death within 3 to 4 days. In dumb form, there is short period of excitement, followed by incoordination and paralysis, dropped lower jaw, dehydration, prostration and death. Incubation period in man generally 1 to 3 months and in dogs 20 to 60 days.

Affected cattle and other ruminants become restless, exited and aggressive. There is abdominal pain, excessive salivation, diarrhoea, itching at the site of bite, paralysis and death after emaciation. The clinical signs in horses are similar to tetanus. In man initially there is fever headache, dilatation of pupils, excessive salivation, perspiration and paralysis of muscles of deglutition followed by death.

Q. 7. Fill in the blanks:

(a) Neurotropic nature of rabies was first demonstrated by .... in 1881.

(b) Infectious nature of saliva from rabid dog was recognised by .... in 1804.

(c) Antirabies vaccination, to a boy bitten by a rabid animal, was first done by .... in 1885.

(d) Viral nature of rabies agent was first demonstrated by its filtrability by .... in 1903.

(e) Intracytoplasmic inclusion bodies in neuronal cells of rabid animal was first demonstrated by .... in 1903.

Ans. (a) Pasteur (b) Zinke (c) Pasteur (d) Remlinger (e) Negri

Select correct answer:

Q. 8. Virus from rabid animal to susceptible animal can be transmitted by:
(a) Inhalation (b) Through intact skin
(c) Through intact mucous membranes of eyes and mouth
(d) Through broken skin (e) Through animal bite
(f) Milk (g) Urine

Ans. (a), (c), (d), (e), (f), (g)

Q. 9. Incubation period of rabies in dogs in most cases is:
(a) 1-2 weeks (b) 2-10 weeks
(c) 3-6 months (d) 6-12 months

Ans. (b)

Q. 10. Rabid dog in dumb form:
(a) Always bites (b) Often bites
(c) Seldom bites (d) Never bites

Ans. (c)

Q. 11. Among following laboratory animals, which animal is most preferred for isolation of street rabies virus?
(a) Rabbits (b) Guinea pigs
(c) Suckling mice (d) White rats

Ans. (c)

Select true or false statements:

Q. 12. An animal/human being when bitten by a rabid dog will have:
(a) Longer incubation period, if bitten on extremities than on face and head.
(b) Shorter incubation period in adults, than in children.
(c) Shorter incubation period, if the bitten wounds are extensive and deep rather than simple and less deep.
(d) No difference in incubation, whether the body size is smaller or larger.
(e) Longer incubation, if the bite is through clothes or body hairs than on bare skin.

Ans. (a) True (b) False (c) True (d) False (e) True

Q. 13. What are 4 different stages of rabies in human beings?

Ans. (a) Prodromal stage (b) Acute neurological stage
(c) Coma stage (d) Death

Select correct answer:

Q. 14. Sylvatic type of rabies is transmitted by:

(a) Dogs (b) Domestic animals
(c) Wild animals (d) Vampire bats

Ans. (c)

Q. 15. From rabid animals, virus is secreted in the following specimens excepts:

(a) Milk (b) Saliva
(c) Blood (d) Tears
(e) Urine

Ans. (d)

Q. 16. Fill in the blanks:

(a) In rabid dogs, dumb form is also known as .... form.
(b) Rabies virus occuring in naturally infected animals is called .... virus.
(c) Rabies vaccines are available in neural and .... forms.
(d) Rabies virus adapted to laboratory or any other animal after brain to brain serial passages is known as .... virus.

Ans. (a) paralytic (b) street (c) nonneural (d) fixed.

Q. 17. Write short notes on:

(a) Rabies street virus (b) Rabies fixed virus

(a) *Rabies street virus*: Isolated from natural human or animal infections is called street virus. This virus when inoculated by any route to any laboratory animal can cause fatal encephalitis after a long but variable incubation period. Intra cytoplasmic inclusions (Negri bodies) can be demonstrated in the brain cells of animal died of street virus. With street virus, the incubation period is long, which may be 20 to 60 days in dogs and 15 to 20 days in rabbits. The virus will invade central nervous system as well as salivary glands.

(b) *Rabies fixed virus:* Serial brain to brain passages by I/C route of street virus into animals like rabbit, sheep, goat etc. yields a fixed virus. Fixed virus does not multiply in extraneural tissues. This virus multiplies faster. Its incubation period is shortened considerably and Negribodies are not produced consistently. Fixed virus is generally used for vaccine production.

Q. 18. Arrange the following laboratory tests in order of preference for the diagnosis of rabies material:

(a) Isolation and identification of rabies virus in young mice by intracerebral injection.
(b) Demonstration of rabies virus antigen in saliva and brain by immunofluorescence, and immunoperoxidase tests.
(c) Demonstration of Negri bodies in the impression smears of brain.

Ans. (b), (c), (a)

Q. 19. The following statements are correct for Negri bodies except:
(a) They are spherical or oval in shape.
(b) Their size may vary from 2 to 10 μm.
(c) In animals died of rabies, Negri bodies are generally found in the ganglion cells of hippocampus of brain.
(d) One large or several variable size inclusion bodies may be present in one neuron.
(e) In all animals died of rabies, Negri bodies must be found in the cytoplasm of neurons.

Ans. (e)

Q. 20. Fill in the blanks:
(a) With Seller's stain the colour of Negri bodies is ....
(b) The colour of basophilic inner structure of Negri bodies is ....
(c) The colour of cytoplasm of neurons is ....
(d) The colour of cell nuclei is ....
(e) The colour of erythrocytes is ....

Ans. (a) cherry red (b) deep blue
(c) blue (d) deep blue
(e) copper coloured

Q. 21. Describe different neural and nonneural antirabic vaccines:

Ans. **Neural antirabic vaccines:**
(a) *Fermi vaccine:* It is fixed virus grown in sheep or goat brain and treated with phenol (0.5%) at 22°C. It is 5% suspension. As the vaccine still contains some residual virus, it is not safe and is not recommended.
(b) *Semple vaccine:* The vaccine was developed at CRI Kasauli (India) by Semple in 1911. It is also 5% sheep brain inactivated by 0.5% phenol at 37°C. This has no residual virus, hence it can be used safely.
(c) *Beta propiolactone (BPL) vaccine:* It is similar to Semples vaccine except that the inactivating agent is BPL. This is supposed to be more antigenic and is widely used in India.

(d) *Vaccine prepared from suckling mouse, rat or suckling rabbit brain using fixed virus:* This type of vaccine is inactivated with phenol or BPL or irradiated with ultraviolet. These animals have non-myelinated neural tissue and will have less encephalitic reaction and can be used safely.

Nonneural vaccines:

(a) *Live attenuated chicken embryo vaccine:* The Flury strain of rabies virus was serially passaged in chicken embryos by yolk sac route to reduce its virulence and to develop an attenuated live vaccine. In this attempt two types of vaccines have been developed. The low egg passage (LEP) vaccine was developed at 40-50 egg passage level and high egg passage (HEP) vaccine at 180 egg passage level. The LEP vaccine is used for dogs and HEP vaccine for cattle and other animals.

(b) *Duck egg vaccine:* This is fixed virus vaccine adapted to grow in duck eggs and inactivated with BPL. This is used prophylactically (preexposure) in human beings and not as post bite vaccine.

(c) *Tissue culture vaccine:* This vaccine was developed in human diploid cell cultures. It is purified and concentrated preparation of fixed rabies virus and inactivated by BPL. It is highly antigenic and only 4-5 infections of 1 ml does are enough for post exposure cases in human beings.

Q. 22. Select true or false statements:

(a) Elephants and rhinoceros are not affected by rabies.

(b) In early stage of the disease, virus can be isolated from blood of the affected animals.

(c) Rabies virus infected Vampire bats, will show symptoms of the disease.

(d) Infected dogs can shed rabies virus in saliva even before showing symptoms of the disease.

(e) All animals which are infected with rabies virus and showed symptoms, will invariably die of the disease.

(f) Puppies are not more susceptible for rabies than adult dogs.

(g) Pasteur for the first time fixed rabies virus, in dogs by intracerebral serial passages.

(h) All dogs infected with rabies, must shed virus in saliva.

Ans. (a) False (b) False (c) False (d) True (e) True (f) False (g) False (h) False

Select correct answer

Q. 23. In a rabies endemic area, if a street dog has bitten a person, the dog must be quarantined for:

(a) At least 3 days (b) At least 5 days
(c) At least 10 days (b) At least 14 days

Ans. (c)

Q. 24. Original source of Flury strain of rabies virus was:

(a) Chicken (b) Dog (c) Human (d) Rabbit

Ans. (c)

Q. 25. From the following rabies vaccines, select one which is free from post vaccinal reactions:

(a) Semples vaccine (b) Duck embryo vaccine
(c) Mouse brain vaccine (d) Human diploid cell culture vaccine

Ans. (d)

Q. 26. Which of the following procedures has been recommended for post bite rabies vaccination in human beings using tissue culture vaccine?

(a) 1 ml S/C injection daily for 5 days.
(b) 1 ml I/D injection daily for 5 days.
(c) 1 ml S/C injection daily for 7 days.
(d) 1 ml S/C injection on alternate days for 14 days.
(e) 1 ml I/M injection on 0, 3rd, 7th, 30th and 90th day.

Ans. (e)

Q. 27. What steps should be taken if a person is bitten by a street dog in an area/country where rabies is endemic?

Ans. 1. If the dog showed symptoms of rabies, take following steps:

(a) Wash and thoroughly flush the wound/bitten part with soap and water, apply some antiseptic like alcohol, tincture of iodine etc. and then cauterise the wound with nitric acid or some other agent. Also give antitetanic serum/toxoid injection.

(b) Start rabies vaccination as per the instructions of the manufacturer.

(c) If the bitten wounds are multiple, deep and near the head and face, inject antirabic hyper immune serum (40 IU/KG wt.) in the tissues on the site of wound (s) and also flood the wound area with antiserum. Antiserum can also be given parenterally.

(d) If the dog can be caught, confine it for further observations. If the animal shows typical symptoms of rabies by its abnormal behaviour and other signs, kill the dog and send brain for confirmation to viral laboratory.

2. If laboratory tests confirm the case of rabies, take complete vaccination schedule. After completing vaccination course blood serum can be tested for antibodies.
3. If the laboratory test is found negative, discontinue rabies vaccination. The dog may be suffering from some other disease.
4. If the dog did not show any symptoms of rabies, confine it for 10 days, if it does not show any symptoms of disease, free the animal and discontinue vaccination.
5. If during confinement, the animal develop symptoms of rabies, send the brain to laboratory for testing and continue or discontinue vaccination schedule as per laboratory result.

31

Family *Arenaviridae*

Q. 1. Give chemical composition and structure of the family *Arenaviridae*

Ans. **Table 31.1:** Showing physical and chemical properties of *Arenaviridae* family

Size (nm)	110-130
Shape	Spherical or pleomorphic
Capsid	Helical type
Envelope	Present, lipoprotein in nature with peplomers
Transcriptase	Present
Replication	Cytoplasm
Nature of genome:	
Type of nucleic acid	RNA
Shape	Linear
No. of strands	Single with ambisense (Some +ve some –ve)
Segments	Segmented with 2 pieces (7.2-3.4 kb)

Q. 2. Name various genera and species of the family *Arenaviridae*.

Ans. 1. Genus: *Arenavirus*

Species:
1. Lymphocytic choriomeningitis virus
2. Junin virus
3. Machupovirus
4. Lassa virus
5. Guanarito virus

Q. 3. Briefly describe the pathogenicity of the lymphocytic choriomeningitis virus.

Ans. The Lymphocytic choriomeningitis virus is generally a rodent parasite, causing persistent infection in natural host. The virus can also infect human beings leading to severe haemorrhagic illness. The virus grows in different cell culture systems including Vero cell line. The virus is zoonotic in nature and causes choriomeningitis and haemorrhagic fever in man. The virus is maintained in rodents in nature and excreted in urine and oral secretions and transmit infection to young ones. There may be vertical transmission in rodents.

Q. 4. Name other arenaviruses causing diseases in human beings.

Ans. Other arenaviruses are:

(a) *Juninvirus:* It causes haemorrhagic fever and has been reported from Argentina.

(b) *Machupovirus:* It is reported from Bolivia and causes haemorrhagic fever in man.

(c) *Guanaritovirus:* It is reported from Venezuela and causes haemorrhagic fever in man.

(d) *Lassavirus:* This virus also causes haemorrhagic fever in man and is reported from West Africa.

32

Family *Bunyaviridae*

Bunyaviridae family contains large number of viruses which are transmitted by arthropod vectors. Other arboviruses contained in *Togaviridae* and *Flaviviridae* families, *Orbivirus* genus of *Reoviridae* and *Vesiculovirus* genus of *Rhabdoviridae* families have already been dealt with in earlier chapters. The name of this family has been derived from Bunyamwera, a place in Uganda from where Bunyamwera group of viruses of this family were isolated. This family contains some group C Arboviruses.

Q. 1. Describe physico-chemical properties of *Bunyaviridae* virus family.

Ans. **Table 32.1:** Showing physico-chemical properties of the viruses of *Bunyaviridae* family.

Size of virion (nm)	90-100
Shape	Spherical
Envelope	Present with glycoprotein peplomers
Capsid	Helical
Transcriptase	Present
Replication	Cytoplasm
Nature of genome:	
Nucleic acid	RNA (13-21 kb)
No. of strands	Single
Whether segmented	Yes, 3 segments (minus sense)
Shape	Linear

The virions contain 4 major proteins, which are transcriptase (L), a nucleoprotein (N), and glycoproteins (G1 & G2).

Q. 2. Name different genera, species and diseases caused by them.

Ans. Genus 1: *Bunyavirus:* The genus has more than 150 viruses, distributed in 18 serogroups. Most of them are mosquito borne. More than

30 viruses are pathogenic to domestic animals and human beings. Akabane disease virus affecting cattle and sheep, occurs in Africa, Australia and Japan.

Genus 2: *Phlebovirus:* This genus contains more than 50 viruses transmitted by *sandflies* and *mosquitoes.* The pathogens include Rift Valley fever virus affecting sheep, cattle and humans in Africa.

Genus 3: *Nairovirus:* This group has more than 30 viruses. Most of these viruses are *tick* borne. Important diseases include Nairobi sheep disease affecting sheep and goats occuring in Eastern Africa. The virus is transmitted by mosquitoes.

Genus 4: *Hantavirus:* This genus has only few viruses. None of them is transmitted by arthropod vectors. Reservoir hosts are rodents. The virus is excreted in urine and saliva. Animals affected are rodents and human beings. These viruses cause haemorrhagic fever in humans and have been isolated from Asia, Europe and America.

Genus *Bunyavirus*

Q. 3. Describe the pathogenesis of Akabane disease in cattle and sheep.

Ans. The virus causes fetal arthrogryposis (hydranencephaly syndrome) and fetal deaths in cattle. It also causes abortions in cattle and sheep. Transmission of virus is through mosquitoes. The disease is reported from South African and South West Pacific region countries. The pregnant cows are affected without any clinical symptoms but may abort with fetal death. Surviving calves develop neurogenic arthrogryposis.

Diagnosis of the disease can be made by clinical symptoms and detection of specific antibodies in serum taken from aborted fetus. Isolation of the virus is difficult.

Inactivated vaccines have been found safe and effective.

Genus *Phlebovirus*

Q. 4. Describe the properties and pathogenicity of Rift Valley fever virus.

Ans. Most of the properties of the virus are those of the virus family. the virus is more resistant than other arboviruses. It gives positive HA test with RBCs of newly hatched chicks, young mice and guinea pigs. The virus multiplies in embryonated chicken eggs by CAM and yolk sac routes. It also grows in kidney cell cultures, Vero and BHK-21 cell lines, and in suckling mouse brain.

The disease is widely prevalent in Africa infecting sheep, cattle, buffaloes and human beings. The virus is transmitted by *mosquitoes.* The disease was first reported from Rift Valley in Kenya. There were many outbreaks of the disease between 1950 and 1978 in Subsaharan Africa including Egypt with large number of deaths in animals and humans. The incubation period of the disease is 3-5 days. Infected sheep develop fever, vomiting, anorexia, nasal discharge and bloody diarrhoea. There may be enlarged spleen, hepatitis and leucopenia. There is very high mortality in lambs and upto 50% in adult sheep. The disease is less severe in cattle. Due to infection in sex organs, there is vertical transmission of infection in fetus. Direct and indirect infection may also take place.

The disease can be diagnosed by clinical symptoms, and isolating and identifying the virus serologically with known hyper immune serum. Testing of paired sera is also helpful.

Q. 5. What preventive measures can be taken to control Rift Valley fever disease?

Ans. (a) Mass vaccination of sheep using attenuated live vaccine before the start of mosquito breeding season and on first indication of spread of disease.

(b) For pregnant ewes, inactivated vaccine should be used.

(c) Extensive use of insecticides over large areas throughout the vector breeding season.

Q. 6. Select true or false statements:

(a) All four genera of the family have arthropod borne diseases.

(b) All the viruses in the family have segmented genome.

(c) Viruses placed in each genus are antigenically related and differentiated by cross neutralization test.

(d) There is no transovarian infection in sheep in Rift Valley fever.

(e) Arthropod vectors in all 4 genera are mosquitoes only.

Ans. (a) False (b) True (c) True (d) False (e) False

Genus *Nairovirus*

Q. 7. Briefly describe the properties and pathogenicity of Nairobi sheep disease virus.

Ans. This is an acute, infectious disease of sheep and goats transmitted by ticks and found in Africa. A closely related virus (Ganjam virus of sheep and goats) has been isolated from ticks and mosquitoes in India. The virus is transmitted by all stages of ticks. There is transovarian infection also in ticks. The virus can be propagated in sheep and goat kidney cell cultures with intracytoplasmic inclusion bodies. The incubation period of the disease is 4 to 12 days. Infected animals show fever with a mucopurulent nasal discharge. There is gastroenteritis with blood tinged diarrhoea. Lymph nodes are congested and enlarged. Abortion may take place in pregnant animals. Mortality may reach upto 50%. Virus may be excreted in urine and faeces. Cattle are not infected with the virus. There is no transmission of virus by contact. Recovered animals possess durable immunity. Mouse brain adapted inactivated vaccine is used for immunisation.

Genus *Hantavirus*

Q. 8. Describe the pathogenicity of hantavirus.

Ans. This virus is excreted from rodents in urine and faeces. Rodents act as reservoir of the virus. Human beings are infected from rodent's excreta and saliva by bites. There is no transmission from person to person and through arthropods. Some animals are also affected by hantavirus. It causes haemorrhagic fever in man. The virus has been isolated from Asia, America and Europe. It causes renal damage in human beings.

33

Family *Retroviridae*

The viruses of *Retroviridae* family consist of RNA tumour viruses and other related agents. The name retro (means reverse) is derived from reverse transcriptase enzyme which is RNA dependent DNA polymerase. Reverse transcriptase enzymes are found in all the members of this family. The family includes some viruses of veterinary importance including the viruses of avian leukosis and avian sarcoma.

Q. 1. Describe the properties of the viruses of *Retroviridae* family.

Ans. Table 33.1: Showing important physico-chemical properties of retroviruses.

Size (nm)	80-130
Shape	Spherical
Envelope	Present with glycoprotein peplomers
Capsid	Incosahedral type
Transcriptase	Present (reverse transcriptase i.c. RNA dependent DNA polymerase)
Replication	Transcription inside nucleus but translation and assembly in cytoplasm
Nature of genome:	
Nucleic acid	RNA (7-10 kb)
No. of strands	Single (diploid in nature which is unique)
Shape	Linear
Whether segmented	Yes, there are 3 segments (+ sense)

Q. 2. In what way the genome of retroviruses differ from the genome of other RNA viruses?

Ans. Table 33.2: Showing differences between the genome of retroviruses and the genome of other RNA viruses.

Genome of retroviruses	Genomes of other RNA viruses
(a) Diploid in nature	Haploid in nature
(b) Transcriptase is RNA dependent DNA polymerase	RNA dependent RNA polymerase
(c) RNA is synthesized by mRNA processing machinery of cell	RNA is synthesized by viral mRNA itself

Q. 3. Classify Retroviruses

Ans. Different members of retroviruses infect human beings, cattle, cats, primates, rodents and avian species. The family has 6 genera out of which only two genera i.e. *Lentivirus* and *Spumavirus* have been recognized officially. Other genera are named provisionally.

The first classification of oncogenic retroviruses was based on their host specificity and virus morphology. Four types of viruses were categorized as type A, type B, type C and type D. All the viruses of veterinary importance are classified under type C group. Lentiviruses differ from other retroviruses in structure and genome. The envelope glycoprotein epitopes (coded by *env* gene) are type specific. The core protein epitopes are group specific (encoded by gene *gag*).

Q. 4. Name different subfamilies, genera and species of retroviruses and diseases caused by them.

Ans. Table 33.3: Showing sub families, genera, and species of *Retroviridae* and diseases caused by them in animals and chickens.

Subfamily	genus	species	host	disease
1. *Oncovirinae*	Avian *Oncovirus* type C	Avian leukosis virus	Chicken	Lymphoma, leukaemia, anaemia, osteopetrosis
		Avian sarcoma virus	Chicken	Sarcoma
	Mammalian *Oncovirus* type C	Bovine leukaemia virus	Bovine	Leukaemia, lymphomas, anaemia, sarcoma
		Porcine sarcoma virus	Swine	Sarcoma
		Feline leukaemia virus	Cat	Leukaemia
		Feline sarcoma virus	Cat	Sarcoma
		Human T cell leukaemia I & II	Humans	Leukaemia

(Contd.)

Subfamily	genus	species	host	disease
2. *Lentivirinae*	*Lentivirus*	Maedi/Visna virus	Sheep	Maedi/Visna
		Caprine arthritis-encephalomyelitis virus	Goat	Arthritis, encephalomyelitis
		Equine infectious anaemia virus	Horse	Anaemia
		Feline immuno-deficiency virus	Cat	Acquired immuno deficiency
		Human immuno-deficiency virus (HIV)	Humans	Acquired immuno-deficiency syndrome (AIDS)
3. *Spumavirinae*	*Spumavirus*	Bovine foamy virus	Cattle	Unknown
		Feline foamy virus	Cat	Unknown

Genus *Oncovirus* type C

Q. 5. Write short notes on oncogenes of retroviruses.

Ans. In some retroviruses the genome is defective. Viruses with nondefective genome carry three oncogenes. The three genes are *gag* gene (codes group specific antigen) encodes capsid protein, *pol* gene encodes reverse transcriptase and *env* gene encodes the envelope glycoprotein. The genome of rapidly transforming retroviruses have fourth gene called viral oncogene (*v-gene*). Presence of this gene is associated with some deletion in the genome (generally *env* gene) with the result, such viruses are unable to replicate and need a helper virus for replication.

Q. 6. Briefly describe how transmission of retroviruses takes place?

Ans. Transmission of retroviruses may take place horizontally or vertically. When it is horizontal, it is transmitted by complete infectious particles as is the case for equine infectious anaemia. In case of caprine arthritis, infection may be via colostrum or milk. Vertical transmission can be through eggs or placenta. The offspring may carry the virus throughout life, will grow normally and will rarely develop leukaemia, but the animal will be a source of exogenous virus which will be transmitted horizontally to other healthy animals or chickens. A provirus integrated in the DNA of host cells will not cause disease endogenously. However, it will pass on to the progeny via ova or sperm.

Q. 7. What is the role of avian exogenous and endogenous viruses in causing leukosis and sarcoma?

Ans. For avian leukosis and sarcoma, three classes of viruses are involved. They are:

(a) *Endogenous viruses:* These viruses occur in the genome of chicken as DNA provirus. Generally, they are not expressed and when expressed, they are non-pathogenic.

(b) *Exogenous viruses which are competent for replication:* They possess *gag*, *pol* and *env* oncogenes in viral genome. Generally, these viruses are also nonpathogenic. A small percentage of birds infected with these viruses may develop leukaemia or lymphoma. Some of these exogenous viruses acquire *c-onc* (cellular oncogene) and then rapidly induce malignant tumours.

(c) *Exogenous viruses which are defective for replication:* Some of the rapidly transforming viruses (as mentioned in (b)) lose part of their genome when they acquire the oncogene (*gag, pal, env*) and become replication defective. They will require a helper virus for their replication.

Q. 8. What are the properties of avian leukosis virus (ALV) and avian sarcoma virus (ASV)?

Ans. These viruses induce a variety of transmissible neoplasms. ALV predominantly affects haematopoietic cells and ASV produces pathological response in fibroblastic cells. Both viruses have common internal antigens. Transmission of disease is mainly vertically but horizontally also in cases of close contact. In both viruses, tumour specific cell surface antigen (TSSA) is present. In sarcoma virus transformed cells, tumour specific transplantation antigen (TSTA) has been demonstrated. There is some immunosuppression due to both these viral diseases. These viruses can be isolated in cell cultures from plasma, serum, tumour tissues or embryos of infected chickens. Rous sarcoma virus induces pocks on CAM of embryonated eggs and produces tumours in embryos by I/V or yolk sac route inoculation. Leukosis virus replicates in chicken embryos by I/V route and kills chicks 1-2 weeks after hatching. Cellular response in avian leukosis is predominantly of B cell type. Removal of bursa, prevents lymphoid leukosis. Major internal antigen is present in supernatant and in the cells of infected cultures which can be detected by Resistance Inducing Factor (RIF) and complement fixation avian leukosis (COFAL) tests. COFAL test is performed to detect subclinical cases of avian leukosis virus infection. The tests is based on principle of C.F. test to detect avian leukosis virus infection in egg albumin, plasma, feather pulp etc. and is quite reliable to detect such non clinical cases of ALV. Marek disease is RIF negative and lymphoid leucosis is RIF positive. Eggs for human vaccine production must be from RIF negative hens.

Q. 9. Briefly describe the pathogenesis of tumours due to exogenous non-defective avian retroviruses.

Ans. Exogenous non-defective avian retroviruses produce tumours, only in birds that are congenitally infected and have a persistent viraemia. There is a high probability of lymphoid cell infection and transformation by leukosis virus. There viruses produce following types of diseases:

(a) *Lymphoid leukosis (Visceral lymphomatosis):* It is the commonest form of avian leukosis and occurs mostly in 4-8 months old birds. The rate of development of lymphoid leukosis is slow. There is lack of feed intake, weakness, emaciation and enlarged abdomen. Leukaemia is not very common. Lymphoblastoid cells are rarely seen in blood circulation. The comb may be pale and shrivelled. Tumours are present in liver, spleen, bursa and in other organs. Removal of bursa in early age arrests development of lymphoid leukosis. This disease is popularly known as big liver disease among farmers. In affected birds, the lymphoblasts may secrete large amounts of IgM, but not other types of immunoglobulins.

(b) *Osteopetrosis (thick leg):* In this form of the disease, bones are affected by uniform or irregular thickening. Generally long bones are affected. In advanced cases, there is osteoma and osteogenic sarcoma. The birds may have anaemia and lesions of lymphoid leukosis.

(c) *Renal tumours:* When renal cells are affected, nephroblastoma may develop which is generally detected at the time of post mortem.

Q. 10. What type of diseases are produced by defective avian leukosis viruses?

Ans. These viruses replicate with the help of non-defective leukaemia viruses (generally exogenous type) and produce a variety of neoplasms. These viruses produce three types of diseases:

(a) *Avian erythroblastosis:* This occurs in two forms: In proliferative form, the virus propagates rapidly and large number of erythroblasts are found in blood circulation. In anaemic from there is anaemia and only a few circulating erythroblasts.

(b) *Myeloblastosis:* In this syndrome, large number of myeloblasts are present in the blood. The symptoms are similar to erythroblastosis. In this disease, leukaemia is a major feature. The incubation period is about 10 days.

(c) *Myelocytomatosis:* In this, the target cells are nongranulated myeloblasts. The symptoms here are also similar to erythroblastosis. Rate of development of the disease is fast. Various mesenchymal cells are affected and lesions produced are those of sarcoma. Tumour growth may extend upto bones.

Q. 11. How will you diagnose a case of avian leukosis?

Ans. History of the disease in the flock, clinical symptoms, gross and histopathological findings are quite sufficient to make a diagnosis. Differential diagnosis should be made with Marek's disease caused by a DNA virus.

Q. 12. How can avian leukosis disease be controlled?

Ans. The disease can be controlled by adopting a strict hygienic measures, elimination of infected flock and starting with a new genetically disease resistant strain. Immunization using inactivated or attenuated live virus vaccines have met with limited success.

Q. 13. Describe the pathogenesis of bovine leukaemia.

Ans. In early twentieth century, the disease was reported from Denmark, Germany and some other European countries. The virus was isolated in 1969 for the first time. It is classified with human T cell lymphotropic Type I and Type II (HTLV I and HTLV II) viruses in *Oncovirus type C* genus. The virus causes both leukaemia and lymphosarcoma in cattle. The incubation period of the disease is 4-5 years. The virus occurs in exogenous form. This is not related antigenically to other mammalian and avian type C oncoviruses, except ovine leukaemia virus.

The disease occurs in following 4 forms in cattle:

(a) adult form (b) skin form (c) thymic form (d) calf form

(a) *Adult form:* It is most common in cattle of 4-8 year old and mostly occurs in lymphosarcoma form. There is persistent lymphocytosis and clinical manifestation of enlargement of lymph nodes, and leukaemic infiltration in various organs and tissues.

(b) *Skin form:* In this form, patches/plaques of 1-2 inches appear on neck, back and thighs.

(c) *Thymic form:* In this form, thymus gland becomes enlarged and swollen along with other forms of clinical symptoms.

(d) *Calf form:* This form is seen in 6-8 months old calves. The calf loses weight along with enlargement of all lymph nodes. B lymphocytes may infiltrate in visceral organs.

Virus can be isolated from lymph nodes in primary bovine or ovine cell cultures. Human and canine cells are also susceptible. It will produce syncytia in cell cultures. The disease has not been produced experimentally. Sheep inoculated with lymphocytes from infected animals, will develop lymphoid tumours in about 2 years.

Under natural conditions, the disease is transmitted horizontally by contact and to new born calves through colostrum. There are reports of transmission by blood sucking insects and congenitally via placenta. The virus is shed in urine and milk.

Diagnosis can be made on the basis of increase of mature and immature lymphocytes in blood circulation and swollen lymph nodes. There is syncytia type of CPE in cell cultures.

Genus *Lentivirus*

Q. 14. What are the properties of Visna and Maedi viruses?

Ans. Maedi and Visna diseases appear to be caused by the same or very closely related lentiviruses (lentus means slow). These diseases were first reported in Iceland in sheep imported from Germany in 1933. During following years, large number of sheep died and equally large numbers were slaughtered to eradicate the infection. The properties of the virus are mentioned below:

The virus is non oncogenic and exogenic. The agents isolated from maedi (causing dyspnoea) and visna (causing wasting disease) are similar morphologically and biologically. Maedi virus produces pneumotropic and visna neurotropic lesions in sheep and goats respectively. The virus is not sensitive to interferons. Both agents are antigenically similar. The mutation rate of these viruses is very high There is considerable antigenic drift in both viruses. The nucleocapsid of these viruses is cylindrical type. There is nucleic acid hybridization between the viruses of maedi and visna indicating they share nucleic acid sequences. These viruses replicate in sheep cell cultures causing syncytial type of CPE followed by cellular degeneration.

Q. 15. Give an account of pathogenesis of maedi in sheep.

Ans. Maedi and maedi like diseases have been reported from several countries in Europe and USA in sheep. In some countries, it is known as ovine progressive pneumonia. In nature, the disease occurs in 3-4 year old sheep. early symptoms of the disease are loss of condition, and increased respiration. Later on, there is dyspnoea, head may be extended with each respiration, nostrils are dialated, and there is slight nasal discharge and cough. Experimentally, incubation period is about

2 years in sheep. The course of the disease is 4-6 months and the animal may survive for about a year. Generally, there are secondary bacterial pneumonia. Macroscopically, lungs are enlarged and diffusely thickened. In advanced cases, lung alveoli are blocked. There may be arthritis and lymphoid tumours in mammary glands.

Q. 16. Describe the pathogenesis and clinical symptoms of visna in sheep and goats.

Ans. Visna virus causes meningo-encephalitis, a chronic progressive neurological disease in sheep and goats affecting CNS. In nature, the virus affects sheep under two years of age. The incubation period after I/C inoculation in sheep and goats is several years and clinical symptoms appear in 2-6 years. The disease starts with weakness of hips and hind limbs. with difficulty in walking. The animal may fall without any apparent reason. There is progressive weight loss, trembling of facial muscles, paralysis and death. The course of the disease is few months to several years. The virus persists in infected animals even though there is humoral and cellular immune response. Isolation of virus is possible during initial stage from leucocytes, brain and cerebrospinal fluid. There is continuous mutation of the virus. The viral antigen may be absent due to stoppage of replication of the virus beyond proviral stage. The virus can be recovered from milk of infected ewes. There is no indication of vertical transmission. Transmission of virus is through contact, by inhalation and ingestion of contaminated faeces and other materials.

Q. 17. How are maedi and visna viruses transmitted from infected to healthy sheep?

Ans. The viruses can be transmitted by:

(a) Droplet transmission when animals are housed in close confinement.

(b) Contaminated feed and water. The virus is excreted in faecal matter and urine.

(c) Lambs can be infected from infected mothers through contaminated milk.

(d) The virus can also be transmitted through biting insects.

Q. 18. Name body fluids which may transmit maedi and visna viruses.

Ans. These viruses can be transmitted by body fluids like blood, tears, nasal discharge, semen, saliva and milk which contain infected cells or free virus.

Q. 19. What are the clinical symptoms of caprine arthritis and encephalomyelitis?

Ans. Arthritis occurs in goats over one year old and encephlomyelitis in kids of 2-4 months old. In older goats, arthritis progresses slowly for months and years. Hock and shoulder joints are swollen and become painful. The disease becomes more severe in winter months. Thickening of joint capsules makes movement difficult. There is synovitis of joints with synovial cell hyperplasia and infiltration of lymphocytes, plasma cells and macrophages. There may be mild interstitial pneumonia. Kids are infected by feeding infected colostrum and milk.

The symptoms of encephalomyelitis in young kids are progressive weakness, trembling and in the later stages, paralysis. Affected goats show progressive wasting. There is no fever and the animals maintain good appetite and eye sight.

Antibodies can be detected by indirect FA, ID and ELISA tests.

Q. 20. Give a detailed account of pathogenesis of equine infectious anaemia.

Ans. The disease is also known as swamp fever, because it mostly occurs in low lying humid and swampy areas where insects are found in large numbers and transmit and disease by biting the horses. The arthropod vectors are tabanid and stable flies and mosquitoes. The disease has been reported in most countries including USA, Central and South America and South Africa. The incubation period of the disease is 7-21 days. The symptoms of the disease, are recurrent fever, anaemia, jaundice, anorexia, progressive weakness, loss of weight and oedema. In acute and subacute cases, there are haemorrhages and enlargement of spleen, lymphnodes and kidneys. There are petecheal haemorrhages on mucous membranes. There is decrease in blood platelets, packed cell volume and RBC count. Tissue macrophages and other cells carry the virus. Cell associated viraemia persists during the entire course of disease which continues life long. This is due to successive antigenic variations in the virus and due to non neutralization of existing antibodies. The virus has a number of immunologically distinct strains. Some animals develop chronic disease showing only mild symptoms. There is infection of lymphocytes, which may have degenerative or proliferative responses.

The disease can spread vertically by transplacental infection and horizontally by consumption of colostrum, milk, saliva and urine. Isolation of the virus can be made by citrated blood, serum, or leucocytes of infected horses in primary equine leucocyte cultures.

The disease can be diagnosed by history, clinical symptoms, examination of blood and pathological lesions. Antibodies in the infected animals may be detected by gel diffusion test with known virus (Coggins tests). Another reliable test is by inoculation of serum or whole blood from infected horse to uninfected susceptible horse.

Q. 21. Select true or false statements:

(a) The virus and antibody exist simultaneously in equine infectious anaemia cases.
(b) There is no vertical infection to foetus in equine infectious anaemia.
(c) Equine infectious anaemia virus is quite stable antigenically.
(d) Different strains of the virus have common group specific antigens but subtypes have different glycoproteins.
(e) Anaemia in equine infectious cases is due to immune mediated RBC destruction and bone marrow suppression during febrile stage.
(f) There is no cell mediated immunity in equine infectious anaemia cases.

Ans. (a) True, (b) False, (c) False, (d) True, (e) True (f) False

Q. 22. Explain why there is poor immune response in *Lentivirus* infections?

Ans. The poor immune response in *Lentivirus* infections is due to:

(a) Death of T helper (Th) cells.
(b) Death of antigen presenting cells (macrophages, dendric cells and B lymphocytes).
(c) Reduced lymphokine production (e.g. interleukin 2 and gamma interferon).
(d) Production of suppressor factors.
(e) Genetic variation affecting viral epitopes.

Q. 23. Write short notes on Human Immunodeficiency virus (HIV).

Ans. The virus belongs to *Lentivirus* genus of *Lentivirinae* sub-family. The virus causes acquired immunodeficiency syndrome (AIDS) in human beings. The discovery of AIDS was made in 1983. It is a generalized chronic debilitating disease. AIDS virus i.e. HIV has similarities with lentiviruses of veterinary importance. A person infected with HIV leads more or less normal life without showing any clinical symptoms for a variable period of time. The incubation period may be from several months to several years. The virus is transmitted to his/her partner by sexual contact, via semen or vaginal fluid. If a female is infected during pregnancy, her newly born child will also be infected. The infection can be transmitted through a contaminated syringe and transfusion of infected blood. Infected person may have progressive weakness, loss of weight, anaemia, fever and flu like symptoms. The virus kills T helper cells (Th) and antigen presenting cells of the body. The immune system of the body is totally broken down which will make the individual susceptible to many other infections. The disease can be diagnosed by ELISA or Western blot tests. Peripheral blood leucocytes may carry virus antigen which can be detected by these tests. So far, there is no vaccine against the disease. Only symptomatic treatment can be carried out.

34

Other Viruses

Majority of important DNA and RNA virus families and their viruses causing diseases of veterinary importance have been described in preceding chapters. There are some other viruses causing diseases in animals and human beings which have been isolated lately and/or have not been studied thoroughly. They are described in this chapter. These viruses belong to the following families or genera.

1. *Filoviridae*
2. *Toroviridae*
3. *Circoviridae*
4. Astroviruses
5. Arteriviruses
6. Delta virus
7. Borna disease virus

Filoviridae

Q. 1. Describe the properties and pathogenicity of *Filoviridae* viruses.

Ans. These viruses are long filamentous rod shaped, single stranded RNA viruses measuring 80 nm in diameter and 800-1000 nm in length. These viruses are enveloped with helical symmetry. The genome is non-segmented with minus (–) sense and linear in shape. The size of genome is 12.7 kb. These viruses have 7 proteins namely L, G, N, VP40, VP35, VP30 and VP24 in addition to transcriptase enzyme.

Genus *Filovirus*

Species: (i) Marburg virus: The virus causes haemorrhagic fever in man. It was first reported in Frankfurt and Belgrade in 1967, from laboratory workers handling monkeys.

(ii) Ebola virus: The virus was isolated from Sudan and Zaire in 1976 from haemorrhagic fever cases in hospitals. Morphologically this virus resembles with Marburg virus but differs antigenically. This virus also causes haemorrhagic fever in man. The virus was responsible for large number of deaths in these countries.

(iii) Reston virus: Morphologically this virus resembles with above two viruses but differs biologically, genetically and antigenically from prototype filovirus. This virus was isolated in USA from monkeys in 1989 showing symptoms of illness and death. In monkeys the symptoms are fever, diarrhoea, depression, prostration, rashes, shock and death.

All these viruses cause haemorrhagic fever in man. Transmission is direct from person to person.

Toroviridae

Q. 2. Write short notes on *Toroviridae* viruses.

Ans. The prototype virus of this proposed family is Berne virus. Berne virus was isolated in 1972 from a horse in Switzerland and another virus named Breda virus was isolated from faeces of calves with diarrhoea in USA. Similar virions have been recovered from faeces of human beings with diarrhoea. The size of these rod shaped RNA viruses varies from 35-170 nm. They are enveloped with helical kidney shaped capsid symmetry. The RNA genome of the viruses is single stranded, non-segmented, linear with plus sense. The size of genome is about 20 kb. Replication of the virus takes place in cell cytoplasm. These viruses can be identified by neutralization and haemagglutination inhibition tests with known antisera. The pathogenic role of these viruses is not clear so far. The Berne virus has been grown in secondary horse kidney cells.

Circoviridae

Q. 3. What are the properties of *Circoviridae* family.

Ans. The name of *Circoviridae* family has been proposed provisionally. The family is proposed to include the viruses of porcine, psittacine beak and feather disease and chicken anaemia circoviruses. The size of these viruses is 15-17 nm with icosahedral capsid. The genome is double stranded DNA, which is non-segmented and circular with minus (–) sense. The size of genome is 1.76 kb. Viral replication takes place in cell nucleus.

Q. 4. Briefly describe the pathogenicity of (a) Porcine circovirus (b) Psittacine beak and feather disease virus and (c) Chicken anaemia virus.

Ans. (a) *Porcine circovirus:* The virus was isolated in Germany in 1974 from a pig kidney cell line. It appears to be non-pathogenic. Specific antibodies against the virus are found among domestic pigs and wild boars in Germany.

(b) *Psittacine beak and feather disease virus:* In Australia psittacine birds permanently lose feathers and develop deformity of claws in captivity. Sections of affected tissues, revealed the presence of a virus, which resembled porcine circovirus in size and genome structure. Birds may die after first appearance of malformed feathers or may live for years in featherless condition.

(c) *Chicken anaemia virus:* This virus was isolated in 1979 in Japan and subsequently reported from other countries. The size of the virus is about 24 nm. Rest of the properties are similar to porcine circovirus. The genomic size of this virus is 2.12 Kb. The virus has a single stranded DNA. The virus has single serotype. Transmission of infection takes place vertically. There is no disease in adult hens due to this virus but 2-3 week old chicks suffer from severe anaemia, atrophy of thymus, bursa and spleen. The disease is more severe, if there are other viral infections. Dual infection with IBD, and Marek's disease will enhance the severity of the disease causing higher mortality.

There is no satisfactory quick diagnostic method. Serum neutralization test may be tried. No satisfactory vaccine is available.

Chicken anaemia virus has genome and virion structure similar to other two circoviruses and classified in this family. The three viruses have no common antigenic determinants and sequence homology.

Astroviruses

Q. 5. Write short notes on *astroviruses*

These viruses were discovered by electron microscopy in the faeces of children with diarrhoea in 1975. Later on they were also found in the faeces of many animals including calves, piglets, lambs, kids, dogs, turkey and ducks. These viruses are spherical, 27-30 nm in size with star shaped surface structure. RNA genome is single stranded, non segmented, linear in shape with plus (+) sense. The size of the genome is 7.2 Kb. The virus can be cultivated in primary embryonic kidney cells but produce no CPE. There is no antigenic cross reaction in the viruses isolated from different animals. These viruses are considered unimportant as they produce no disease.

Arteriviruses

Q. 6. Describe the properties of arteriviruses.

Ans. These viruses were formerly classified under *Togoviridae* family. As they differed considerably from *Togoviridae* viruses, they were removed from that family and described separately. Arteriviruses are spherical, 60-70 nm in size, enveloped, with icosahedral capsid. They multiply in cytoplasm. The genome of the virus is RNA (12Kb.) type, single stranded, linear and non segmented with (+) sense. Transcriptase enzyme is not present. These viruses have one genus named *Arterivirus.*

Q. 7. Name species of *arteriviruses*.

Ans. Species: Equine arteritis virus
Simian haemorrhagic fever virus
Lactate dehydrogenase elevating virus
Lelystad virus

All above mentioned species, grow fast and infect macrophages. The infection persists in the hosts without showing any symptoms and may cause severe disease in certain circumstances.

Q. 8. Briefly describe the pathogenesis of Equine arteritis virus:

Ans. The Equine arteritis virus is transmitted by contact. It is reported from many countries. The virus causes generalised infection, abortion and respiratory disease in equines. The animal suffers from fever, acute depression, leucopenia, anorexia, oedema of head and legs and conjunctivitis. Generally the disease is not fatal. If stallions are infected, they transmit infection to mares through semen. There is necrosis of small arteries in certain parts of the body. Transmission can be by contact with aborted foetus and placenta. This virus replicate in primary equine kidney cells without any CPE.

Attenuated live virus vaccine of cell culture origin gives good results. In view of rare occurrence of clinical disease vaccination of only valuable animals is recommended.

Q. 9. Write short notes on (a) simian haemorrhagic fever virus and (b) Lelystad virus.

Ans. (a) *Simian haemorrhagic fever virus*: The virus causes haemorrhagic fever in monkeys. The transmission is by contact and fomites. The disease was first reported in 1964 in monkeys imported in Russia and USA from India. The disease is reported in many other countries. In monkeys there is early fever, facial oedema, diarrhoea, dehydration and haemorrhages on skin. There is very high mortality reaching upto 100%.

Control of the disease is by separation of infected colonies from healthy and by following strict hygienic practices.

(b) *Lelystad virus:* The virus causes epidemic abortion and respiratory disease in swines. The disease was first reported in USA and Canada in 1987 and by 1990 the same disease was reported from several other countries. Dutch workers proposed the name of the disease 'Porcine epidemic abortion and respiratory syndrome'. The clinical symptoms of the disease are similar to pseudorabies with incubation period of 4-7 days. The colour of ears and abdomen of infected sows become blue. There are still births, abortion and infertility. Piglets develop neurological and respiratory symptoms. The virus can be isolated with lung and tonsillar tissues in swine alveolar macrophages.

Delta Virus

Q. 10. Describe the properties and pathogenicity of Delta Virus.

Ans. This virus is also called hepatitis D virus. This virus requires the help of hepatitis B virus of human beings for replication and assembly. The size of the virus is 35-37 nm. It is single stranded RNA virus with nonsegmented and circular genome with a size of 1.75 Kb. In conjunction with hepatitis B virus the disease becomes more severe and causes greater mortality. The virus has not been classified so far.

Borna disease virus

Q. 11. What are the properties and pathogenicity of the virus causing Borna disease in horses?

Ans. The disease is a rare encephalopathy of horses which occurs sporadically in Germany and Switzerland. This was first reported from a place named Borna in Germany. The virus is single stranded RNA, enveloped, and less than 100 nm in size. It is sensitive to ether and labile to heat and acid. Serologically it is uniform and not related to any other virus. The disease can be acute, chronic or inapparent. The virus causes encephalomyelitis in horses. Natural infection is also reported in sheep. Incubation period of the disease is from several weeks to several months. In acute form, there is fever, pharyngeal paralysis and muscle tremors. There is incoordination, lithargy, paralysis and death within 2-3 weeks after the onset of symptoms. Brain lesions indicate perivascular cuffing and degeneration of ganglion cells. There are intranuclear inclusions in brain cells. The disease is mediated by T-cell dependent immunopathological reactions. Experimentally several laboratory animals like mice, guinea pigs and hamesters can be infected intracerebrally. Virus can be grown in monkey kidney cells without showing any CPE.

Diagnosis of the disease can be made, on the basis of virus specific antibodies by ELISA or FA test with infected cells. Antibodies in serum and cerebrospinal fluid are demonstrated by binding assays. They do not neutralize infectivity. The infectious virus could not be detected in the brain cells of affected animals. Viral antigen is easily demonstrated in the sections of brain cells. The virus is cell associated and is not released.

35

Agents Causing Subacute Spongiform Encephalopathies

There are some submicroscopic infectious agents whose structures are not similar to viruses. These agents cause subacute spongiform encephalopathies in humans and some animals. The incubation period of these diseases is very long, sometimes extending upto several years. The prototype of these degenerative neurologic diseases is scrapie disease of sheep.

Q. 1. What are the properties of infectious agent(s) causing subacute spongiform encephalopathy?

Ans. On the basis of filtration, the size of these agents is about 30-50 nm. Examination of the sections of infected brain by electron microscopy, these agents reveal no structure similar to viruses. The infectivity of the agents shows high resistance to heat, chemical agents, nucleases and UV light. These agents have some resemblances to 'viroids' another less studied agents, causing infectious diseases in plants. The spongiform encephalopathy agent differ in some respects from 'viriods'.

Q. 2. What are different views about the nature of spongiform encephalopathy agents.

Ans. There are three different theories about the nature of spongi-form encephalopathy agents. Some consider them virus like, others believe in virino theory while others consider them prion like.

Those who believe that they are virus like, consider that the particles have not been visualized because they are very small and have a strong tendency to aggregate and associate with fragments of plasma membranes. There is inaccuracy of assays which depend on production of the disease after a long period. They believe that the agent is small, otherwise a conventional virus.

Other scientists believe in virino theory, which suggests that the nucleic acid of spongiform agents is too small to code for any protein, but it serves a regulatory function. According to this theory, the protein component of the agent is host derived. This theory is not very convincing.

In the prion theory, it is believed that prion which is a pure protein particle and has no nucleic acid, could infect a host, replicate and cause neurological damage. This view is supported by some studies on scrapie disease. By careful examination of scrapie brain material, containing high titre infectivity, has revealed the presence of prion protein which is a cell surface constituent of neurons that is encoded by a single gene. This theory of transmissible infectivity by prion like agent in absence of nucleic acid, is most acceptable hypothesis.

Q. 3. Write short notes on:
(a) Prions (b) Virino (c) Viroid

Ans. (a) *Prions:* Prions are transmissible agents causing degenerative changes in central nervous system. They are composed of glyoproteins but do not contain nucleic acid. Prions are capable of multiplication but do not evoke any immune response. They cause slow virus diseases having very long incubation period. The diseases are characterised by degenerative neurological changes. Prions are also known as atypical or unconventional viruses. They are sensitive to proteases. They are proteinacious infectious particles and cause diseases like scrapie in sheep.

(b) *Virino:* The nucleic acid in virino is too small to code any protein but it serves a regulatory function. The protein content is derived from the host.

(c) *Viroid*: The term 'viroid' was introduced by Diener in 1971, a new agent without any extracellular phase and having much smaller genome. Viroids have no protein coat. The RNA is of much low molecular weight. They are resistant to heat and other organic solvent but sensitive to nucleases. They are known to cause some diseases in plants.

Q. 4. Name diseases caused by agents responsible for subacute spongiform encephalopathy.

Ans. These diseases are:
(a) Scrapie disease of sheep
(b) Bovine spongiform encephalopathy (BSE)
(c) Transmissible mink encephalopathy (TME)

(d) Wasting disease of mule deer
(e) Mad cow disease
(f) Kuru disease in humans
(g) Creutzfeldt-Jacob disease in humans.

All above mentioned diseases are slow and have long incubation period.

Q. 5. What are the properties of the agent causing scrapie disease of sheep?

Ans. Scrapie is a slow, progressive disease of central nervous system of sheep and occasionally of goats. The disease had been reported in USA and some European countries since 1940s. In 1965 the agent/virus could be transmitted to mice and then to other experimental animals. The agent is filtrable through a 40-50 nm filter. It is resistant to boiling, UV irradiation, formalin treatment and exposures to strong acids and alkalies but it is susceptible to phenol and ether. It is not affected by nucleases. The agent is intimately associated with host cell components. There are 2 distinct strains of scrapie disease agent. The agent could not be grown in cell cultures. It has no structure similar to virions. The agent has no nucleic acid but only protein which may be drawn from host. Prion has been given the name of the agent, which is non immunogenic.

Q. 6. Describe the pathogenesis of scrapie disease agent.

Ans. The incubation period of the disease in sheep is 2-3 years naturally and 6-9 months experimentally by I/C inoculation. Sheep and goats can be infected by all routes of inoculation with infected brain tissue. The disease is generally seen in sheep and goats of 3 years and older. Infection in sheep by contact is uncommon but verticle transmission is common. The infected animals show nervous sign, staggering gait and then unable to move and die after some months. There is irritation on the skin which leads to rubbing against a post, thus suggesting the name scrapie. There is spongiform degeneration and vacuolation of neuronal cytoplasm. The agent/virus in mice is maximum in spleen and brain, after some weeks of I/C inoculation. Diagnosis of the disease can be made, only on the basis of I/C inoculation in sheep with infected brain material. No diagnosis can be made on the basis of serological and virological procedures.

Q. 7. Write short notes on bovine spongiform encephalopathy (BSE).

Ans. This disease was first diagnosed in Great Britain in 1986. Subsequently it was reported from Ireland, Switzerland, France and some other European countries. Majority of the cases were reported in dairy cows.

The cases of spongiform encephalopathy were also reported in zoo animals, cats and pigs. The symptoms of the disease and lesions in brain, were similar to scrapie. Diagnosis of the disease is difficult. Confirmation is only made by examination of sections of infected brain tissues. For control measures, the infected animals are recommended for slaughter. It is also recommended that meat and bone meal from affected animals should not be mixed as feed supplement. The agent is very resistant to sterilization by various means. BSE epidemics have raised public concern about human health hazards associated with eating of beef and drinking of milk from such animals.

Q. 8. Write briefly what you know about: (a) Transmissible mink encephalopathy, (b) Kuru disease, (c) Creutzfeldt—Jacob disease and (d) Mad Cow disease.

Ans. (a) *Transmissible mink encephalopathy:* This disease resembles scrapie disease of sheep and is reported to be transferred to minks by feeding scrapie infected meat of sheep.

(b) *Kuru disease:* This disease is reported in tribals, inhabiting Eastern part of New Guinea. It is mostly seen in women and children. Incubating period of the disease is about 5-10 years. The symptoms of the disease are tremors and cerebral ataxia. Once the symptoms are developed, the patient dies within 3-6 months. The disease is believed to be due to eating Kuru disease infected dead bodies without cooking.

(c) *Creutzfeldt-Jacob disease*: The disease is characterised by progressive incoordination due to spongiform degeneration of brain of human beings infected by scrapie like agent. Death occurs in about a year after the onset of symptoms. The disease has been transmitted experimentally in chimpanzees.

(d) *Mad cow disease:* This disease was reported in cows in England in 1999-2000. This appears to be similar to BSE. The country has suffered huge losses on account of slaughter of infected cows and prohibition of beef export.

36

Additional Miscellaneous Questions

Q. 1. Match column A with column B

Column A	Column B
(a) Ribavirin	(i) Marek's disease
(b) Pearl eye disease	(ii) Influenza virus
(c) Panters	(iii) Avian encephalomyelitis
(d) Epidemic tremor	(iv) FMD
(e) Button ulcers	(v) Canine distemper
(f) Hard pad disease	(vi) Hog cholera

Ans. (a) (ii), (b) (i), (c) (iv), (d) (iii), (e) (vi), (f) (v)

Q. 2.

Column A	Column B
(a) Earthernware candles	(i) Cellulose nitrate
(b) Membrane filters	(ii) Keisulguhr
(c) Equilibrium density gradient	(iii) An inhibitor of viral entry in cells
(d) Amantadine	(iv) Cesium chloride

Ans. (a) (ii), (b) (i), (c) (iv), (d) (iii)

Q. 3.

Column A	Column B
(a) Vaccinia virus	(i) Antigenic shift/drift
(b) Influenza virus	(ii) Pasteur
(c) Rabies vaccine	(iii) Reverse transcriptase

(d) Japanese encephalitis	(iv) Ribavirin
(e) Avian leukosis virus	(v) Pig

Ans. (a) (iv), (b) (i), (c) (ii), (d) (v), (e) (iii)

Q. 4.

Column A	Column B
(a) Hard pad disease	(i) Equine infectious anaemia
(b) Gumboro disease	(ii) Rabies
(c) Lyssa bodies	(iii) Immuno suppression
(d) Stable cough	(iv) Canine distemper
(e) Swamp fever	(v) Equine influenza

Ans. (a) (iv), (b) (iii), (c) (ii), (d) (v), (e) (i)

Q. 5.

Column A	Column B
(a) Infectious bulbar paralysis	(i) Infectious canine hepatitis
(b) CELO virus	(ii) Aujeszky's disease
(c) Pink eye disease	(iii) Aviadenovirus
(d) Rubarth disease	(iv) Infectious bovine rhinotracheitis

Ans. (a) (ii), (b) (iii), (c) (iv), (d) (i)

Q. 6.

Column A	Column B
(a) Hepatitis A	(i) *Hepadnavirus*
(b) Hepatitis B	(ii) *Picornavirus*
(c) Hepatitis C	(iii) *Deltavirus*
(d) Hepatitis D	(iv) *Calicivirus*
(e) Hepatitis E	(v) *Hepatovirus* (*Flaviviridae*)

Ans. (a) (ii), (b) (i), (c) (v), (d) (iii), (e) (iv)

Q. 7.

Column A	Column B
(a) Malignant catarrhal fever	(i) Sheep
(b) Louping ill	(ii) Cattle
(c) Marek's disease	(iii) Swine
(d) Pseudorabies	(iv) Poultry
(e) Ectromelia	(v) Dog
(f) Parainfluenza virus 2	(vi) mouse

Ans. (a) (ii), (b) (i), (c) (iv), (d) (iii), (e) (vi), (f) (v)

Q. 8.

Column A	Column B
(a) Avian pneumoencephalitis	(i) Marek's disease
(b) Infant paralysis	(ii) Paramyxovirus
(c) MATSA	(iii) Slow virus disease
(d) Contagious pustular dermatitis	(iv) Poliomyelitis
(e) Visna-Maedi	(v) Orf virus disease

Ans. (a) (ii), (b) (iv), (c) (i), (d) (v), (e) (iii)

Q. 9.

Column A (disease)	Column B (specimen)
(a) Rabies	(i) Spleen tissue
(b) Influenza	(ii) Saliva
(c) Marek's disease	(iii) Throat swab
(d) Rinderpest	(iv) Vesicular fluid
(e) Foot and mouth disease	(v) Feather follicle

Ans. (a) (ii), (b) (iii), (c) (v), (d) (i), (e) (iv)

Q. 10.

Column A	Column B
(a) Small pox	(i) *Rubivirus*
(b) Herpes simplex	(ii) *Morbillivirus*
(c) Measles	(iii) *variolavirus*
(d) Rubella (German measles)	(iv) *Herpesvirus*

Ans. (a) (iii), (b) (iv), (c) (ii), (d) (i)

Q. 11. Select true or false statements:

(a) *Papovavirus* may be mechanically transferred by arthropods.
(b) Fowlpox virus is not transferred by arthropods.
(c) There is congenital transovarian transmission in hog cholera.
(d) *Pneumovirus* possess neither haemagglutinins nor neuraminidase enzyme.
(e) The birds infected with avian leukosis virus do not lay infected eggs.

Ans. (a) True, (b) False, (c) True, (d) True, (e) False

Q. 12. (a) Hog cholera disease is non arthropod borne.
(b) Japanese encephalitis occurs in Japan and South East Asian countries including India.

(c) Blue tongue disease occurs in India.
(d) African horse sickness emerged in India around 1960s but eradicated within few years.

Ans. (a) True, (b) True, (c) True, (d) True

Q. 13. (a) Swine fever and African swine fever are caused by one and the same virus.
(b) Swine fever and hog cholera are two different diseases.
(c) African swine fever also occurs in countries other than Africa.
(d) Louping ill, African swine fever and equine encephalomyelitis are not reported from India.
(e) Kyasanur forest disease occurs in India.

Ans. (a) False, (b) False, (c) True, (d) True, (e) True

Q. 14. (a) In general, spherical viruses have icosahedral symmetry and elongated viruses have helical symmetry.
(b) Most of the viruses are haploid in nature.
(c) The genome of all RNA viruses is linear.
(d) Single stranded viral RNA molecule when functions directly as mRNA is designated as positive (+) sense.
(e) Single stranded RNA viruses with negative (–) sense must first replicate to form a complementary strand to function as mRNA.

Ans. (a) True, (b) True, (c) False, (d) True, (e) True

Q. 15. Fill in the blanks:
(a) Japanese encephalitis is primarily a disease of .... infecting .... accidentally by mosquitoes.
(b) Three well known rinderpest strains are ...., ... and ....
(c) When one virus enhances the growth of second virus, the phenomenon is called ....
(d) The virus of Louping ill is transmitted through ....

Ans. (a) humans, equines (b) Kabete 'O', Nakamura III, Mukteshwar
(c) exaltation (d) ticks

Q. 16. Which of the following viruses are often called orphans?
(a) *Echovirus* (b) *Rhinovirus*
(c) *Arbovirus* (d) *Aphthovirus*

Ans. (a)

Q. 17. Name structural proteins of the following viruses:

(a) Ranikhet disease virus (b) Rinderpest virus
(c) Rabies virus (d) Foot and mouth disease virus

Ans. (a) L, HN, F, P, NP and M and five other minor proteins.

(b) P, N, L, H, F and M. Out of these major immunological factors are H and F.

(c) Nucleoproteins N and NS; glycoprotein G and membrane proteins M_1 and M_2.

(d) VP_1, VP_2, VP_3 and VP_4.

Q. 18. What is the mechanism of antiviral chemotherapeutic agents of Amantadine, Iodouridine Ara-A, Rifamycins and Interferons on viruses?

Ans. Table 36.1: Showing probable mechanism of their antiviral activity

Drug	Probable point of action	Action on
Amantadine	On penetration or uncoating of viruses	Influenza A_2 virus
Iodouridine Ara-A	Replication of DNA	DNA viruses
Rifamycins	Reverse Transcriptase	Leukoviruses
Interferons	Transcription or translation	All viruses

Some antiviral compounds act by preventing penetration of viruses inside the cells, others by preventing transcription and/or translation of mRNA, still others by preventing the replication of DNA/RNA nucleic acids.

Q. 19. Name clinical stages/forms of the following diseases:

(a) Rinderpest (b) African horse sickness
(c) Malignant catarrhal fever (d) Infectious bovine rhinotracheitis
(e) Equine rhinopneumonitis (f) Rabies in dogs
(g) Fowl pox (h) Newcastle disease

Ans. (a) (i) Incubation phase (ii) Prodromal phase
(iii) Mucosal phase (iv) Convalescent phase

(b) (i) Very mild form (ii) Acute or pulmonary form (Dunkop)
(iii) Subacute or cardiac form (Dikkop) (iv) Mixed form

(c) (i) Peracute form (ii) Alimentary form
(iii) Head and eye form (iv) Benign form

(d) (i) Respiratory form (ii) Genital form

(iii) Conjunctival form (iv) Abortion inducing form
(v) Encephalitic form

(e) (i) Respiratory form (ii) Abortion form
(iii) Genital form/Equine coital exanthema form (iv) Neurological form

(f) (i) Furious form (ii) Dumb form

(g) (i) Cutaneous form (ii) Comb and wattle form
(iii) Diphtheretic form

(h) (i) Doyle's form (Asiatic) (ii) Beach's form (pneumoenteritis)
(iii) Beaudettes form (respiratory) (iv) Hitehner's form (mild inapparent form)

Q. 20. Name common viruses causing abortion/still birth in:
(a) Bovines (b) Equines (c) Swines

Ans. (a) IBR virus, bovine enterovirus, bovine virus diarrhoea, blue tongue virus, Riftvalley fever virus and para-influenza virus.
(b) Equine herpesvirus 1-3, equine arteritisvirus.
(c) Porcine parvovirus, porcine herpesvirus, African swine fever virus, porcine enterovirus, vesicular exanthema virus.

Q. 21. Name virus families in which viruses can transform infected cells.

Ans. *Adenoviridae, Papovaviridae, Poxviridae, Herpesviridae, Retroviridae.*

Q. 22. Name common viruses causing diarrhoea in:
(a) Cow and buffalo calves (b) Foals (c) Piglets

Ans. (a) Bovine parvovirus, bovine rotavirus, bovine coronavirus, bovine adenovirus type 3. Diarrhoea in bovines is also caused by other viruses including rinderpest, bovine virus diarrhoea, blue tongue disease and malignant catarrhal fever.
(b) *Rotavirus*
(c) Porcine enterovirus, rotavirus, hog cholera virus, African swine fever virus, transmissible gastroenteritis virus.

Q. 23. The following viruses cause congenital infections except:
(a) Infectious bovine rhinotracheitis virus
(b) Bovine virus diarrhoea virus
(c) Bovine leukaemia virus
(d) Blue tongue disease virus
(e) Pseudorabies virus
(f) Avian leukosis virus

(g) Canine distemper virus
(h) Equine herpesvirus-1

Ans. (g)

Q. 24. What is the incubation period of the following diseases?

(a) Newcastle disease
(b) Equine influenza
(c) Rinderpest
(d) Canine distemper
(e) Foot and mouth disease
(f) Rabies in man
(g) Rabies in dog
(h) Blue tongue disease
(i) African horse sickness
(j) Swine fever
(k) Infectious bovine rhinotracheitis
(l) Malignant catarrhal fever

Ans. (a) 5-6 days
(b) 1-3 days
(c) 4-9 days
(d) 5-8 days
(e) 2-5 days
(f) 21 days to 2-3 months
(g) 3-10 weeks
(h) 6-7 days
(i) Paracute type 3-5 days
(j) 3-8 days
(k) 4-6 days
(l) Upto 8-9 weeks

Q. 25. Name causative agents of:

(a) Cattle plague
(b) Duck plague
(c) Fowl plague
(d) Human plague
(e) Fowl cholera
(f) Hog cholera
(g) Human cholera
(h) Avian diphtheria
(i) Human diphtheria

Ans. (a) Rinderpest virus
(b) Duck herpesvirus type-1
(c) Avian influenza virus
(d) A bacterium *Yersinia pestis*
(e) A bacterium *Past. multocida*
(f) Hog cholera virus
(g) A bacterium *V. cholerae*
(h) ILT virus
(i) A bacterium *C. diphtheriae*

Q. 26. Name causative agents of:

(a) Red nose in cattle
(c) Pink eye in cattle
(c) Pink eye in equines
(d) Ring sores in cows
(e) Sleeping sickness in equines
(f) Swamp fever in equines
(g) Hepatitis blue eye in dogs
(h) Hard pad disease in dogs
(i) Blue comb disease in turkeys
(j) Blue tongue in sheep
(k) Epidemic tremor in chickens
(l) Big liver disease in poultry
(m) Mad itch disease in swine
(n) Mad cow disease

Ans. (a) Respiratory form due to bovine herpesvirus
(b) Conjunctival form due to bovine herpesvirus

(c) Arteritis virus
(d) Pseudo cowpoxvirus
(e) Eastern equine encephalomyelitis virus
(f) Equine infectious anaemia virus
(g) Infectious canine hepatitis virus
(h) Canine distemper virus
(i) Turkey enteritis virus
(j) Orbivirus of *Reoviridae*
(k) Avian encephalomyelitis virus
(l) Avian leukosis virus
(m) Porcine herpes virus-1
(n) A slow virus infection causing spongiform encephalopathy.

Q. 27. Give full forms of the following abbreviations:
(a) FAT (b) ELISA (c) PAGE (d) CIEP
(e) MATSA (f) TSTA (g) TSSA (h) COFAL
(i) RIF

Ans. (a) Fluorescent antibody test
(b) Enzyme linked immunosorbent assay
(c) Polyacrylamide gel electrophoresis
(d) Counter immune electrophoresis
(e) Marek's associated tumour specific surface antigen
(f) Tumour specific transplantation antigen
(g) Tumour specific cell surface antigen
(h) Complement fixation for avian leukosis
(i) Resistance inducing factor

Q. 28. (a) PCR (b) REA (c) cDNA
(d) mRNA (e) tRNA (f) rRNA

Ans. (a) Polymerase chain reaction
(b) Restriction endonulcease
(c) Complementary deoxyribonucleic acid
(d) Messenger RNA
(e) Transfer RNA
(f) Ribosomal RNA

Q. 29. (a) ICTV (b) PPRV (c) CELO (d) AAV (e) QBV
(f) MCFV (g) ICHV (h) EBV (i) TMV (j) ILTV
(k) IBV (l) EDS_{76} (m) SV40

Ans. (a) International Committee on Taxonomy of Viruses
(b) Peste des Petits Ruminants virus

(c) Chicken embryo lethal orphan
(d) Adeno Associated Virus
(e) Quail bronchitis virus
(f) Malignant catarrhal fever virus
(g) Infectious canine hepatitis virus
(h) Epstein Barr virus
(i) Tobacco mosaic virus
(j) Infectious laryngo-tracheitis virus
(k) Infectious bronchitis virus
(l) Egg drop syndrome $virus_{76}$
(m) Simian $virus_{40}$

Q. 30. Name the year when the following emerging viral diseases were first reported in India.
(a) Infectious laryngotracheitis in poultry
(b) Infectious bronchitis in poultry
(c) Infectious bursal disease
(d) Avian encephalomyelitis
(e) Egg drop syndrome due to EDS_{76}
(f) Marek's disease
(g) Duck plague
(h) Inclusion body hepatitis in poultry
(i) Blue tongue disease
(j) Infectious bovine rhinotracheitis
(k) Peste des petits ruminants (PPR) virus disease.
(l) Diarrhoea due to rotavirus in calves
(m) African horse sickness
(n) Equine herpes virus 1
(o) Equine influenza
(p) Equine infectious anaemia

Ans. (a) Singh *et al* in 1964 (Poult. Sc. 43, 492).
(b) Verma in 1964 (Cited by Verma *et al* (1968). Ind. J. Vet. Sci. 38, 418).
(c) Mohanty *et al* in 1971. (Current Sci. 40, 181).
(d) Mohanty *et al* in 1971 (Proceeding of seminar on poultry research and breeding arranged by Venkateshwara Hatcheries, Poona, on 9th January 1982).
(e) Mohanty *et al* in 1980. (Ind. Poult. Rev. 11, 29)
(f) Mohanty *et al* in 1970-71. (Proceeding of Seminar on poultry research and breeding arranged by Venkateshwara Hatcheries, Poona, on 9th January 1982).

(g) Punnoose and Abdulla in 1976 in Kerala.
(h) Ajinkya in 1985. (XI Annual Conference and symposium IAVMI held at Bikaner on 26-28 Dec. 1990).
(i) Sapre in 1964 in Maharastra (Ind. Vety. Rev. (M & B) 15, 69.
(j) Mehrotra *et al* in 1976. (Ind. J. Vet. Path. 1, 70)
(k) Outbreak in sheep in Tamil Nadu in 1988 cited by S. Ramachandra- XII, Annual Conference and symposium IAVMI held at Tirupati on Sept. 12-14, 1991).
(l) Panday and his associates in 1986 (Ind. j. Virol. 2, 164).
(m) The disease was reported in 1960 and was eradicated in 1963.
(n) Jain *et al* in 1976 (Vet. Rec. 99, 57).
(o) Uppal and Yadav in 1987, NRC on equine at Hissar.
(p) Uppal and Yadav in 1987 at Hissar (on the basis of serological reaction).

Q. 31. Describe the changes produced by the following viruses in embryonated chicken eggs. Also mention the age of the embryos used and the route of inoculation.
(a) Ranikhet disease virus
(b) Infectious bronchitis virus
(c) Infectious laryngotracheitis virus
(d) Marek's disease virus

Ans. Table 36.2: Showing changes in embryonated chicken eggs due to RD, IB, ILT and MD viruses.

Name of virus	Age of embryos	Route of inoculation	Changes produced in embryos
(a) Ranikhet disease virus	9-12 days	Allantoic cavity	Death of embryos, haemorrhagic on skin of embryos, production infective virus and haemagglutinins in allantoic fluid.
(b) Infectious bronchitis virus	9-12 days	Allantoic cavity	Curling and dwarfing of embryos
(c) Infectious laryngotracheitis virus	10-12 days	CAM route	Pock lesions on CAM and intranuclear inclusion bodies in infected cells
(d) Marek's disease	10-12 days	CAM route	Pock lesions on CAM and intranuclear inclusions and rarely intra-cytoplasmic inclusion bodies.

Q. 32. Name important emerging diseases of:

(a) Bovines (b) Equines
(c) Swines (d) Sheep and goats
(e) Poultry (f) Dogs

Ans. (a) Bovines: IBR, bovine leukosis, blue tongue, diarrhoea due to corona and rota viruses, bovine virus diarrhoea, bovine para-influenza.

(b) Equines: Equine rhinopneumonitis, equine influenza, Japanese encephalitis, equine infectious anaemia, African horse sickness, equine arteritis disease, equine parainfluenza.

(c) Swines: Hog cholera, Japanese encephalitis, pseudorabies, swine vesicular disease, vesicular exanthema, vesicular stomatitis, diarrhoea due to rotavirus, swine influenza.

(d) Sheep and goats: Blue tongue, caprine arthritis-encephalitis, maedi/visna, pesti des petits ruminants, rotavirus diarrhoea.

(e) Poultry: Marek's disease, IBD, ILT, IB, AE, EDS76.

(f) Dogs: Parvovirus infection, infectious canine hepatitis, canine parainfluenza, diarrhoea due to coronavirus, canine parainfluenza.

Q. 33. Name at least ten viral zoonotic diseases.

Ans. FMD, Ranikhet disease, Rift valley fever, vesicular stomatitis, rabies, pseudorabies, swine vesicular disease, swine influenza, vaccinia Kyasanur forest disease, most of the encephalitic diseases.

Q. 34. Name the virus which may be suspected to cause the following disease condition in an animal species or poultry.

(a) A poultry flock showed gasping and uro-genital involvement, producing misshapen eggs and roughened or soft shell eggs. The agent also produced dwarfing and curling of the embryos when inoculated in 10 day old embryonated chicken eggs by allantoic route.

(b) A puppy showing coryza, diphasic fever, respiratory distress, nervous symptoms and hard foot pads. Smears of conjuncti‸al epithelium revealed intracytoplasmic inclusions.

(c) This is an acute, febrile disease of ruminants characterized by a rapid course and a high mortality. Hill and exotic breeds of cattle are more susceptible. The fever generally precedes other symptoms by 1 or 2 days and seldom lasts for more than 1 or 2 days. The animal suffers from severe diarrhoea and with its onset, temperature subsides to normal or below normal. Mouth lesions appear on inside lower lips and gums. The conjunctivitis and mucous membranes become reddened and haemorrhagic. Discrete small necrotic lesions develop in mouth and sometimes in nasal and vaginal mucosa. There is general septicaemia. The virus grows abundantly in lymphoid tissues. There is dehydration and emanciation. Death occurs within 5-8 days.

(d) The disease is arthropod borne and primarily infect sheep but can also infect cattle. The disease is marked with fever, depression, anorexia, salivation, discharge from eyes and nose. There is diarrhoea, ulcers on tongue, dental pad and lips. Tongue is swollen, cynotic and purple blue. Incubation period is about a week. Virus grows in chicken embryos by yolk sac method and in a variety of cell cultures including BHK_{21} and Hela cell lines when inoculated with lymph node and spleen inoculum. Virus gives HA test with sheep RBCs.

Ans. (a) Infectious bronchitis virus
(b) Canine distemper virus
(c) Rinderpest virus
(d) Blue tongue disease virus

Select correct answer:

Q. 35. Virus neutralization test is a preferred diagnostic test for the following diseases except:
(a) Japanese B encephalitis (b) Blue tongue disease
(c) Foot and mouth disease (d) Bovine virus diarrhoea

Ans. (c)

Q. 36. Complement fixation test is a diagnostic test for the following diseases except:
(a) Rinderpest (b) Rabies
(c) Foot and mouth disease (d) Japanese B encephalitis

Ans. (b)

Q. 37. Haemagglutination inhibition test is a diagnostic test for the following diseases except:
(a) Ranikhet disease (b) Influenza
(c) Canine hepatitis (d) Mumps

Ans. (c)

Q. 38. Immunity is life long in the following diseases after recovery except:
(a) Rinderpest (b) Swine influenza
(c) Swine fever (d) Foot and mouth disease

Ans. (b) and (d).

Q. 39. Name the disease in which local immunity is important:

(a) Influenza (b) Fowl pox
(c) Parvovirus infection (d) Diarrhoea due to *rotavirus*

Ans. (a) and (d)

Q. 40. Which of the following is the main advantage of a genetic probe in Microbiology?

(a) Rapid detection of microbes
(b) Detection of microbes directly in specimens
(c) To study toxigenicity of microbes
(d) To study antigenicity of microbes

Ans. (a) and (b)

Q. 41. The following are the disadvantages of a genetic probe except:

(a) Needs isotopes (b) Isotopes are costly
(c) Half life of some isotopes is short (d) Specificity

Ans. (d)

Q. 42. The labelling of fragments of DNA/RNA with ^{32}P for genetic study is known as:

(a) Prion (b) Virion
(c) Virino (d) Probe

Ans. (d)

Q. 43. Name virus families in which viruses can transform infected cells.

Ans. DNA virus families: *Papovaviridae, Adenoviridae, Herpesviridae, Poxviridae.*
RNA virus families: *Retroviridae*

Q. 44. Name viruses which produce inclusion bodies in infected cells.

Ans. (a) Viruses producing intranuclear inclusion bodies:
Parvoviruses, adenoviruses, herpesviruses, Rift valley fever virus.
(b) Viruses producing intracytoplasmic inclusion bodies:
Poxviruses, reoviruses, rabies virus
(c) Viruses producing both intranuclear and intracytoplasmic inclusion bodies:
Marek's disease virus, African swine fever virus, canine distemper virus, rinderpest virus

Q. 45. Give the number of serotypes of the following viruses:

(a) Blue tongue disease virus
(b) FMD virus
(c) Vesicular stomatitis virus
(d) African horse sickness virus
(e) Venenzuelan equine encephalomyelitis virus
(f) Equine herpesvirus
(g) Bovine herpes virus
(h) Rabies and related virus
(i) Bovine Adenovirus
(j) Canine adenovirus
(k) Porcine enterovirus
(l) Vesicular exanthema virus
(m) Dengue fever virus
(n) Arenareovirus
(o) Infectious bronchitis virus
(p) Human influenza virus

Ans. (a) 24, (b) 7, (c) 7, (d) 9, (e) 7, (f) 4, (g) 4, (h) 4, (i) 9, (j) 2, (k) 11, (l) 13, (m) 4, (n) 11, (o) 8, (p) 3.

Q. 46. Name viruses which produce pock lesions on CAM of embryonated chicken eggs.

Ans. They are: Pox viruses, ILT virus, Marek's disease virus, pseudorabies virus, vesicular stomatitis virus and avian reovirus.

Appendix

Preferred Specimens and Host Systems for Isolation of the Virus from Viral Infections in Animals

Viral disease	Specimens	Host system
1. Fowl pox	Skin, feather follicles, comb lesions	Cultivation in chicken embryos on CAM
2. Infectious laryngotracheitis	Trachea and lungs	Cultivation in chicken embryos on CAM
3. Infectious bronchitis	Trachea and lungs	In chicken embryos by allantoic cavity route
4. Newcastle disease	Lung, spleen, kidney, brain, proventriculus, intestine, liver and heart	Cultivation in chicken embryos by allantoic route
5. Avian ence-phalomyelitis	Brain	Cultivation in day old chicks by intracerebral route
6. Marek's disease	Intact cells from buffy coat, spleen, tumour tissues, lymphoid cells	In chicken embryo by CAM route and chicken kidney cell culture
7. Avian leukosis	Plasma, serum, tumour tissues like liver, spleen, kidneys etc. or embryos from infected chicken	In chicken embryo fibroblast cell culture
8. Avian influenza	Nasal swabs, trachea, lung	In chicken embryos by allantoic route
9. Infectious bursal disease	Bursa of Fabricius	In embryonated eggs by CAM route
10. Infectious bovine rhinotracheitis	Bronchial lymphnodes, nasal and vaginal swabs, trachea, lung, kidney, foetal liver and kidney	In calf kidney and testes cell culture

(Contd.)

Viral disease	Specimens	Host system
11. Rinderpest	Blood at the height of temp., faeces, intestinal lymph glands, spleen	In calf kidney cell culture, Vero cell culture
12. Bovine virus diarrhoea	Nasal and faecal swabs, spleen, lymph nodes, intestine, buffy coat	In bovine and ovine kidney and testes cell culture
13. Bovine para-influenza	Nasal swabs, lungs	In bovine kidney and testes cell culture
14. Foot and mouth disease	Lymph from tongue and buccal cavity vesicles, foot and tongue lesions	In suckling mice, guinea pig foot pad, BHK21 cell line and calf kidney cell culture
15. Cow pox	Lymph from teat vesicles	In calf kidney cell culture
16. Malignant catarrhal fever	Thyroid and buffy coats of leucocytes	In cell culture of suspected tissue
17. Calf diarrhoea rota virus	Faecal swabs, infected intestine and lymph glands	In calf kidney and testes cell culture
18. Bovine entero-virus infection	Nasal and faecal swabs	In cell culture of bovine origin
19. Equine rhino-pneumonitis (equine abortion)	Nasal swabs, vaginal swabs, lung, fetal lung and liver	In equine kidney cell culture and PK15 cell line
20. Equine influenza	Nasal swabs, lung	In chicken embryos by allantoic route
21. Equine ence-phalomyelitis (all forms)	Brain	In PK15 cell line, chicken embryos, various routes in suckling mice I/C
22. Vesicular stomatitis	Saliva and vesicular fluid and vesicular epithelium	In chicken embryo on CAM and most cell system
23. Equine infectious anaemia	Whole blood, leuco-cytes, serum	In primary horse leuco-cytes cell culture
24. African horse sickness	Lymph nodes, spleen, lung	In Vero cell line and mon-key kidney cell line
25. Sheep pox	Scabs from skin lesions	In lamb kidney and testes cell culture

(Contd.)

Viral disease	Specimens	Host system
26. Blue tongue disease	Blood at height of temp., saliva, swabs from eyes and nasal discharges, faecal swabs, lung, spleen	In chicken embryos by yolk sac route, in bovine and ovine kidney and testes cell culture, BHK21, Hela cell lines
27. Contagious pustular dermatitis	Skin lesions and scabs	In lamb kidneys and testes cell culture
28. Hog cholera	Spleen, mandibular & pharyngeal, lymph nodes, blood nasal and eye swabs in dry ice	In pig kidney, spleen, testes, lymph node cell cultures and PK15 cell line
29. Pseudorabies	Brain, tonsil, lung, kidney & a piece of spinal cord	In pig kidney cell line, in rabbit by S/C route
30. Transmissible gastroenteritis	Intestine	In primary pig kidney cell culture
31. African swine fever	Blood, tissue fluid, internal organs, eye and nasal swabs	In yolk sac of chicken embryos, pig, bovine and chicken kidney cell culture
32. Rabies	Brain	In suckling mice, chicken embryos (egg adapted), many cell lines including BHK21
33. Canine distemper	Lung, urinary bladder, cerebellum	In chicken embryo fibroblast cell culture, primary and continuous dog and ferret kidney cell culture
34. Canine hepatitis	Liver, kidney and lung	In canine kidney cell culture
35. Canine parvovirus disease	Intestinal scrappings, lymph nodes, spleen, liver, faecal samples	In canine foetal kidney, testes and lymph node primary cell culture
36. Scrapie	Cerebrum, spleen and lymph node	Intracerebral inoculation in sheep and mice

List of Textbooks

1. Ananthanarayan, R. and Jayaram Paniker, C.K. (1986). *Textbook of Microbiology.* 3rd Edn. Orient Longman Ltd., 160 Anna Salai, Madras.
2. Andrews, C.H., Periera, H.G. and Wildy, P. (1978). *Viruses of Vertebrates,* 4th Edn. Bailliere-Tindall, London.
3. Braude, A.1. (1986). *Infectious Diseases and Medical Microbiology,* 2nd Edn. W.B. Saunders, Philadelphia.
4. Buxton, A. and Fraser, G. (1977). *Animal Microbiology,* Vol. 2, Oxford, Black-well Scientific Publications.
5. Collee, J.G., Duguid, J.P., Fraser, A.G. and Marmion, B.P. (Eds). (1989). Mackie and McCartney's *Medical Microbiology* (Cruick Shank). ELBS, Churchill Living stone.
6. Davis, B.D., Dulbecco, R., Eisen, H.N., and Ginsberg, H.S. (1980). *Microbiology,* 3rd Edn. Harper and Row, Hagerstown, MD.
7. Dimmock, N.J. and Primrose, S.B. (1994). *Introduction to Modern Virology.* 4th Edn. Blackwell Science Inc., MA, USA.
8. Fenner, F. (1974). *Biology of Animal Virology.* 2nd Edn. Academic Press New York.
9. Fraenkel-Conrat, H. and Kimball, P.C. (1982). *Virology.* Printicc-Hall, Englewood Cliffs, N.J.
10. Freemen, B.A. (1985). *Burrows, Text Book of Microbiology,* 22nd Edn. W.B. Saunders, Philadelphia, 1985.
11. Harper, D.R. (1993). *Virology.* LabFax series, Bios Scientific Publishers Ltd., Oxford U.K. and Academic Press, USA.
12. Jawetz, E. Melnick, J.L. and Adelberg, E.A. (1987). *Reviews of Medical Microbiology,* 17th Edn. Appeleton and Lange, Norwalk CT.
13. Joklik, W.K., Willett, H.P. and Amos, D.B. (1984). Zinsser *Microbiology,* 18th Edn. Appleton-century crofts, New York.
14. Luria, S.E., Darnell Jr. J.E., Baltimore, D. and Campbell, A. (1978). *General Virology,* 3rd Edn. Wiley, New York.
15. Mahanty, S.B. and Dutta, S.K. (1981). *Veterinary Virology,* Lea and Febiger, Philadelphia.

16. Mims, C.A. and White, D.O. (1984). *Viral Pathogenesis and Immunity.* Blackwell, Oxford.
17. Parker, M.T. and Collier, L.H. (1990). Topley and Wilson's *Principles of Bacteriology, Virology and Immunity.* 8th Edn., Vol. I-IV, Edward Arnold Publishers, Hodder and Stoughton, London.
18. Pelczar, Jr. M.J., Chain, E C.S. and Krieg, N.R. (1986). *Microbiology,* 5th edn. Mc Graw-Hill Int. Edn. Singapore.
19. Prescott, L.M., Harley, J.P. and Klein, D.A. (1996). *Microbiology.* 3rd Edn., WMC Brown Publishers, New York.
20. Rott, R. and Goebel, W. (1988). *Molecular Basis of Viral and Microbial Pathogenesis.* Spinger-Verlag Publishers Pvt. Ltd., New York.
21. Stryer, L. (1988). *Molecular Design of Life.* W.H. Freeman and company, New York.

Index

D

E

F

G

H

I

J

K

L

M

N

O

P

Q

R

S